"Where are the snows of yester-year?"

Be a Poet!

by

NANCY BOGEN

with original illustrations

19 80

The Twickenham Press
NEW YORK

Published by The Twickenham Press, 31 Jane Street, New York, NY 10014-1982; http://www.twickenhampress.com.

Library of Congress Cataloguing-in-Publication Data

Bogen, Nancy, 1932-
Be a poet / by Nancy Bogen, with original illustrations. —1st edition.
p. cm.
Includes bibliographical references and index.
ISBN 978-0-936726-07-6 (pbk. : alk. paper)
1. Poetry–Authorship. I. Title.
PN1059.A9B63 2007
808.1—dc22

2007007350

Edited by Susan Walker
Designed by Karla Kraus
Cover by Lisa Tait of Silvertop Graphics and Karla Kraus

For my dear friend Brent Bouldin

And I made a rural pen,
And I stain'd the water clear,
And I wrote my happy songs
Every child may joy to hear.

Who said that?

Table of Contents

Illustrations

Be a Poet!

Introduction

This is not a conventional textbook or, in fact, a textbook at all. I can't think of anything sillier and potentially more boring than a bunch of rules and regulations in so many pages that purport to teach a person how to engage in so personal an activity as writing poetry. And if that's what you're after, good luck to you elsewhere! Rather than plague folks in that fashion, what I have opted to do in this book is act as a guide — a big sister, if you will — who is very free with advice, which you, naturally, as a hopeful would-be or budding poet may feel free to accept or reject.

What makes me qualified to act as such a guide? Purely and simply a sense that I have of what the needs of an aspiring poet are, which I derive from many years of leading poetry workshops at various college and graduate school levels — albeit not always conventionally. Oh yes, I've written a bit of poetry myself, especially in my youth, and some of it was even published and in fairly decent little mags, I'll have you know. Also, various friends and admirers have remarked at times that passages here and there in my three novels seem to dissolve into verse. Dip into the most likely candidate — *Klytaimnestra Who Stayed at Home* — and see for yourself.

So much for my credentials; now let's turn to you. What does it take to become a poet or be a better poet than you are at present — that is, beyond a persistent yearning to? Well, first of all, regardless of your age or the stage you're at in life, you're going to have to decide on who you want to be or are as a poet. Another way of putting it: what special things do you want to say that are better said in verse than in prose? Closely related to this — like the opposite side of a coin — you're going to have to spell out to yourself what style or, more precisely, what voice you'll be choosing or have opted to write in. And ultimately you'll have to decide what form or forms you want your poems to be in or to take stock of how they've shaped up so far. Finally, comes the most gut-wrenching part of the whole process: giving everything a good, long, hard look to see if you like the mix and / or you're comfortable with it.

Don't be surprised if some or perhaps all of your answers are slow in coming. Indeed, at times you may find yourself feeling as if you're in a virtual Chinese restaurant, forever trying to match a delicious something from Column A with other desirables from Column B and Column C that aren't quite compatible. Don't be surprised, also, if you find yourself changing your mind about some things, like your poetic voice, and then changing it again. . .and again.

On the other hand, it may turn out that you're one of the few to whom right answers flow — like lava — and they all turn out to be golden. (Golden lava?) Anyway, that's what happened to the nineteenth-century poet William Wordsworth at the outset of his career. He was coming home from an all-night party early one morning, and there being no public transportation where he lived up there in the north of England, he decided to walk rather than ask someone for a ride, and while he was so doing, a curious thing happened:

> The morning rose, in memorable pomp,
> Glorious as e'er I had beheld — in front,
> The sea lay laughing at a distance; near,
> The solid mountains shone, bright as the clouds,
> Grain-tinctured, drenched in empyrean light;
> And in the meadows and the lower grounds
> Was all the sweetness of a common dawn —
> Dews, vapours, and the melody of birds,
> And labourers going forth to till the fields.
>
> Ah! need I say, dear Friend! that to the brim
> My heart was full; I made no vows, but vows
> Were then made for me; bond unknown to me
> Was given, that I should be, else sinning greatly,
> A dedicated Spirit. On I walked
> In thankful blessedness, which yet survives.

To get the full effect of this passage, try reading it again aloud, slowly, pausing at every punctuation mark so as to savor each detail by itself and cumulatively. Here's a thought: why not follow up with a walk of your own? Like tomorrow? Make it early in the morning if you can, but don't be a ninny and just put one foot in front of the other — take a good, long look at everything as you're stepping along, and listen, smell, even touch and taste, and above all, feel!

One of your most critical decisions will be concerning form. Before the latter part of the nineteenth century, this was a relatively simple matter. Everyone learned the various standard forms, like the sonnet and ballad, at school and as ingenue poets went on to choose whichever ones suited his or her temperament, fancy, and/or subject matter, devising variations as the need arose. In fact, far from being a necessary burden, both the poets and their audiences considered such established forms a pleasure and a delight. But then sometime in the early twentieth century, something happened in the world of poetry in English; one might almost say, something snapped. A number of leading poets seemed to become weary of tradition and began creating works that were independent of the forms, writing in what they termed free verse, which as we shall see has its own set of rules — like restrictions. Happily, poets nowadays, including yourself, can do as they please, write a poem either in one of the traditional forms or in free verse — or in both. There's only one bottom-line rule of thumb to be followed: there must be some kind of correspondence between what you are saying and how you are saying it.

A few words remain to be said about how to use this book. One fact not to lose sight of is that it doesn't contain any magic formulas or quick fixes. What I've tried to do is gather together various essential things that I feel you should zero in on. If you're already aware of them, fine and good; I'll just be reminding you. If you're not and it's all "Greek" to you, how nice; think of the riches that await you! Feel free to use this book alone or with one or more friends or in a formal group like a poetry club; it can also work well as a textbook in a classroom setting with a teacher. As for how to proceed in it, you can do so conventionally, beginning at the beginning and systematically going through it to the end, which, of course, would be extremely gratifying to me, the author. But if you feel the need to concentrate on a particular aspect — like sound correspondences — and sort of give yourself a mini-intensive course in it, that's just fine; do it. Another possibility is simply to flip through the pages and now and then stop and browse whenever something of interest catches your eye, and do or not do the exercises. In fact, there's nothing wrong with doing all or some of the exercises without reading a word of the text.

Be advised that the exercises are all of my own devising and I hope will turn out to be fun, which was my intention. A word to the wise, meaning teachers of creative writing and leaders of poetry workshops in an academic setting: do not under any circumstances grade students on them! If you do and I hear about it, I'll haunt you in your dreams, so help me!

If you're planning to go through the book alone or with a friend or friends or to use it in a small group without a leader and anticipate that you'll need some kind of guidance, I'll be happy to oblige. Yes, do feel free to write me and even send me poems if you wish. But bear in mind that I'm only human like everyone else, meaning don't take my word alone for anything. Also not to be forgotten: I'm temporally-challenged — meaning old — as perhaps some of you are, so have a heart and don't send more than three: <nancyrbogen@cs.com>.

Some folks may be wondering how I, in my dotage, came to write this book. Well, the fact is there were two earlier versions. I began working on the first, titled "So You Want to Be a Poet," in the mid-1970s and, quite satisfied with it, had gone so far as to make a list of publishers likely to be interested in it, draft a query letter, and even type up a few. But then suddenly, within the space of a few months, both of my parents died, and then quite unexpectedly someone I cared for very deeply. Bowled over by shock and grief, I stuck the manuscript away with all the materials pertaining to it and totally forgot about it.

One night fifteen years later, I woke from a deep sleep and suddenly remembered it. But where was that manuscript, what the devil had I done with it? It wasn't in my apartment, I felt sure, and somehow anticipating that it would turn up in my office, which was located in a small college I'd been teaching at, I headed for there early the next morning with the express purpose of finding it — if it was to be found. Standing on the threshold, I took everything in for a good, long moment, from the file cabinets to the bookshelves crowded with books, wondering, where oh where could it be? Then, sort of sleepwalking to my desk, I got down on my hands and knees, and pulling open the bottom drawer, a file drawer packed full of stuff, stuck my hand way in to behind the last folder — and it came upon something that seemed like a bulky manila envelope. Yanking it out, I tore it open, and there indeed it all was, replete with those query letters to editors — and three-cent stamps on the envelopes! It was like taking part in an archeological dig and suddenly stumbling on a time capsule with another me inside!

I began reading the manuscript and couldn't help but be charmed — and the rest is history. Simon & Schuster published it as an Arco manual under their title *How to Write Poetry*, and it went through a second and a third edition via Macmillan and Peterson's. This current book is based on the same principles as that work, but contains many fresh insights and much new material that I gained from additional years of teaching.

The time has come, the walrus said — for giving thanks. First and foremost, I wish to express heartfelt gratitude to my dear friend and assistant David Lutzer for his absolutely necessary service in behalf of this book in a tale too long to be told here. I'm also much beholden to my students, both of the past and of recent years, and to our three guest poets, whom you'll be meeting shortly: Ruth Fainlight, Nina Cassian, and Jeffrey Greene. Thanks are also due to my teachers at Columbia University's wondrous English Department in the Graduate School of Arts and Sciences, namely to Carl Woodring, Marshall Suther, Marjorie Hope Nicolson, James Clifford, and Elliott Van Kirk Dobbie, who instilled in me their uncompromising love of timeless things. More distantly I am also grateful to M. L. Rosenthal, Lillian Hornstein, Eda Lou Walton, John Varney, Warren Bower, and George Maitland of New York University's Washington Square College for sometimes making school a home away from home.

On the production end, let me begin by blowing kisses to my editor Susan Walker (sbwalker@hvc.rr.com), whose sensible presence abounds in every line. Thanks also go to Lisa Tait of Silvertop Graphics (http://www.silvertopgraphics.com), David Bergsland of Bergsland Design (http://www.bergsland.org), friend-in-need Wray Rominger of the Purple Mountain Press (http://wwwcatskill.net/purple/category.htm, and the folks at our printer McNaughton & Gunn, who were always ready with sound advice. Finally, let me here pay tribute to Dan Poynter of Para Publishing (http://www.parapublishing.com) and Len Fulton of Dust Books (http://www.dustbooks.com/), each in his own area a leader in the small press movement, for being among the first to show everyone the way.

Should anyone be curious, the manuscript was typed in WordPerfect and designed and typeset in Adobe's InDesign. The full-page illustrations are black-and-white translations of colored digital images created by me from my own photographs and material in the public domain. The other graphics are my transmogrifications, via Adobe's Photoshop, of materials encountered in a nineteenth-century book of German poetry picked up at Vienna's Naschmarkt and in various Dover books.

1

Whither Wilst, Wit

We all know who we are on a day-to-day basis, but one's identity as a poet is an entirely different matter, and that has to be our first concern. Once you have a better idea of yourself as such, there are certain essential things — tools of the trade, if you will — that you should have or least be aware of regardless of your level of achievement.

WHO are You-ou-ou?

The Whys and Wherefores

When it comes to defining yourself as a poet, bear in mind that it's not like doing a problem in math; there's no right or wrong answer. In essence, it means asking yourself why you want to write poetry or are trying to write it, but some folks find it easier to deal with this when the question's rephrased into something more personal, like: for whom do you want to write (or, if you're already doing so, are you trying to write)?

I'm a great believer in mirrors. They never lie; indeed, they're the ultimate — and perhaps only — truth-tellers in our society. Go find one and pose that question to yourself while looking yourself straight in the eye: *"For whom do you want to write (or are you trying to write)?"* If you're working in a group, you might want to take turns in the bathroom or a bedroom, or do this part at home alone in advance of the meeting.

Now go and get a pen or pencil and a sheet of paper, and write your answer down, and then look at the three statements below to see if yours in any way matches or resembles one of them.

1. *I don't want to write (or I'm not trying to write) for anyone or anything, or for a reason; I just want to write.*

2. *I want to write (or I'm trying to write) for myself as I see myself.*

3. *I want to write (or I'm trying to write) for a faceless audience that I visualize hovering in the air before me.*

Meditate on your answer for a while, and then take up your pen and pencil again and elaborate on it. In other words, if you chose number 1, what do you mean by "*I just want to write?*" If you opted for number 2, how do you see yourself? And if number 3, what is distinctive about that faceless crowd you envision?

It is possible that you came up with an answer other than 1, 2, or 3, and that's okay. It simply means that you're on your own when it comes to expanding, and for that reason, you may find yourself compelled to explain at greater length in order to satisfy your Burgeoning Poetic Self.

Sometimes when one's confronted by a thorny question, it helps to look over another guy's shoulder and see what he or she's got to say on the subject, and there are always members of your group to do that with if you're in one. But some of you are going it alone, so I decided for the sake of our all being in step to pose the question *For whom do you write?* to three established poets — Ruth Fainlight, Nina Cassian, and Jeffrey Greene — and in fact to make them our invited guests. You can find brief bios of each with a representative poem and a recent photo in the appendix to this chapter, and a list of their books in my bibliography in the back of this book. Suffice it to say here that Ruth, a senior, is among my oldest friends; Nina, another senior, is the wife of a friend; and Jeffrey, younger by a generation, is a second cousin. Additionally, it seems important to note that they're quite a cosmopolitan group: Ruth was born here in the Unites States but has resided in England for most of her life; Nina, a Romanian, has been living in exile here; and Jeffrey, another American, has made France his home for a fair number of years.

Ruth chose number 2 — *I write for myself as I see myself* — as her answer, but do take note of how she qualified it in her elaboration:

> If I concentrate on the question For whom do you write? the first image of a reader which comes into my mind is someone rather like I imagine myself when young: a serious young person (gender is immaterial here, either a young woman or young man) who loves poetry and probably writes it also; who responds intensely to everything in the world about them: landscape and living beings, animal and human; works of art: painting, sculpture and music; someone who ponders those spiritual and metaphysical questions which power scientific enquiry as much as they inspire art. But of course I don't imagine my readers as a group of "Ruth-clones." Many people who don't write poetry read and love it. And ideally, this reader would also be interested in poetry as a craft, and know enough about its form and structure — prosody, etc. — to appreciate that aspect of my work.

Nina chose number *1 — I don't write for anyone or anything, or for a reason; I just write* — but note how she turned her elaboration into a mini-autobiography:

> Poetry came to me naturally, like breathing, when I was five years old. Later, in adolescence, I realized that this "emanation" of mine, which was both a necessity and a pleasure, could be called a "vocation" and, therefore, a burden itself with practice, growing pains and responsibility. Of course, I write in order to express myself and the surrounding world — and, above all, to communicate, to free myself of selfishness and other interior demons, as in an exorcism!

Jeffrey, who chose number *3 — I write for a faceless audience that I visualize hovering in the air before me* — also most interestingly individualized himself in his elaboration:

> I write for an audience I imagine in the air, but I imagine an audience of one. Muriel Rukeyser calls this more eloquently "the audience of the individual." Since poems are spoken, I'm acutely aware of an intrinsic rapport between a speaker and a listener/reader. I write primarily lyric poetry, which by its nature is intimate. I imagine my audience of one overhearing and experiencing the turns and intrigues of thought and feeling. Perhaps the most rewarding experience I've had as a poet is when my poems have been recited back to me completely by surprise, or sung. I'm aware when writing of trying to create a speaker who moves someone, not so different from song.

Now let's get back to you. If you yourself wrote something, go back to it now and look it over and see if you want to add or delete anything. If you didn't write anything yet, try again now. But if you still can't, not to worry. Sooner or later you will, okay? So don't be concerned about your degree of commitment. The mere fact that you opened this book and got into it this far is an indication of sufficient interest and seriousness of purpose.

What-what-what?

Another, related question that you should ask yourself concerns subject matter. Is there some topic or theme that you would like to focus on (or are focusing on) in your poetry? In other words, would you like to have (or do you indeed have) an agenda as a poet? Some possibilities are *love, nature,* and *politics* or a more narrowly defined form of one of them, like *free love* and *forests.* When one thinks about it, quite a few poets of the past wrote with an agenda like that in mind. For instance, the Italian poet Petrarch devoted a humongous number of sonnets to his love for someone named Laura, and in his more mature poetry, English poet John Milton sincerely sought to "justify the ways of God to man."

Sounding out our three guest poets about the matter, I found Ruth to be solidly against the idea of an agenda, and she was quite adamant about it:

> I do not have an agenda as a poet, and find it hard to understand how a poet can claim to have one. Perhaps I should specify that I use the word poet in this context to mean lyric poet — my definition of a lyric poet being someone open to the reality of both the inner and outer worlds, as well as to the spiritual realisations called inspiration. This demands total attention and acceptance and self-forgetting: a state of mind quite the reverse of one already primed to make a certain point.

Nina, charmingly, straddled the fence:

> "No" — that is to say, I have never had an overall agenda! If anything, I suppose one could say that each poem has its own agenda. Just as each poem dictates its own form.

Clearly, Jeffrey likes the idea of agendas and indeed recognizes them in his work, though "themes" would seem to be a better word for what he describes:

> I have issues that continually make their appearance in my work and may in part be responsible for my need to write. Some of my earliest memories growing up out in the country involve falling asleep at night and having a sudden, horrifying recognition that life is finite and we are all individually alone in an unfeeling universe. As a six-year-old, I would make up running sentimental fantasies to protect myself from reaching this thought, which still found ways to penetrate my defenses and took on other forms of recognition, such as the inevitable loss of loved ones. Now that I'm well into midlife, I find the indifference of nature consoling in many ways, the antithesis of evil, and the coldness of the human heart unnerving. And yet I agree with Wallace Stevens in "Art as Establisher of Value" when he states that the poet's function "is not to lead people out of confusion" or to be a moral arbitrator but "to see his imagination become the light in other people's minds." Paradoxically, while the subjects vary, I find myself trying to recreate a piercing recognition on the page that one feels almost physically.

Now it's your turn. Get hold of your pen or pencil again, and grab a fresh sheet of paper. Will you have or do you feel you have something special to concentrate on as a poet? And if so, what will it be or is it? If not, why not? When you have finished, set what you've written aside with your answer to the previous question regarding audience, if you have one.

That Mysterious Thing Called Style

In the wild and woolly days of my youth, literary folks were forever exercising their vocal cords over something they called style, and they generally agreed that there were three levels of same: *formal*, *informal*, and *colloquial*. A *formal style* was characterized by long, complicated sentences, a sophisticated vocabulary that avoided contractions like "isn't," and a strict adherence to grammatical rules; one employed it for essays on ultra-serious subjects, printed invitations to fancy affairs, and so on. The earmarks of a *colloquial style* were simple sentences with a limited vocabulary consisting largely of short words, contractions, and slang, and a loose grammatical structure; its use was reserved for letters to close relatives and friends, and such like. A style that was somewhere between those two extremes was considered *informal*, and this was to be used for everything else. Here's a set of examples to make the distinctions between those three levels of style clear:

Formal: a passage from George Santayana's book *The Sense of Beauty:*

> There are, indeed, other objects of desire that if attained leave nothing but restlessness and dissatisfaction behind them. These are the objects pursued by fools. That such objects ever attract us is a proof of the disorganization of our nature, which drives us in contrary directions and is at war with itself. If we had attained anything like steadiness of thought or fixity of character, if we knew ourselves, we should know also our inalienable satisfactions.

Informal: my translation of same:

> We all have foolish desires. We want things which do not satisfy us when we get them. We are subject to conflicting desires and want to go in opposite directions at the same time. If we had a clearer understanding of our own needs and purposes, we would know what course was best for us.

Colloquial: my translation of same:

> We all have dumb ideas. The things we want we don't dig once we get them. We're full of urges, and they don't agree with each other. If we knew what was freaking us out, everything'd be okay.

The notion of there being three levels of style has largely passed by the wayside, but I've found them helpful when it comes to poets further defining themselves. So-o-o:

Exercise 1

To drive home the distinctions among the three styles, do the following with respect to each paragraph: count up the number of long and short words, the number of words in each sentence, the number of sentences, and the number of simple (subject-verb) and involved (more than one subject-verb) sentences, and write your results down in three parallel columns. The difference is startling, isn't it?

Well, knowing is doing, and doing is knowing, I say. So let's take things one step further.

Exercise 2

There used to be a popular song that began "I got along withoutcha before I metcha, gonna get along withoutcha now." Try your hand at coming up with formal and informal versions of it. However, be forewarned: if you're unaccustomed to using long words and fancy phrases, your version of formal may turn out to be amusing to some folks — as trying on Mom's high heels or Dad's fancy pants was when you were a kid. Pay them no mind; this is just an exercise.

So much for fun and games. It's time now to get serious. Below is a passage from *Paradise Lost* by John Milton (1608-1674) in which he encapsulated Satan's descent from Heaven to Hell. By the way, in case you're not aware or it's slipped your mind, *Paradise Lost* is about the fall of Adam and Eve in the Garden of Eden and took place in the never-never land of Milton's imagination:

....Him the Almighty Power
Hurl'd headlong flaming from th' Ethereal Sky
With hideous ruin and combustion down
To bottomless perdition, there to dwell
In Adamantine Chains and penal Fire,
Who durst defy th' Omnipotent to Arms.
Nine times the Space that measures Day and Night
To mortal men, hee with his horrid crew
Lay vanquisht, rolling in the fiery Gulf
Confounded though immortal: But his doom
Reserv'd him to more wrath; for now the thought
Both of lost happiness and lasting pain
Torments him; round he throws his baleful eyes
That witness'd huge affliction and dismay
Mixt with obdúrate pride and steadfast hate:
At once as far as Angels' ken he views
The dismal Situation waste and wild,...

Read it through to yourself, noting that it consists of five statements (or sentences, if you will), so pause significantly after "Arms," "immortal," "Torments him," and "hate." Read it through again, this time aloud, putting the emphasis where you think it should be. If you're in a group, this can be done together; if alone, before the mirror. Either way, try to put some feeling into it, and get your body involved, especially your arms.

Now look at this other passage below. It's one of the high points of a long poem by William Wordsworth (1770-1850) titled *The Prelude* in which he spoke of crossing the Alps on foot as a young man:

....The immeasurable height
Of woods decaying, never to be decayed,
The stationary blasts of waterfalls,
And in the narrow rent at every turn
Winds thwarting winds, bewildered and forlorn,
The torrents shooting from the clear blue sky,
The rocks that muttered close upon our ears,
Black drizzling crags that spake by the way-side

As if a voice were in them, the sick sight
And giddy prospect of the raving stream,
The unfettered clouds and region of the Heavens,
Tumult and peace, the darkness and the light–
Were all like workings of one mind, the features
Of the same face, blossoms upon one tree;
Characters of the great Apocalypse,
The types and symbols of Eternity,
Of first, and last, and midst, and without end.

This passage consists of a single statement or sentence. Do the same thing with it: read it through to yourself for the sense, and then again aloud to hear how it sounds.

***Exercise** 3*

Analyze each passage stylistically on the basis of its vocabulary.

Which passage do you identify with more? Here's another question, a sneaky one: if you had a choice, which poem would you like to read more of? Bear in mind that this is not a test, nor is your answer cast in cement. Also, your decision should not be made on the basis of your ease of understanding.

***Exercise** 4*

I don't suppose you could write a short piece, in prose or verse, imitating the passage you identify with, could you?

The following excerpts from poems are both closer to home, so to speak, in that they were both written closer to us in time:

I heard a Fly buzz – when I died –
The Stillness – in the Room
Was like the Stillness in the Air
Between the Heaves of Storm –

The Eyes around – had wrung them dry –
And Breaths were gathering firm
For that last Onset – when the King
Be witnessed – in the Room –

From Emily Dickinson, "I Heard a Fly Buzz"

> Let us go then, you and I,
> When the evening is spread out against the sky
> Like a patient etherised upon a table;
> Let us go, through certain half-deserted streets,
> The muttering retreats
> Of restless nights in one-night cheap hotels
> And sawdust restaurants with oyster-shells:
> Streets that follow like a tedious argument
> Of insidious intent
> To lead you to an overwhelming question ...
> Oh, do not ask, "What is it?"
> Let us go and make our visit.
>
> From T. S. Eliot, "The Love Song of J. Alfred Prufrock"

As with the passages by Milton and Wordsworth, read through each one silently to yourself for the sense, then do so aloud.

Exercise 5

Analyze each passage for its vocabulary.

Again let me ask: do you lean more toward Dickinson or Eliot stylistically? And again let me sneakily inquire: which poem would you like to read more of?

Exercise 6

How about it, can you write a short piece, in verse or prose, imitating the one you lean toward? I dare you!

You can almost guess what's coming next, yes?

Exercise 7

Take something you've written recently. A poem is best, but if you don't have one or don't want to use one, choose something else, like an entry from a diary. Just make sure that it's not too short or too long; around fifty words is best. Analyze it stylistically just as you did the paragraph by Santayana and my informal and colloquial renderings of it in Exercise 1, that is, for its vocabulary, sentence length, and sentence complexity. If you feel squeamish about doing this and you're in a friendly group, do exchange your "specimen" with someone else.

So where does your piece stand stylistically. If it's informal, in which direction does it lean?

Taking Stock

In school textbooks, reviews of material covered in a chapter are usually pro forma; they're there because they've got to be there. This one, on the other hand, has a genuine purpose; I'm suggesting that you do what follows so as to learn more, poetically speaking, about who you are, where you're heading, and what your next stop or stops along the way might be.

Your first step is that first question I asked: For whom do you want to write or are you trying to write? If you were able to answer it, carefully read over what you wrote and adjust it in terms of content and style. In fact, consider going over it until it says exactly what you want it to in the way you want it to, and if it turns out you're still not altogether satisfied with it, consider, possibly, rewriting it from scratch. Of course, if you weren't able to answer it earlier, now's the time to take another whack at it. But if it still doesn't come, not to worry; it will, sooner or later.

Now do the same with regard to your statement about the potential subject matter of your poetry. That is, tidy it up or possibly do it over.

Also to be examined anew by you are your preferences with respect to the passages by John Milton and William Wordsworth, and Emily Dickinson and T. S. Eliot. Are they really so, or do you want to reconsider?

Next, return to your stylistic analysis of a piece of writing by yourself. Meditate on that analysis long and hard in the light of your statements regarding whom you are writing for or are trying to write for and your preferred subject matter, and your preferences with respect to Milton and Wordsworth and Emily Dickinson and Eliot.

Finally, look at all five items (or as many as you have) together as a single statement. It may not seem like much at first. But clearly you're further along toward defining yourself as a poet than you were at the beginning of this chapter, wouldn't you say? It's a start.

And now, how about it, let's take some time out for a little celebration!

Exercise 8

Various folks in your group or you alone should get hold of the following items: an ordinary candle and something to stick it on, like an old saucer; a red rose and a water-filled receptacle for it, like a cream-pitcher; a decent (but not necessarily expensive) bottle of red wine and a glass or glasses. Open the wine and let it stand for a bit, put the rose in the water, and light the candle. Finally, when the wine's aired out, you or someone should pour, and either everyone should clink or you should salute yourself in your mirror. Sip.

P. S. If you'd rather hold off on celebrating until the end of the chapter or even of the book, fine and good. Just be aware that there'll be other occasions for libations like this along the way.

The English poet Samuel Taylor Coleridge claimed that his truly magnificent poem "Kubla Khan" was unfinished. According to his account, the whole thing came to him in a dream and he was rudely torn from writing it all down by the sudden appearance of a visitor, hence his subtitling it *A Vision in a Dream. A Fragment.* I for one think that Coleridge was full of beans (to put it politely), but it really doesn't matter one way or another for our purposes here. What I do want to emphasize is that while poems may write or seem to write themselves in your head, setting them down so that you and others can read them requires that you have a special place to work and a writing implement and something to use it on that belong to you and you alone, plus a few books on a shelf or just piled up near at hand that you may need or want to consult or just browse through from time to time.

Your Special Place

Ideally there should be somewhere in particular where you live, no matter how small and humble, to do your serious composing in, and it should be associated in your mind as such. A whole room would be ideal, but where conditions are cramped, a part of one, like a corner, will do or have to do. If you live with someone, Your Place should be respected as such — indeed, considered Holy Ground, in other words, should be off limits.

It goes without saying that Your Place should contain some kind of table to sit at and write on and a comfortable chair, with decent lighting over them. In a pinch, any old thing like a kitchen or dining-room table can serve as a desk. Failing these, an easy chair with a board across its arms or just a clipboard in your hand or on your crossed knees can do the trick, as can a bed, though the latter can lead to perpetual balancing acts if you're not accustomed to working in or on one.

If it's impossible to establish such a Place where you live, your best alternative will probably turn out to be a library, especially one with cozy nooks and chairs that don't have the feel of electric chairs. The library of a nearby college or university would be ideal because of their extended hours, and some offer annual user's cards in exchange for a donation. But, of course, one can't become overly attached to a particular spot in a library, as it might not always be available, so best to have a number of alternative spots built into your mind-set of Your Place.

If you live where it's warm all year round, somewhere outdoors, like a park bench, is also possible. A big advantage is that you can sit for a while, then walk, then sit again. Try this sort of thing if you've never done so before, but take your time when you walk — I mean, move along slowly so that your creative juices can flow unimpeded by the hard breathing and muscle fatigue that come with physical exertion. A painter at an art colony I was once in residence at remarked that you can always tell poets from a distance because they stroll, whereas other kinds of writers, composers, and visual artists like himself always seem to be in a big hurry.

While we're on the subject, strolls are best taken alone, but if you've got a special friend who is also a poet with whom you'd like to share your walks, by all means do so. You never can tell what might come of it. While the composition of poetry is generally considered a solo activity, there've been a number of notable exceptions. For instance, William Wordsworth (1770-1850) and his friend Samuel Taylor Coleridge (1772-1834) hiked together in their mid-twenties, and the fruits of their jaunts were published in *The Lyrical Ballads,* which included two of their greatest works, Wordsworth's very moving ode "Tintern Abbey" and Coleridge's ballad-like tale of crime and punishment "The Rime of the Ancient Mariner."

Whatever you do, be sure that Your Place is quiet; I can't emphasize this enough. You need to be fully in touch with your own sounds and rhythms, and in order to do so, you need to be insulated from background noise, especially cheap commercial music with a steady beat, even if you have a predilection for it or think that it helps you. Imagine silence as the equivalent of an astronaut's spacesuit when he or she's up there.

I couldn't resist sounding out our three guest poets about their special places. Interestingly, Ruth's specifications as to place were particularly bound up with her mode of composition:

> I prefer to work at a table rather than on my lap or the arm of a chair; for me that is the best position, when I can be comfortable enough to forget my body and let my mind follow the inspiration of the emerging poem wherever it leads.
>
> It doesn't matter too much which table, as long as I have a reasonable chair and a flat surface to lay my papers or notebook on — usually separate sheets of paper; if I suddenly realise that what I am writing in my notebook has the possibility to become a poem, I copy out the "germ" lines onto a sheet of paper, rather than continue working in the notebook. (The first few drafts of a poem are written like that — mostly with pen and ink, though sometimes with pencil. At a later stage I type it onto my computer, and then keep printing it out, making alterations by hand, printing again, etc., etc. — a process which can continue for days or weeks or months.)
>
> But my desk, in my study, is the best place, because it is where I do most work, the room is isolated and quiet, etc. The desk is a very nice piece of furniture, nineteenth century if not older, with a dark leather top and a long drawer underneath, and four drawers on each side. I was able to buy it for far less than its value, I'm sure, from a friend who was moving abroad.
>
> Of course I have worked at many other tables and desks in different circumstances, but I do like to have one special place to work, so when I am at home, that is where it is.

Wouldn't you know it, Nina was, predictably, full of surprises, pleasant ones:

> Whenever I get serious about working on a poem, I do so wherever I happen to be at that particular moment! Thus it could happen on a train, on a plane, in the subway, between meals, at sunset, in town, out in the country, anywhere — no matter how inconvenient, uncomfortable, unpromising the site may be — whenever I have a moment to myself in this hectic life. However, curiously enough, I never actually work on it at a desk, but rather on a couch!

And Jeffrey begins with a longing for a better place but then, quixotically, goes on to particularize about each and every item in the one he has:

> I wish I had a small studio to escape to, since my study often serves as a guest room. Space in Paris, as in NYC, is precious.
>
> It is remarkable how ritualistic poets are, some writing on paper scraps at a kitchen table and others composing in public places like Wendy's. When I am seriously at work, I read poetry before falling asleep and then get up before dawn and begin writing at a small wooden desk in a corner of our cramped Paris apartment. It is the only private space available to me. The walls there are cluttered with photographs, paintings, and prints while the surface of the desk around my computer has a silver birth cup holding pens and pencils, a tortoise shell laden with coral from the Great Barrier Reef, a plastic box full of sand from the Sahara, a jar with volcanic flakes that look like gunpowder, and finally, a stamp-size picture of my first dog. I have a window that looks out on a towering chestnut tree and the neighboring apartments in the courtyard, all mercifully quiet. By lunchtime, I am invariably required to free myself from a semicircle of poetry and reference books that seem to pile themselves up around me.

Writing Implements

I recommend that you use a pen rather than a pencil. The writing from both has a tendency to smudge, but with pencils one has the added burden of keeping them sharpened or having a supply of lead forever on hand and within easy reach. I myself prefer ballpoint pens, but I choose mine with extreme care, making sure that I can write with them lying down and standing up as well as sitting, and that they'll glide — and I mean glide! — across the paper without my having to bear down. I buy my pens in large quantities and distribute some not only on and in my desk but also beside my bed, in my car, and even in the kitchen and bathroom.

Not surprisingly, our poets have characteristic views about these matters. Ruth, for instance, is as particular about her writing implement as she was about her space:

> I usually write by pen — a Rotring Artpen (a sort of fountain pen, but in shape like an old "dip pen" usually used for drawing). If there's no choice, I'll use an ordinary ballpoint pen, though I prefer a Papermate "Non-stop" pencil.

As with her spatial requirements, Nina is absolutely unparticular about her writing implement:

> When working on a poem, I write with whatever implement is at hand — pen, pencil, or chalk if necessary! If it's a pen, naturally I'd prefer a good fountain pen. But sometimes I just write with them in my mind as I imagine them.

Jeffrey prefers to use a computer keyboard for a perfectly understandable reason:

> Typing provides a formality or visual concretion to my generally chaotic thinking and moods. My handwriting, which is disturbingly bad, only seems to enhance chaos.

Paper

While working on his famous Ninth Symphony late one night, Beethoven is said to have run out of paper and continued making musical notes on the white window sill of his study, much to the annoyance of his housekeeper the next morning. A word to the wise, always have a goodly supply of whatever paper you use on hand.

For making notes, I myself prefer a stenopad rather than a loose-leaf binder because it's easily packable in anything. Whenever I begin in a new pad, I put the date with a hyphen on the cover, and when I reach the last page, I add that day's date after the hyphen. For drafts of works in progress, I use the blank sides of old 8 ½ x 11-inch sheets, which I fold sideways so they are the same size as the stenopad. From time to time I cut out a passage from one of those sheets and staple it onto a blank page of my current stenopad. I have a few clipboards of that size, which come in handy for both the folded sheets and the pad when I'm working in bed.

Whatever size notebook and loose sheets you decide to use, there's one cardinal rule I urge you to follow: always write on one side of the sheet only! The reason should be apparent at once: if you destroy a page with writing on both sides, you might unintentionally do away with something precious and irreplaceable on the second side.

When it comes to paper, Ruth, predictably, prefers:

> Single sheets much more than a notebook. A poem may arise from a notebook entry — but as soon as I am aware this is likely to happen, I move to sheets of paper.

Although of the same generation as Ruth, Nina went to the other extreme, leaving one to wonder to what extent she was influenced by her experiences in Romania during the Cold War era:

> Whatever paper is at hand — single sheets, pages of a notebook, scrap paper, backs of envelopes, even paper napkins.

Concerning his drafts on the computer screen and use of paper, Jeffrey explained:

> Before the computer was available, I would type drafts on single sheets of paper, often replacing a whole sheet when making even small changes. I had a low tolerance for too many revisions on a draft page and was shamefully wasteful. Fortunately, with the computer, it is very easy to conserve drafts, and I will only from time to time print a poem to read over and pencil in the corrections to be made.

Reference Books

You should own a small collection of such books and keep them within reach near Your Place so you don't go crazy searching for one of them at some critical moment. Be sure to consult my bibliography for specific titles and publication data where I don't supply any below.

First and foremost, you need a *dictionary,* to check on both the meanings of words and their spelling. I recommend a standard hard-covered desk dictionary such as college students use, which you can usually find in any chain bookstore. You don't need the latest version or even a brand-new one, so if you happen to come upon an older one or a used one, or both, that is in good condition and the price is right, go for it. If you have some particular interest in the history of words, you might consider also acquiring a copy of the shorter version of the *Oxford English Dictionary,* commonly known as the OED.

Roget's Thesaurus, which provides formidable lists of synonyms, could prove to be a good supplement to your dictionary, especially when you're trying to find the right word that is also right-sounding. If rhyming is your thing, you should acquire a rhyming dictionary as well, and there are any number of them on the market. Also possibly useful is a book that deals with correct usage, and at the very least that means Strunk and White's *Elements of Style.* The *sine qua non* is Fowler's *Modern English Usage,* and there's an American version of it by Margaret Nicholson.

If you're interested in literary terminology and the like, may I recommend Harmon and Holman's *Handbook to Literature* and Corbett and Connors's *Classical Rhetoric for the Modern Student.* There are a number of other works dealing with poetic terminology alone, the best of which seem to be Paul Fussell's *Poetic Meter and Poetic Form* and Joseph Malof's *Manual of English Meters.*

Your little library of essential books should also include at least one anthology of poetry that goes back to Day One, like the Norton; this work, it should be understood, is not for reading from cover to cover but for browsing through as you would the shelves of a bookstore or a library. You might feel that you should have an anthology of contemporary poetry as a supplement to this, but be forewarned: "contemporary" is a relative term and, besides being rife with biases, such works quickly become outdated. To your anthology or anthologies might be added several volumes by your favorite poet or poets, and it wouldn't hurt to have others by some of our great writers of lyrical prose, especially those of the recent past like Thomas Wolfe and Marcel Proust.

I have promised a certain someone that I would here add another "plug" for my own work, *Klytaimnestra Who Stayed at Home,* which I do with extreme humility.

Our Guest Poets

Photo by David Sillitoe

RUTH FAINLIGHT was born in New York in 1931. Her mother came from the eastern borders of the Austro-Hungarian Empire; her father was English. Both he and her younger brother Harry were also poets. When Ruth was five, the family moved to London; with the outbreak of World War II, she returned to New York with her mother and brother. She returned to London for good when she was fifteen, and her education was completed at the Birmingham and Brighton Colleges of Art. She is married to English writer Allan Sillitoe, and they have two children and six grandchildren.

Ruth began writing poetry when she was five or six years old. She has thirteen books of poetry to her credit. Individual poems have been included in numerous anthologies, and two books have appeared in French and Portuguese translations. She was Poet in Residence at Vanderbilt University in 1985 and 1990, and the recipient of the Cholmondeley Award for Poetry in 1994.

Ruth's other credits include translations of two books of the works of Portuguese poet Sophia de Mello Breyner and another of Lope de Vega's play *All Citizens Are Soldiers* with Alan Sillitoe; two collections of short stories; and libretti for two chamber operas, *The Dancer Hotoke* by Erika Fox, which was nominated for the Lawrence Olivier Award, and *The European Story* by Geoffrey Alvarez, and for the TV opera *War Cries* by Robert Jan Stips.

Ruth and I met on Majorca in 1955; we were both writers and around the same age and instantly became friends and mutual admirers of one another's work. Because the tone of her poems seems matter-of-fact, readers sometimes miss their passion and compassion to say nothing of their artistry.

One of my favorite poems by her is titled "Love-Feast":

> Sulphur-yellow mushrooms like unlaid, unshelled eggs
> inside a chicken's stomach when my mother cleaned it.
> This morning, mushrooms on the lawn made me remember.
> Bright as dew on the grass and silver with air-bubbles,
> a stream of water splashed from the dull brass tap against
> the side of the sink and over her red-chilled fingers when she
> opened the carcase and laughed to show me how some were
> almost
> ready — yolks only needing their coating of lime and mucus,
> while others were still half-formed, small as pearls or seeds.
>
> Always, once the chicken was plucked and quartered and
> boiling,
> my mother would take those eggs, marked with twisting coils of
> crimson threads like bloodshot eyes, and the liver put aside
> on the draining-board in a chipped old china saucer, and fry
> them
> with an onion to make our private treat. In the steamy
> kitchen, the two of us would eat, and love each other.

Photo by Mihai Cucu

NINA CASSIAN was born in 1924 in rural Romania, and at age eleven, she moved with her family to Bucharest, where she attended the *gymnasium* and then went on to study music at the Conservatory and liberal arts and philology at the University. She was married to Romanian writers Vladimir Colin and A. I. Stefanescu. In 1985, she came to the United States as a Visiting Professor and sought political asylum here; she is currently married to American writer and actor Maurice Edwards.

Nina thinks of herself as a poet and a composer. Her first poem dates from her fifth year, and she now has to her credit fifteen books of poetry in her native Romanian, five of which have appeared in English translation. A sixth, *Take My Word for It*, consists largely of poems written in English. Nina has been the recipient of many prizes in Romania; here in the United States, she has received the New York

Public Library Lion Literary Award and was recently honored by the Poetry Society of America.

Nina's other literary works include three novels and five children's books. She has translated Shakespeare, Molière, Brecht, and many others into Romanian. Her musical compositions have been performed extensively in Romania.

I particularly like and relate to her poem "Night Must Fall":

> I was walking one evening on a country road.
> It was a dry spring without fragrance,
> and my footsteps were muffled by the dust.
> Such strange scenery! I said to myself, watching
> the motionless branches, the earth
> still unruffled by even the premonition of grass.
> The light was calm.
>
> Suddenly on the horizon there appeared
> a form: gross, heavy, tenacious.
> Was it a cloud shaped like a camel?
> I asked an invisible Polonius.
> When the form drew nearer –
> it was an ox.
> It was a quiet ox
> sinking its silent hooves in the dust,
> with its skin the color of stone,
> with its bleached symmetrical horns,
> with its square forehead.
>
> I hoped for an instant – only for an instant –
> that I was wrong, that I would make out
> the reassuringly full maternal udders
> or else recognize the virile muscular neck
> of a bull. But it was useless.
> It was only a neutered, passionless ox.
>
> He stopped in front of me. He looked at me –
> the wise white ox.
> The falling evening framed the countryside.
> I tried to avoid that messenger of solitude
> by walking on through the dust.
> But turning after me, with its indifferent stare,
> serene death followed.
>
> Translated by Dana Gioia

Photo by Mary Weiss

JEFFREY GREENE was born in Wilton, Connecticut in 1952. His mother, Gretchen née Van Blaricom, an eighth-grade dropout, became a senior research associate at Yale; his father, J. Edward Greene, and Jeffrey's older brother Wayne are both photographers. Jeffrey received a B.A. from Goddard College and an M.F.A. in creative writing from the University of Iowa, where he studied under Donald Justice. He went on to earn a Ph.D. from the University of Houston and after teaching briefly in Hartford, moved to Paris, where he now lives with his wife, Mary Weiss, a molecular biologist.

Jeffrey began writing poetry at age fifteen, and a number of his poems were accepted and published in little mags when he was in his early twenties. His first volume of poems, *To the Left of the Worshiper*, was published in 1991. His second volume, *American Spirituals*, won the 1998 Samuel French Morse Prize. He is also a winner of the Discover / The Nation Award and the Randall Jarrell prize. His poems have appeared in *The New Yorker*, *Parnassus*, *Boulevard*, *Ploughshares*, and many other journals and anthologies.

Jeffrey's father and I are first-cousins on our mothers' sides. I remember him as a spirited, fun-loving little boy with a vivid imagination and mind of his own.

One poem of his that has stuck in my mind for ever so long is titled "La Cluza":

Evening is a shift in weight.
Mountains grow harder.
Skiers, at last, have only to descend
on final runs.
They leave so little proof
of paths behind them,
and then all the wheeling lifts
come to a halt.
After the day on the deck
and the hot wine,
we approach the village directly
and climb the steep wooden stairs
to our room.
We make love still
in our white sweaters.
Then that too is over.
Beyond the small window
the village is beautiful.
Even the Luftwaffe
flew here harmlessly,
the planes racing up the pass
to climb the slopes
where ground soldiers
dressed in white
hardened into snow-covered bushes.

Words, words, words

When I was a child, my friends and I used to taunt one another with sayings like "Sticks and stones can break my bones, but words will never harm me!" But as we all well know, this isn't so. Indeed, the mere fact that such sayings existed shows how very potent words can be. Without a doubt, words make the greater world go round, and where poetry is concerned, a healthy command of them, meaning knowing how to choose and use them with a master's hand — and even, as we shall see, abuse them! — is absolutely essential.

But there's more to it than that. You as a poet or a potential poet have to be fond of words, indeed have to be mad about them, even at times drunk with them, or at least find them irresistibly delicious, as is the case with practicing poets, or at least some of them.

On the other hand, too much of a good thing can present a problem, too. You have to take care not to swing so far the other way with words as to lose sight of what you're saying or want to say. Yes, being in love with them to such an extent is as fraught with danger as being mentally constipated and declaring, I have enough words, I don't need any more.

The Evocative Power of Words

Regardless of how much or little schooling we've had, all of us humans share the ability to evoke vivid and powerful feelings in people around us with words — indeed, oftentimes with just a few words, and sometimes with only a single one. Think of your own knee-jerk reaction if someone walking behind you on a street should suddenly yell "Watch out !" or "Help!" Or if, where you least expect it, you should come upon a sign in big, bold lettering reading "Danger!" or "Keep out!" or even "Beware of Dog!" A scream-headline in a newspaper can have the same effect — "Man Bites Dog!"

Not to be forgotten are passwords, once powerful for getting one into a speakeasy or a meeting of a secret society and now all important for protecting our privacy in cyberspace. And think of the effect that mantras and other devotional words, like "amen," have on us, to say nothing of incantations, like a stage magician's "Abracadabra!" as he waves an ordinary conductor's baton, which he calls a "wand," over a seemingly ordinary black top hat.

Also highly effective is our hoard of naughty words to chew folks out with, like the "F"-word. Nothing is more intimidating when enunciated once or even twice in a loud voice with a belligerent look. But after that, it becomes utterly boring, like who cares.

Exercise 1

I'm sure that you have your very own favorite evocative word or phrase, like everyone else, no? Write it down and read it aloud — with a matching look on your face. If you're alone, try doing it before the good old bathroom mirror.

Equally potent — indeed, one of our uniquely human activities — is our giving names to things, whether it be people, like a new baby, or places, like a new home, or things like a car. By naming someone or a thing, we delineate or define it and thus distinguish it from all others of a like nature, and in a rarefied sense we thereby exercise a kind of control over it. Nicknames, like "Slim" and "Whitey," refine what has already been defined. Interestingly, according to the Bible, one of God's first activities after the Creation was to name things, beginning with "day" and "night," and Adam, created in his image, in turn gave names to "all the cattle, and to the fowl of the air, and to every beast of the field."

Exercise 2

Look about you and find something that needs a name or a new name. Give it one, a good one, or rename it and then address that thing by its new name and give it a little lecture. Oh, what a power trip, no?

Short, pithy statements can also turn out to be real point makers. Consider "He that troubleth his own house shall inherit the wind" from the *Book of Proverbs* in the Bible. My favorite is "Damn braces, bless relaxes" from the "Proverbs of Hell" by William Blake (1757-1823). Proverb-like statements in speeches can be extremely effective in politics, helping people with a common cause to bond together and bury differences. Think of the very real "This day shall live in infamy!" that President Franklin Delano Roosevelt pronounced in a speech before Congress on the day after the Japanese attack on Pearl Harbor.

Exercise 3

Find a statement to your liking in the ***Book of Proverbs*** *or Blake's "Proverbs of Hell" (which you'll find in his* ***Marriage of Heaven and Hell****). Say it aloud to your partners in crime or to yourself you know where.*

Slogans are short, catchy statements that are given in the form of commands urging action of some kind. They are the stock-in-trade of political groups and business enterprises. "Bring it on!" and "Stop the War!" are all too familiar to us from recent times.

Exercise 4

Come up with a slogan for your group or class if you're in one and vote on the best one. If you're alone, make up a slogan for yourself that relates to your personal course of study based on this book.

Mottoes are short written statements that pertain to an organization and have been selected and adopted to define it and inspire loyalty and camaraderie in its membership. "In God We Trust," which appears on our coins, is a good example. There's a certain snob appeal in devising mottoes in other languages, like Latin or French. Let "E Pluribus Unum" (one out of many), which also appears on our coins, and "Semper Fidelis" (always faithful), watchword of our Marine Corps, serve as examples.

Exercise 5

Devise a motto for your group and vote on the best one, or if you're alone come up with a motto for yourself with respect to your self-devised course of study based on this book. For more fun, cast your motto in Latin or French — or fractured Latin or French, if you don't know either.

Repetitions of words and/or sounds can add real spice to proverbs, slogans, and mottoes. Consider Franklin Delano Roosevelt's other famous pronouncement "We have nothing to fear but fear itself," and such commonplaces as "Once a thief, always a thief" and "A stitch in time saves nine," to say nothing of "Better dead than red" and "We're here, we're queer." We'll be covering *sound repetitions* of all kinds in chapter four. Meanwhile:

Exercise 6

Take your slogan or motto of Exercises 4 and 5 or make up a new one, and give it that added edge with a little jingle. This can be great fun, but if you can't hack it, don't sweat it. Just move on or, if you're in a class or with friends, borrow a tasty tidbit from someone else.

Sound-repetitions in speeches, particularly political ones, can also be effective, making them almost proverb- or slogan-like. The opening sentence of Abraham Lincoln's Gettysburg Address immediately comes to mind: "Four score and seven years ago our fathers brought forth, upon this continent, a new nation, conceived in Liberty, and dedicated to the proposition that all men are created equal." What American wouldn't recognize it? Why would we? What in particular helps to make it memorable? The answer: the repeating hard *c*'s plus *d*'s, *e*'s, *f*'s, *l*'s, *n*'s, *p*'s, *r*'s, and *s*'s.

Exercise 7

Read Lincoln's sentence aloud several times, slowly, to see how these work for yourself.

Also memorable in this respect is the slogan-like refrain that Shakespeare put in the mouth of Mark Antony when he was giving forth with his moving funeral oration for Caesar in *Julius Caesar:*

> Friends, Romans, countrymen, lend me your ears.
> I come to bury Caesar, not to praise him.
> The evil that men do lives after them;
> The good is oft interred with their bones.
> So let it be with Caesar. The noble Brutus
> Hath told you Caesar was ambitious.
> If it were so, it was a grievous fault,

And grievously hath Caesar answer'd it.
Here, under leave of Brutus and the rest —
For Brutus is an honorable man;
So are they all, all honorable men —
Come I to speak in Caesar's funeral.
He was my friend, faithful and just to me;
But Brutus says he was ambitious,
And Brutus is an honorable man.
He hath brought many captives home to Rome,
Whose ransoms did the general coffers fill.
Did this in Caesar seem ambitious?
When that the poor have cried, Caesar hath wept;
Ambition should be made of sterner stuff.
Yet Brutus says he was ambitious,
And Brutus is an honorable man.
You all did see that on the Lupercal
I thrice presented him a kingly crown,
Which he did thrice refuse. Was this ambition?
Yet Brutus says he was ambitious,
And, sure, he is an honorable man.
I speak not to disprove what Brutus spoke,
But here I am to speak what I do know.
You all did love him once, not without cause.
What cause withholds you then, to mourn for him?
O judgment! Thou art fled to brutish beasts,
And men have lost their reason. Bear with me;
My heart is in the coffin there with Caesar,
And I must pause till it come back to me. (*Italics mine.*)

Of course, since Brutus was the leader of Caesar's assassins, Mark Antony means just the opposite, doesn't he?

Exercise 8

Read this speech aloud. If you're in a group or class, the most effective way of doing this for our purposes here is to have one person read the arguments, the other the refrains. If you're alone, try different voices, as if you are two different people.

Let me not fail to mention here the evocative power of spoken prayer. Indeed, can anything be more moving, even to one who isn't religious, than the sight of a whole congregation repeating "Our Father who art in Heaven, Hallowed be Thy name" with bowed heads? Here's a piece of food for thought: does anyone know what *amen* means?

Of course, as you poets or poets in the making know or will come to know, words can evoke far subtler feelings besides extremely positive or negative ones. A good example is the phrase "sylvan Wye," which occurs in William Wordsworth's celebrated ode "Tintern Abbey." The word "sylvan" means "woodsy" in case you didn't know, but unlike plain old "woodsy," Wordsworth's "sylvan" conjures up a whole range of delightful forest sights, sounds, and smells.

Exercise 9

Don't take my word for it. Pronounce "O sylvan Wye" aloud and then follow it with "O woodsy Wye."

Did you hear the difference? It's hard to believe that you wouldn't. I should add here that I seem to remember a guy I once knew who was so in love with Wordsworth's phrase that he named his child Sylvan Wye. What can one say? It takes all kinds, yes? Be that as it may, it's now time to become a trifle more abstract (and physical) and do your stuff.

Exercise 10

Write down each of the following words: cannibal, restitution, scarecrow, soporific, torrential, obtuse, barleycorn, protrude. Slowly and clearly pronounce each one aloud — and act it out! By which I mean, pronounce it with arm movements and other kinds of body language.

Ooh La-La! How English Is & Got that Way

When it comes to richness, English has to be unique among languages. If you're a native speaker, you're indeed lucky. If you're also aware of its richness, you're more fortunate yet. And if you can, in addition, tap into that richness with ease and use it unselfconsciously, count yourself a king or queen among communicators.

How did English get to be like it is, you may be wondering? Let me give you a quick-and-dirty sketch. In the fifth and sixth centuries A.D., three Germanic tribes called the Angles, Saxons, and Jutes invaded England and displaced the native folk, who were Celtic. It wasn't long before the dialect of German spoken by the Saxons predominated, and eventually it changed to such an extent as to become a separate language, which is referred to nowadays as Old English. Like the Old High German of the Saxons — and indeed like German today — Old English was heavily inflected; that is, every noun had a gender — masculine, feminine, or neuter — along with gender-markers, and four cases with distinctive case-markers, and the adjectives followed suit. Further, verbs were either strong or weak, indeed as they've remained until today, being either of the sing-sang-sung or walk-walked-walked variety.

So that you can see what I mean, here's a hymn in Old English written by a seventh-century monk named Caedmon, along with an interlinear translation, which you'll observe at once is absolutely necessary:

Nū wē sculan herian heofonrīces Weard
(Now we shall praise Heaven-kingdom's guardian,)

Metodes mihte ond his mōdgeþonc
(*God's power and His understanding,*)

weorc Wuldorfæder, swā hē wundra gehwæs
(*work of the Glory-Father as He of each wonder,*)

ēce Dryhten, ord onstealde.
(the eternal Lord the foundation laid.)

He ærest gescēop eorðan bearnum
(*He first created for men's children*)

heofon tō hrōfe, hālig Scyppend;
(*Heaven for a roof holy Creator;*)

ðā middongeard moncynnes Weard,
(*the middle earth mankind's guardian,*)

ēce Dryhten æfter tēode
(*the eternal Lord after made*)

fīrum foldan Frēa ælmihtig.
(*for men, the earth Ruler almighty.*)

It's important to note for future reference that all polysyllabic words were accented on the first syllable, indeed as is still, by and large, the case with German today.

Exercise 11

How many words in this passage are still in our language, do you imagine? Count them up and compare notes with someone if you're in a group or class.

In 1066, the English were beset by Norman-French invaders and defeated at the celebrated Battle of Hastings. Norman kings held sway in England for the next two hundred years, and French — first Norman French, then Parisian French — became the language of court and city, while English hung on in the backwaters, where it was much modified. Chaucer (ca. 1343-1400) spoke French and read Latin, the language of learning and the Church, but he wrote his universally celebrated work *The Canterbury Tales* in the English of his day (which we today refer to as Middle English). Here are the opening six lines of his Prologue to that work. Note how much less "foreign" it looks than the selection from *Caedmon's Hymn* above:

Whan that Aprill with his shoures soote *sweet*
The droghte of March hath perced to the roote,
And bathed every veyne in swich licour *such / liquid*
Of which vertu engendred is the flour;

Whan Zephirus eek with his sweete breeth *also*
Inspired hath in every holt and heeth.... *grove / field*

Exercise 12

How many words are there in it of French origin?

Here is the answer; don't peek, okay?

Seven: perced, veyne, licour, vertu, engendred, flour, inspired.

The Renaissance began reaching England from Italy via France in the sixteenth century. Because it brought with it a renewed interest in Greek and Roman antiquity, a large number of Latin words, along with some from Greek, were imported into English; at the same time, many of the old Middle English forms fell into disuse. The result was a verbally richer and more flexible version of English, which we today refer to as Early Modern English. These lines from Shakespeare's *Macbeth*, with quite a few words of Latin origin, pretty much tell the story:

Canst thou not minister to a mind diseas'd,
Pluck from the memory a rooted sorrow,
Raze out the written troubles of the brain
And with some sweet oblivious antidote
Cleanse the stuff'd bosom of that perilous stuff
Which weighs upon the heart?

Exercise 13

Get hold of your dictionary and look up each word of two syllables or more to see which ones are of Latin origin.

In case you're too lazy or have other troubles, here are the answers:

There are 13 in all: minister, diseas'd, memory, sorrow, raze, written, troubles, brain, oblivious, antidote, cleanse, bosom, perilous

The end result of all that importation — first from French and then from Latin and Greek — is that we now have a language abounding in synonyms, sounds, and rhythms, and a built-in receptivity to new ones. We shall be looking more closely at sounds and rhythms in chapters four and five. Where synonyms are concerned, it's important to note that they allows us to fine-tune both our spoken and written utterances according to the audiences they're intended for. To put it more precisely, we have a general vocabulary for use in everyday situations, a collection of Latinate words that we hold in readiness for more formal situations, and another collection of colloquialisms and slang that we can trot out for chats with relatives and friends. In practical terms, we're likely to say "I would like to buy a stove" to a salesperson at a store, while to someone at a fancy store, we'd announce "I am interested in purchasing a replacement for my stove," and to a parent or spouse, confide "I'd like to get a new stove."

It seems that we're back to the three levels of style again, aren't we? Fancy that! But that's only part of the story where the richness of English is concerned. Also of note is that, because of all the French, Latin, and Greek accretions, we're blessed with an unusually large number of alternatives for expressing many ordinary ideas — indeed, larger than is to be found in any other language on Earth, I bet. Consider, for instance, the verb "to divide" with its meaning of "to render in parts." *Roget's Thesaurus* lists the following sets of synonyms:

– *sunder, subdivide, sever, dissever, cut, chop, saw, snip, nip, cleave, rive, rend, rip, split, splinter, chip, crack, snap, break, tear, burst*
– *wrench, rupture, hack, hew, slash, slice, carve, quarter, dissect, anatomize*
– *partition, parcel.*

Now I ask you, isn't that mind-blowing?

Exercise 14

Just for the fun of it, why not take a verb from each category of synonyms and use it in a sentence of your own — but not just any old sentence, I mean a good one.

One single hop, skip, and a jump lands us very close to composing, doesn't it?

Exercise 15

How many synonyms for the following can you come up with off the top of your head: "make love," "old man," "old woman," "small," "to shoot," "girl," "husband," "businessman," "beautiful," "ugly," "shy," "amusing," "dead man," "dog," "wife," "flower"? Think of those big (learned) words as well as teeny simple ones. P. S. If you get stuck somewhere, I guess it's okay to take a peek in your **Thesaurus** *you know, cheat a little. After all, what's it on your bookshelf for anyway?*

You can almost guess what's coming next.

Exercise 16

Take two of your synonyms and use them in stylistically appropriate sentences. Yes, of course, write them down!

One truly remarkable thing about present-day English is that in spite of its humongous vocabulary and wide variety of ways of saying things, it's still open — wide-open as other languages like French are not — to foreign imports. To give an example, not long ago, English acquired the German word *angst.* Since we English-speakers already had "anxiety" (to say nothing of a variety of related ills), why we needed it is anybody's guess. But acquire it we did, and that was that. (Amusingly, the Germans, in their turn, adopted our noun "stress" and went so far as to create the adjective *gestresst* from it, meaning "all stressed out.")

Exercise 17

Want to have some real fun? Get hold of someone who is foreign-born, like a friend or fellow student or maybe a neighbor or shopkeeper, and ferret out a word in his or her language that's really evocative! Adapt it into your everyday vocabulary and see if you can pass it on to others <g>.

Another remarkable feature of English is the variety of its verbal forms, which we as native speakers take for granted almost from the time we're born and which foreigners all too often wearily shake their heads at. Consider, for instance, the verb "to phone":

one phones
one is phoning
one phoned
one was phoning
one has phoned
one has been phoning
one has been phoned
one had phoned
one had been phoned
one had been phoning
one will phone
one will be phoning
one will have phoned
one will have been phoned
one will have been phoning
one would phone
one would be phoning
one would have phoned
one would have been phoned
one would have been phoning
one should phone
one should have phoned
one should have been phoned
one may phone
one may be phoning
one may have phoned
one may have been phoned
one may have been phoning
one might phone
one might be phoning
one might have been phoned
one might have been phoning

Tell me, is that not awesome? Imagine a situation in which someone close to you, like a spouse or Significant Other, reprimands you for not calling when you said you were going to and you want to smooth things over; which form or forms from the above would you choose?

Exercise 18

Come up with a sentence involving one or more of the above forms. The important thing here is to create a full-blown situation or scene. Kids love to do this one, so if you find yourself bogged down or even floundering around, do consider drafting one of those delightful creatures to give you a hand. Of course, you needn't stick to the verb "to phone" <sniff>.

As if the many forms of its verbs weren't enough, English has several other most unusual features, one of which involves everyday verbs like "get" and words we call prepositions. When such a verb is combined with a preposition, a new, unique meaning is the result. For instance, look at what happens when one adds different prepositions to this particular humdrum verb:

get above
get across
get around
get behind
get below
get in
get into
get inside
get on
get through
get under
get up

Electrifying, isn't it? We've got a whole new word hoard, and we didn't have to do much to bring it about.

Exercise 19

Think of a situation in which you'd use one of the get-phrases above with a noun and make it the basis of a sentence — I mean a good, long, involved one. Here, let me show you what I mean: "The sky was grey when the plane took off, but the pilot needed only a moment to get above the clouds." Once you've composed your sentence and made adjustments for sense and sound — why, what else? Try acting it out.

The verb "get" plus other words can be used in specific situations. For instance, when we're angry with someone and want that person to leave, all we have to do is raise an arm, point to the door, and say, "Get out!" Here's a list of such get-phrases to chew on:

get about
get after
get along
get angry
get anywhere
get away
get down
get even
get going
get home
get over
get sick
get somewhere
get together
get wind of

Exercise 20

Think of a situation in which you'd use one of the above with a noun and make it the basis for a sentence. Here's mine: "As soon as the temperature turns to freezing and the first winter snow comes, I want to get away as fast as I can." Not to neglect acting it out, please.

Another unusual feature of English involves creating compounds, by which I mean joining two existing words together to form a new word with a new meaning. The example I like to use is "bookcase." At some distant point in time, humans began to manufacture books, and when there got to be too many of them in households, it occurred to their owners that a piece of furniture was needed to put them all in, a "case" in other words. The two words, "book" and "case," were probably separate at first, but then as the concept took hold and more and more folks began having that new piece of furniture built for them, the two words were joined by a hyphen — "book-case"— and eventually run together into our present word.

Early on, compounding became a favorite stratagem for accommodating English to a new concept, and so it has remained, as recent additions to our vocabulary like "email," "keyboard," "headset," and "website" bear witness. Interestingly, as if a throwback to the distant past, every new compound retains its accent on the first syllable.

I can't help hearkening back here to those distant days when I was still in the classroom. Every now and then I used to get a composition from a student in which he or she wrote about "hardwork," which always conjured up in me feelings ranging from irritation at their not having bothered to check out the spelling in a dictionary to sadness at the thought that the two ideas should be so closely associated with one another by someone at so early an age as to give rise to that sad coinage.

While we're still on the subject, let me remind you here that our compounding instinct sometimes leads us to form a new word to cover our forgetfulness or ignorance, like "thingumajig," "dojigger," and "whatchumacallit."

Exercise 21

How about it, would you like to try your hand at creating a new compound? Good, thought you would. But don't just find two words and bring them together; use your very own compound in a sentence — a juicy one.

So much for some, but by no means all, of the peculiarities of that most trying, still fascinating language of ours. Let our guest poet Nina Cassian, who is Romanian-born, you'll recall, have the last word here. Her frustration is well recorded in the following, titled *Invitation au voyage:*

Compared to my struggle with English,
Hercules was a honey child...

Not to acquire vocabulary,
not to tickle the idioms,
not to amaze oneself that Kansas
doesn't rhyme with Arkansas
— but to breathe, to emanate beings, organic
creatures —

Can I lose my doom, my limit,
the skin, tight as a straitjacket, of my native language?
Can you, my new friends and neighbors, tolerate my
intrusion?
Acknowledge my reincarnation?

My child, my sister, my brother,
and the sweetness of living together. . .

Let's try this for an encore.
For which I need a rehearsal
on using a viceversal
score.

One can well commiserate with her and, of course, with all other foreign-born poets. Just imagine if you were compelled by circumstances beyond your control to write in one of their languages.

WITH WORDS 101

In the latter part of the nineteenth century, English writer Lewis Carroll took joining words to a whole new level by inventing nonsense compounds, which he called *portmanteau* words. His celebrated poem "Jabberwocky," which appears amidst Alice's adventures in *Through the Looking-Glass,* is chock full of them:

'Twas brillig, and the slithy toves
Did gyre and gimble in the wabe:
All mimsy were the borogove
And the mome raths outgrabe.

"Beware the Jabberwock, my son!
The jaws that bite, the claws that catch!
Beware the Jubjub bird, and shun
The frumious Bandersnatch!"

He took his vorpal sword in hand:
Long time the manxome foe he sought —
So rested he by the Tumtum tree
And stood awhile in thought.

And, as in uffish thought he stood,
The Jabberwock, with eyes of flame,
Came whiffling through the tulgey wood,
And burbled as it came!

One, two! One, two! And through and through
The vorpal blade went snicker-snack!
He left it dead, and with its head
He went galumphing back.

"And, hast thou slain the Jabberwock?
Come to my arms, my beamish boy!
O frabjous day! Callooh! Callay!"
He chortled in his joy.

'Twas brillig, and the slithy toves
Did gyre and gimble in the wabe:
All mimsy were the borogoves,
And the mome raths outgrabe.

Not only that, with tongue in cheek, Carroll provided a kind of gloss in Humpty Dumpty's discussion of the finer points of the poem with Alice:

"'*Brillig*' means four o'clock in the after-noon — the time when you begin *broiling* things for dinner."

"That'll do very well," said Alice: "and '*slithy*'?"

"Well, '*slithy*' means 'lithe and slimy.' 'Lithe' is the same as 'active.' You see it's like a portmanteau — there are two meanings packed up into one word."

"I see it now," Alice remarked thoughtfully: "and what are '*toves*'?"

"Well, '*toves*' are something like badgers — they're something like lizards — and they're something like corkscrews."

"They must be very curious-looking creatures."

"They are that," said Humpty Dumpty: "also they make their nests under sundials — also they live on cheese."

"And what's to '*gyre*' and to '*gimble*'?"

"To '*gyre*' is to go round and round like a gyroscope. To '*gimble*' is to make holes like a gimlet."

"And '*the wabe*' is the grass-plot round a sundial, I suppose?" said Alice, surprised at her own ingenuity.

"Of course it is. It's called '*wabe,*' you know, because it goes a long way before it, and a long way behind it —"

"And a long way beyond it on each side," Alice added.

"Exactly so. Well then, '*mimsy*' is 'flimsy and miserable' (there's another portmanteau for you). And a '*borogove*' is a thin shabby-looking bird with its feathers sticking out all round — something like a live mop."

"And then '*mome raths*'?" said Alice. "I'm afraid I'm giving you a great deal of trouble."

"Well, a '*rath*' is a sort of green pig: but '*mome*' I'm not certain about. I think it's short for 'from home' — meaning that they'd lost their way, you know."

"And what does '*outgrabe*' mean?"

"Well, '*outgribing*' is something between bellowing and whistling, with a kind of sneeze in the middle: however, you'll hear it done, maybe — down in the wood yonder — and, when you've once heard it, you'll be quite content."

Additional notes of the same ilk turn up in Carroll's other writings and correspondence, as well as those of some of his ingenious explicators:

Jabberwock — "the result of much excited discussion," a combination of "jabber" and "wocer" or "wocor," the Anglo-Saxon word for "offspring" or "fruit."

Jubjub — a name. Possibly "jub" is a sound that the bird makes. The *Oxford English Dictionary* lists "jug" as an imitation of one of the notes of the nightingale.

frumious — a *portmanteau* of "furious" and "fuming."

Bandersnatch — a name combining "snatch" and "bander," possibly Carroll's word for "band," short for "hairband."

vorpal — possibly a *portmanteau* of "verbal" and "torpid."

manxome — could be related to Manx, the Celtic people of the Isle of Man.

Tumtum — used to describe a stringed instrument being monotonously strummed.

uffish — a *portmanteau* of "gruffish," "roughish," and "huffish."

whiffling — "blowing unsteadily in short puffs."

tulgey — possibly a *portmanteau* of "bulging" and "turgid."

burbled — a variant of "bubble," also used as a verb meaning "to perplex, confuse, or muddle."

galumphing — a perfect *portmanteau* of "gallop" and "triumphant."

beamish — a variant of "beaming."

frabjous — very likely a *portmanteau* of "fabulous" and "joyous."

Callooh — the call of a species of arctic duck so named.

But of course we can't leave it at that, can we?

Exercise 22

Here are three portmanteaus created by me:

> *"Spricket" — a combination of "sprinkle" and "thicket "*
> *"Dollger" — a combination of "doll" and "tiger"*
> *"Baltice "— a combination of "balloon" and "entice "*

Now where are yours?

I can't help mentioning here that once upon a time, in a satire on contemporary culture titled *Bagatelle • Guinevere,* I invented a language that included quite a few *portmanteaus,* among which was " bagaba," a combination of "bargain" and "garbage," which had as its meaning "a trendy work of art." Friends of mine made it into a fad word for pieces of "artistic" trash that very likely got noticed in the media in exchange for cash on the barrel.

P. S. In case you're wondering what "Jabberwocky" is all about, here it is in a nutshell. An older person cautions a younger one to be on his guard against three evils: the Jabberwock, the Jubjub bird, and the Bandersnatch. The Jabberwock comes, there's a fight between it and the younger person, who ends up slaying it and returning with its head to the older person, who is overjoyed.

Fun with Words 102

There used to be a popular song that went, "My Time Is Your Time." Well, that time has come, dear Readers. It's time to kick some words around, by which I mean your words and your words alone.

First things first, do you have a favorite word? If you do, fine and good. Keep it in readiness. If you don't, it's about time you acquired one — like now. Think about it, and when you have it, write it down. But if thinking doesn't do the trick, go and get your dictionary and open it to a page, and then close your eyes and plunk your finger down, and *voilá* — that's IT!

The first thing you want to do is pronounce it, that favorite word of yours, but don't just say it like it's any old word. Do it slowly, letting it roll-ll-ll around in your mouth like a piece of candy, so it sort of melts on your tongue. Pronounce it again and again like that. It's quite wonderful, isn't it? And just think of it, you've got your own favorite word, like a pet of your own.

Exercise 23

Use your pet in a sentence — I mean, a GOOD one!

Sometimes, when you've got a real pet, it becomes necessary, because of a heavy workload, to acquire a second one to keep it company. Do so — acquire a second swinging pet word and make it as good as the first.

Exercise 24

Now use both of your pets in a sentence, and as before, make it one of substance.

Is this a trifle mad? You think so? Good. But you're not done yet, noooooo, not by a long shot. For the next three exercises, you're going to need a whole kennel of pets — like ten nouns, ten verbs, and ten adjectives. So get going with your dictionary or *Thesaurus*, and if one of them doesn't do the trick, try one of your unfavorite textbooks or a newspaper or magazine. Opt for words that are bizarre and unusual, for example, words that sound funny, like "pullulate," or look funny, like "coccyx."

If you're in a group or class and find yourself stuck after a while, lean over and see what the guy next to you has been up to. Maybe you two can make a deal to swap a few. If you're going it alone, this might be a good time to call up a friend: "Hi, I need some crazy words. You got any?"

Also, don't just settle for the first pets you come up with. Keep discarding and adding new ones to each category till you've got what seem like the best choices. Okay? Ready, set, go!

Exercise 25

Choose from among your new pets in the three categories and fill in the blanks:

He __________ the __________ __________.
verb adjective noun

The important thing here is to eschew (how do you like that one?) sense. So read your sentence over to yourself, and if it sounds too rational, keep working on it. Onward, we're not done yet. Close, but not yet.

Exercise 26

Again, making selections from among your recently acquired pets, fill in the blanks:

If the __________ __________ __________ the
adjective noun verb

__________, then the __________ __________ __________
noun adjective noun verb

the __________ __________.
adjective noun

As before, read your sentence over, and if it doesn't sound totally loony, keep working on it until it does. Being somewhat of an old hand at this by now, you'll feel it when it does reach that point.

If you're in a group or class, a contest is definitely in order here, with a vote for the wackiest. If you're going it alone, I suggest trying yours out on something live, even a real pet — even just a turtle — and as always, be sure to get your body involved or you'll miss half the fun. A neighbor, cleaning person, janitor, handyman, or shopkeeper at a place where you buy a lot of stuff are also possibilities.

Now what about your other pets? What are you going to do with them? One can't just kick them out into the cold and let them fend for themselves, can one?

Once again, in this exercise, don't just settle for your first choices. Try out the various words from the different categories till the whole thing seems "right." Remember Coleridge's "Kubla Khan," that so-called fragment I mentioned in the previous chapter? Consider how it begins:

> In Xanadu did Kubla Khan
> A stately pleasure-dome decree:
> Where Alph, the sacred river, ran
> Through caverns measureless to man
> Down to a sunless sea.

Now where is this exactly? Do you have any idea? Does it interfere with your enjoyment of what's to come in the poem if you don't know?

Exercise 27

> *Get up a dialogue between two friendly strangers who encounter one another one night in a dark alley in some metropolis. One is an earth person, the other an alien, and both have recently escaped from lunatic asylums. Needless to say, feel free to use sentences from the last two exercises as well as new crazies of your creation.*

The rest is silence. (Where does that come from?)

Well, maybe not. Before you go on to the next chapter, may I suggest that you take a deep breath here and begin developing a closer relationship with our language if you haven't done so already. Not only read-read-read, but when you can, do so out loud — and I mean LOUD!

Also, listen to people when they talk, indeed as you never have before. And listen not only to What they're saying but also to How they're saying it. Ask yourself and keep on asking yourself, Why that way? Why not some other? Yes, make the world around you your textbook. And then? And then, I'd go a bit further.

Exercise 28

Get hold of a favorite poem — a short one works best — and give it a long and hard look not only for what it's saying and how it's saying it, but also and especially for its words.

There, did that hurt? I hope not.

Exercise 29

Now look at a piece of your own in the same way.

Now is silence, yes? Well, yes and no. I can't quite leave it there. A little bit remains to be said here about communication without words, namely, nonverbal utterances and silences. The former, involving the vocal apparatus, can take a variety of forms, such as murmurs, mumbles, sighs, yawns, sniffs, coughs, moans, groans, sobs, cries, and screams. These and others can be used to considerable effect if your poetry works well orally, and indeed we as humans have a considerable repertoire of body language to define or refine such utterances. Pauses, short and long — in other words, downright silences — can also add something to a text, as indeed they do in music, and they can sometimes be as important to the meaning of a poem as the words themselves. As we shall see when we come to deal with free verse later on in this book, such silences can truly turn out to be magical ingredients.

Exercise 30

Turn back to "Friends, Romans, Countrymen" on pages 53-54 and read it aloud with some nonverbal utterances and body language, then again with short and long pauses, and finally utilizing all of these together.

Now silence for sure.

SPECIAL EFFECTS

—WITH WORDS—

There are a certain number of skills and tools that I feel poets and prospective poets should be acquainted with and know how to use, and this goes for everyonc, no matter how old or young you are and/or different you may think you are or anticipate being.

This is as good a place as any to say something about being far out — that is, abstract, vague, obscure, or even cute and clever. If that's the direction you're heading in or you've been told is your bent, be forewarned: success with it, by which I mean first and foremost self-satisfaction, doesn't come easily; it will certainly not be achieved by dashing something off. Making oneself difficult to understand or fully appreciated by only a chosen few requires practice, like anything else. As the Dadaist-Expressionist painter George Grosz is rumored to have said to a pretentiously way-out student, "Before you dump everything overboard, you have to get something on board first."

Describing

First and foremost among the skills and tools that a poet should have is the ability to describe. By this, I mean the ability to describe everything, whether it be how someone or something looks and behaves, or how you feel and what you're thinking.

Consider how, with a few strokes of the pen (if that was his writing implement), Carl Sandburg (1878-1967) was able to conjure up this picture of fog rolling in, settling on an urban area, and then going elsewhere:

The fog comes
on little cat feet.

It sits looking
over harbor and city
on silent haunches
and then moves on.

While the concepts in this poem and its language are not at all complex, each word was chosen with care.

Exercise 1

I feel that it's important that you demonstrate this to yourself, so take up your Thesaurus and find synonyms — simple ones, mind you — for "comes," "little," "sits," "silent," and "moves." Invariably a few people will feel squeamish about doing this; if you're one of them, take a peek at my version:

The fog moves
on tiny cat feet.

It stays looking
over harbor and city
on quiet haunches
and then goes on.

With one or both versions in hand, point made? If not, do-o-o look again at Sandburg's original and my Jake-the-fake and take to heart. Now you see it, yes? Good, now let's turn to your own descriptive abilities and see if they can be honed a bit.

Describing Appearances

As we all learned early on in our lives, the workhorse part of speech to use when describing a person, place, or thing is the adjective. Consider how bare, flat, and downright boring the following statement is without such a descriptive word to help us form a precise picture of the person and / or his possession:

The man looked at his watch.

Now see what happens when two ordinary adjectives are applied to him and it:

The old man looked at his gold watch.

Immediately our mental image is sharpened; it's almost as if we'd fine-tuned a scene we'd been observing with a pair of binoculars. Yes, adjectives are truly invaluable when it comes to describing what someone or something looks like, as well as sounds, feels, etc. They are the jewels of verbal adornment! (How's that?)

Exercise 2

Think up ten adjectives that one might apply to "man" instead of "old." Read each one aloud between "the" and "man" slow-ow-owly, and note how your mental picture of the person changes with each one. It's something like looking at him in a kaleidoscope, and then shaking it and looking again, and then again, isn't it?

By the way, your person needn't be old; that's part of my mind-set. You can make him any age and in any physical condition or situation you want, like young or decrepit or poor. In fact, he can even be a she, can't he?

Exercise 3

Do the same with "watch." Think up ten adjectives that can be used between "his" and "watch" instead of "gold." Again, slowly read each adjective aloud with "his watch," noting how your mental picture constantly changes.

Needless to say, the same thing holds for his watch as for the man. You can make the object looked at just about anything you want.

Exercise 4

Now look your two lists over and choose an adjective from Column A and another from Column B — that is, those you think go best with your mental pictures of the man and his watch, or what you will. Write your new sentence down and read it aloud several times, noting how much richer and more specific your picture has become.

There are a few things that I must caution you against regarding your handling of adjectives. First, unless you have a conscious, well-thought-out reason for using workhorses like "beautiful" and "gorgeous," to say nothing of "good," "nice," "great," "cool," "hot," "awesome," and "weird," avoid them like the plague. Why? They're so overused that they just aren't of much help in creating pictures anymore — certainly not the one-of-a-kind pictures that you as a poet want to paint with words. But don't simply take my word for it; as an acid test, try each of these old shoes out with "watch" and then compare your results with your ten good combinations from Exercise 2.

A second no-no where adjectives are concerned is never to pile them on, that is, unless, as with using the workhorses noted above, a situation calls for it. Just picture a person loaded to the gills with junk jewelry or cheap makeup, or reeking with 99-cent-store perfume — or rotgut booze — and you'll see what I mean.

Adding an adverb to an adjective can sometimes provide a much-needed, albeit minuscule, descriptive touch.

Look at what happens when I add "very" to the adjectives in our original scene:

> The very old man looked at his old watch.
> The old man looked at his very old watch.
> The very old man looked at his very old watch.

Exercise 5

Right on, add "very" or another qualifying adverb to one or both of your adjectives in your sentence from Exercise 4.

If you like the small touches that adverbs can produce, be sure to avoid "sort of" and such like, which can produce unintended awkwardness and even amusement — for example, "they were sort of married"; "he was sort of dead."

Adjectives, with and without qualifying adverbs, are not the only parts of speech that can be used to describe appearances. Nouns themselves — that is, more visually descriptive ones — can also be employed toward that end and can be especially effective when paired with descriptive adjectives. Note what happens to our model when I find new nouns to replace "man" and "watch":

> The old gentleman looked at his very old timepiece.
> The old geezer looked at his very old ticktock.

Electrifying, wouldn't you say? Like, who needs a piece of canvas on an easel and a palette of paints? And when I discard "old" and "very old" in favor of a few really descriptive adjectives, presto-chango:

> The elderly gentleman looked at his rare, gold timepiece.
> The ancient geezer looked at his tarnished ticktock.

Exercise 6

Using descriptive adjectives and nouns of your choosing, fine-tune your picture of Exercise 5.

But that's not the end when it comes to choosing words to describe; you might think it is, but it isn't, not by a long shot. Verbs, too, can be enlisted to serve in the cause.

Look at what happens to my models, for instance, when I substitute a verb that's more appropriate for each individual for "look," which is rather bland:

> The elderly gentleman consulted his rare, gold timepiece.
> The ancient geezer peered at his tarnished ticktock.

Exercise 7

Return to your sentence of the previous exercise and try out different verbs until you hit on one that does the trick. Here's an occasion where you might want to consult your dictionary or your ***Thesaurus****.*

Now for a really nifty touch, the addition of qualifying adverbs to go with my new verbs:

> The elderly gentleman nervously consulted his rare, gold timepiece.
> The ancient geezer cautiously peered at his tarnished ticktock.

Exercise 8

Do yourself a favor: get out that sentence again and find a nice, new qualifying adverb to go with your verb.

Another descriptive tool where individual words are concerned is the prepositional phrase, which we all use every day in every way without realizing it but have trouble defining. Let me take a whack at it. A basic no-frills-type prepositional phrase consists of two words: a part of speech called a preposition (such as in, into, above) plus a noun or pronoun. The noun is usually preceded by "a," "an," or "the" — for example, "in a hurry," "above an entrance," "into the woods." And of course an adjective or adjectives can be added to the noun for added color.

Here's the delightful thing about prepositional phrases: they can function either as adjectives or adverbs. For example, in the following —

> The elderly gentleman in the green coat nervously consulted his rare, gold timepiece —

the phrase "in the green coat" is descriptive of the elderly gentleman; hence, it functions as an adjective. In the following sentence—

> The ancient geezer peered at his tarnished ticktock
> in a strange way—

the phrase "in a strange way" indicates how the old geezer peered, so its function is adverbial. Note that I deleted "cautiously" because it would have added unwanted redundancy to my sentence, and, in addition, my sentence would have become top-heavy with adverbs, which I didn't want to happen either. Be advised, however, that occasions may arise when one would want redundancy and possibly adverbial overload like that.

Exercise 9

Let's get it over with in one fell swoop: add an adjectival prepositional phrase and an adverbial prepositional phrase to your sentence of Exercise 8. Be sure to eliminate adjectival and adverbial overloads.

As you may or may not have realized, being served up models and creating imitations based on them has one glaring drawback: they're just that and have nothing to do with reality—yes, that awful word. So let me provide you with an example of describing appearances from the real world—the real world of fiction! This is from Shakespeare's *Antony and Cleopatra;* someone is here describing Cleopatra's meeting with Antony:

> The barge she sat in, like a burnish'd throne,
> Burnt on the water. The poop was beaten gold;
> Purple the sails, and so perfumed that
> The winds were love-sick with them; the oars were silver,
> Which to the tune of flutes kept strokes, and made
> The water which they beat to follow faster,
> As amorous of their strokes. For her own person,
> It beggar'd all description: she did lie
> In her pavilion — cloth-of-gold of tissue —
> O'er-picturing that Venus where we see

The fancy outwork nature. On each side her
Stood pretty dimpled boys, like smiling Cupids,
With divers-color'd fans, whose wind did seem
To glow the delicate cheeks which they did cool,
And what they undid did.

Begin by looking up the meanings of any words you're unsure of in your dictionary. Then read the passage aloud several times, first for the major ideas and then for how the whole thing holds together.

Exercise 10

Underline the passage's adjectives and other descriptive words and phrases.

Read the passage aloud again, giving special emphasis to your underlined words and phrases. Now that's how to paint a scene verbally, wouldn't you say?

Exercise 11

To put it to the proof, let's try our old game of substituting. Insert the following changes in the first seven lines: "boat" for "barge"; "was" for "sat"; "golden" for "burnish'd"; "ocean" for "water"; "quicker" for "faster"; "amorous" for "love-sick."

Now read the passage two more times, first with the changes and then as is. It all really begins to come alive — to acquire a life of its own — doesn't it?

We should, at this point, try our own hands at describing appearances from scratch. What do you say? Are you up to it? I hope so. Let's creep up on it, okay?

Exercise 12

Think of someone you know who has memorable eyes or take a good look at your own in the mirror and — what else? — describe. Remember to include all the devices we've covered so far: descriptive adjectives, descriptive nouns, descriptive verbs, adverbs to qualify the adjectives and verbs, prepositional phrases, the whole schmeer.

It's like a graduation exercise, no? But don't worry if things don't come out quite the way you would have liked them to. Good description takes a lot of practice. Very likely, the Bard himself didn't become so proficient at it overnight.

Up to this point, I've dwelt only on describing how things look, and by extension how they sound, feel, smell, etc. But, of course, there are also states of mind to reckon with, which sometimes require elaboration as well. As a case in point, consider how John Keats (1795-1821) handled the devastating thought that he might soon die, which indeed he did not long after he wrote this poem:

> When I have fears that I may cease to be
> Before my pen has glean'd my teeming brain,
> Before high-piled books, in charactery,
> Hold like rich garners the full ripen'd grain;
> When I behold, upon the night's starr'd face,
> Huge cloudy symbols of a high romance,
> And think that I may never live to trace
> Their shadows, with the magic hand of chance;
> And when I feel, fair creature of an hour,
> That I shall never look upon thee more,
> Never have relish in the faery power
> Of unreflecting love; — then on the shore
> Of the wide world I stand alone, and think
> Till love and fame to nothingness do sink.

Begin, as with the passage from Shakespeare earlier, by reading the whole thing through both for the poet's sense and his arrangement of ideas.

Exercise 13

Underline the key words and units of thought or phrases in the last two and a half lines.

Read those lines alone, perhaps several times, emphasizing those key words and phrases.

Exercise 14

Make the following substitutions: "vast" for "wide"; "globe" for "world"; "am" for "stand"; "zero-plus" for "nothingness."

Read the whole poem through with the substitutions, then as is. Enough said, wouldn't you say?

Describing Actions

It almost goes without saying that the workhorses of describing action are verbs, by which I mean action-verbs like "throw" as opposed to linking-verbs like "is" and seeming-verbs like — well — "seem." Here's yet another utterly bland sentence:

> The man threw the ball.

"Threw" is the key word here. But look at what happens when I substitute more colorful verbs for it:

> The man tossed the ball.
> The man hurled the ball.
> The man lofted the ball.

Not only has our mental picture of the ball sailing through the air become more clearly delineated but also the stance and arm movement of "the man."

As with describing appearances, actions can be fleshed out by adjusting other elements in a sentence, first and foremost by showing how a person or thing looks while in the midst of an action. Notice, for instance, what happens to our picture of lofting when we add an adjective or two to the thrower:

> The decrepit old man lofted the ball.

And do notice how very different that picture is if we change the subject and its modifiers:

> The handsome young man lofted the ball.

Each picture can be further rounded out by the addition of a few adjectival brush strokes to the ball:

> The decrepit old man lofted the brand-new soccer ball.
> The handsome young man lofted the mud-bespattered tennis ball.

Bear in mind that we have yet to flesh out our verb with adverbs, as we did above in describing the elderly gentlemen and the ancient geezer. Watch what happens when we do that here:

> The decrepit old man painfully lofted the brand-new soccer ball.
> The handsome young man carelessly lofted the mud-bespattered tennis ball.

Not only do we see more clearly delineated actions in our minds but we're also inclined to intuit possibly unintended consequences: before long, the old man may be rubbing his shoulder with liniment, while the young man's clothing may be headed for the neighborhood dry cleaner or the washing machine.

Finally, as before, prepositional phrases, used either as adjectives or adverbs, can be applied to round out such scenes even further:

> The decrepit old man painfully lofted the brand-new soccer ball into the stands.
> The handsome young man in the pink shirt carelessly lofted the mud-bespattered tennis ball.

Exercise 15

Create your own picture in a sentence of someone throwing a ball. Be sure to color it with adjectives, nouns, adverbs, and prepositional phrases as well as your choice of a verb. Don't be easily satisfied here; try out different combinations until you get something distinctive. However, beware of overload, or you'll have an unintended comedy on your hands.

As the saying goes, a picture is worth a thousand words, and that goes as well for verbal pictures. The following passage, from the *Nun's Priest's Tale* in *The Canterbury Tales* by Geoffrey Chaucer (ca. 1340-1400), has got to be one of the all-time great action sequences in literature. The setting is a barnyard belonging to a widow and her two daughters. The cock, who has just been tricked by the fox, is being carried off on the fox's back, and the hens, the cock's wives, have just sent up a cry of alarm:

This sely wydwe and eek hir doghtres two *innocent*
Herden thise hennes crye and maken wo,
And out at dores stirten they anon, *leaped*
And syen the fox toward the grove gon, *saw*
And bar upon his bak the cok away,
And cryden, "Out! harrow! and weylaway! *help*
Ha! ha! the fox!" and after hyim they ran,
And eek with staves many another man.
Ran Colle oure dogge, and Talbot and Gerland,
And Malkyn, with a dystaf in hir hand;
Ran cow and calf, and eek the verray hogges,
So fered for berkying of the dogges *frightened*
And shoutyng of the men and wommen eeke,
They ronne so hem thoughte hir herte breeke. *ran*
They yolleden as feendes doon in helle;
The dokes cryden as men wolde hem quelle; *ducks / kill*
The gees for feere flowen over the trees; *flew*
Out of the hyve cam the swarm of bees.
So hydous was the noyse, a, *benedicitee*! *bless me*
Certes, he Jakke Straw and his meynee *company*
Ne made nevere shoutes half so shrille
Whan that they wolden any Flemyng kille,
As thilke day was maad upon the fox.
Of bras they broghten bemes, and of box, *trumpets / boxwood*
Of horn, of boon, in whiche they blewe and powped, *bone*
And therwithal they skriked and they howped. *shrieked / whooped*
It seemed as that hevene sholde falle.

Did you notice how economical Chaucer was in his use of verbs at first? Not only did he show the women running but also "many another man," the three dogs, Malkin the servant with a stick in her hand, and the cow, calf, and hogs. There was a method to his madness; he used "run" exclusively there, so that he could surprise his readers with the added touches of the frightened geese flying over the trees and the bees swarming out of their hive. Notice also how he used sound-making to reinforce all that movement; besides crying out, everyone is barking, shouting, yelling, or blowing and pooping on horns. Finally, to realize the scene fully, he inserted allusions at key places: the hogs ran as if their hearts would break and yelled like fiends in hell; the clamor that everyone made surpassed that of Jack Straw and his men when killing Flemish folk; and, with the added noise of the various horns, it sounded as if heaven would fall.

Exercise 16

> *Think of a profession — let's say, teaching — and make a list of verbs connected with it, like "talking," "lecturing," "correcting," "grading," "nagging," "sighing," etc. Write a brief description of someone who would perform those actions, and then put it all together in a paragraph.*

So much for describing, except for this. Bear in mind that when revising pieces of your own — which will surely involve striving to be more explicit — you'll be doing advanced versions of these exercises.

Handy Tools

There are any number of verbal tools that can prove useful to a poet or prospective poet. At the top of the list are the *metaphor* and its cousin, the *simile*, along with a considerable range of possibilities involving them. While you may know what they both are, consciously using them to effect — especially *metaphors* — is another matter. And that you should be able to do, or at least you should be aware of their expressive possibilities for future reference.

Metaphors

In case you never realized it, human language is, by its nature, metaphorical. No matter what culture one comes from, one employs *metaphors* every day in a variety of ways. "What a jackass I am!" — is one. "Where did the time go?" — is another. In case you're wondering, there's no such thing as a fixed number of *metaphors;* on the contrary, people are constantly inventing new ones, just as new forms of life are forever evolving here on Earth.

We all learned what a *metaphor* is in school, but for the sake of our all marching together with this, let's call it plainly and simply an identification of a person, place, or thing — A — with something else — B — in order to elucidate or cast new light on that person, place, or thing — A. For instance, in the two trite examples above, the "I" is equating himself or herself with that colossally stupid creature, the jackass, and time is being viewed as something that can move, like a train.

There are two secrets to creating effective metaphors. First, B should be familiar enough to people so that they can easily recreate it in their minds. Second, B should provide readers — indeed, electrify them — with a new dimension or insight into the thing being identified A. I can't think of a better example than the opening of "Portrait d'une Femme" by Ezra Pound (1885-1972), but of course, all is lost if you don't know what the Sargasso Sea is; ideally you do or will look it up:

> Your mind and you are our Sargasso Sea,
> London has swept about you this score years
> And bright ships left you this or that in fee:
> Ideas, old gossip, oddments of all things,
> Strange spars of knowledge and dimmed ware of price.

Note how the sea *metaphor* is bolstered by "bright ships left you this or that in fee" and broadened by "strange spars of knowledge and dimmed wares of price."

Exercise 17

Let's begin by thinking of a loved one, a good friend, a pet, or even a favorite plant and then of a magical someplace or something to equate your individual with. Now, with pen in hand, address that individual as Pound did: "You are. . . ." Note: beware of synonyms (for example, "You are my friend") and simple comparisons ("You are like a brother").

In "London," William Blake sought to enumerate the ills of English society, and the *metaphor* he adopted is that of himself going for a walk in the city. Note the very logical order to the "I"'s activities in these first two stanzas: he wanders, and as he does so, he sees and hears.

I wander thro' each charter'd street,
Near where the charter'd Thames does flow,
And mark in every face I meet
Marks of weakness, marks of woe.

In every cry of every Man,
In every Infants cry of fear,
In every voice: in every ban,
The mind-forg'd manacles I hear.

"Charter'd" refers to the *Magna Carta,* which granted rights to every Englishman; it's used here negatively, Blake having believed that all men are born with them. The "I"'s position becomes clear with the mention of "mind-forg'd manacles," or thought control, a relatively new idea in the late eighteenth century. The "I" hears these manacles in men's and children's voices, whereas one normally hears a prisoner rattling real chains in a real prison.

Exercise 18

This is a tough act to follow, but let's take a whack at it anyway, okay? Decide on a subject like, say, "lovemaking," and make a list of metaphors with respect to it.

A metaphor can sometimes be quite long, in which case it's called an *extended metaphor* or a *conceit.* The whole of Blake's "Garden of Love" is one:

I went to the Garden of Love,
And saw what I never had seen:
A Chapel was built in the midst,
Where I used to play on the green.

And the gates of this Chapel were shut,
And Thou shalt not writ over the door;
So I turn'd to the Garden of Love,
That so many sweet flowers bore,

And I saw it was filled with graves,
And tomb-stones where flowers should be:
And Priests in black gowns, were walking their rounds,
And binding with briars, my joys & desires.

The story told in this poem goes as follows: I went to see someone I deeply cared for, who seemed to care as much for me, only to discover that she's become falsely religious and smothered her true feelings with what to me are mindless pious observances.

Exercise 19

Choose one of your metaphors from the two previous exercises and try developing it further.

There are longer works yet both in verse and prose, sometimes occupying many hundreds of pages, that are considered *extended metaphors.* For instance, in telling the story of a human soul on the road to fulfillment or redemption, Chaucer's *Canterbury Tales* surely qualifies as such and indeed can be classified as one grand *exemplum* or *moral tale*, a specialized form of *extended metaphor.* Sir Edmund Spenser's *Faerie Queene*, in which the characters are persons who represent abstractions, is an example of an *allegory*, another kind of *extended metaphor.* Yet one more kind of *extended metaphor* is the *fable*, a brief moral tale usually involving animals, like *Aesop's Fables.* You should dip into these works, if for no other reason than to get some idea of the possibilities that *extended metaphors* offer you as a writer — and do consider reading that glorious work *The Canterbury Tales* in its entirety.

"Eek, the lights screamed!" That's a *mixed metaphor,* in case you're not in the know, and something remains to be said about them. When I was a kid in public school, the teachers were always warning us to avoid using them, and this attitude seems to prevail in certain lofty academic circles today (including, alas, Corbett and Connors's celebrated *Classical Rhetoric,* which is otherwise on target). Later in college, I learned that mixing *metaphors* was a venerable trick of the literary trade. For what could be more respectable than Hamlet's reflecting on whether or not to "take arms against a sea of troubles." No, there's nothing really wrong with mixing *metaphors,* and don't let anybody tell you differently. As with everything else, it's all in how and on what occasion you do so.

No better example of the use of *mixed metaphors* exists than in the last two stanzas of Blake's "London," where they come thick and fast, and at the same time become increasingly dense, as if the "I" has quickened his pace:

How the Chimney-sweeper's cry
Every black'ning Church appalls,
And the hapless Soldiers sigh,
Runs in blood down Palace walls

But most thro' midnight streets I hear
How the youthful Harlots curse
Blasts the new-born Infants tear,
And blights with plagues the Marriage hearse.

Note how black and red, the colors of Church and State, predominate. In four terse lines, the cry of the Chimney-sweeper, himself blackened by the work that society compels him to do, appalls (a negatively blackening word) an already smoke-begrimed church, and the sigh of the wounded Soldier in his red coat runs in blood down Palace walls. In the final stanza, the young Harlot's curse, blighting and blasting in a fashion akin to that of the deity of the Old Testament, brings the plague of venereal disease, and its targets are infants and marriage, itself a detestable priest-ridden institution, which is seen as deadening, a hearse in other words.

Exercise 20

> *How's this? Get hold of some whiskey and soda and mix your own! Seriously, try giving it a whirl, will you? Create your own mixed metaphor — and make it a really good one! But don't be surprised if you find yourself having to work at it. Yesirreebob, even doing something "wrong" — that is, with finesse — takes practice.*

There's a specialized form of *mixed metaphor,* called an *oxymoron,* that you should be aware of. It became all the rage some years ago, but in case you're not in the know, be advised that it has nothing to do with livestock or intelligence. Rather, it's the pairing of an adjective and a noun that are contradictory — for example, "sweet pain" and "cheerful pessimist." Blake's "marriage hearse," his final blast in "London," is one. And so too is Milton's glorious, one-shot blow against the gold-grasping clergy of his time as "blind mouths" in *Lycidas.*

Exercise 21

> *They're cool, try one. Maybe two, they're small.*

Similes

Like the *metaphor,* the *simile* involves two unlike things, A and B, and its purpose is to elucidate or cast light on A. But the *simile* is a comparison, whereas the *metaphor* is an identification. A *simile* always includes the comparing word "like" or else "as," where grammatically appropriate; sometimes it occurs with the verb "seemed," and in that case, "like" or "as" is sometimes omitted and understood. "Jane eats like a bird" and "Jack is as slow as molasses" are examples of *similes* from our daily life.

It is sometimes said that *similes* are specialized forms of *metaphors* or are really *metaphors* with the addition of "like" or some other comparison word. However, this is not really so; *similes* and *metaphors* rarely translate well into one another. For instance, "How like a jackass I am!" lacks the pizzazz of "What a jackass I am," and the same can be said regarding Jane and her anorectic tendencies — that is, "Jane eats like a bird" has far more punch to it than "Jane is a bird when it comes to eating." Nevertheless, the secret of writing an effective *simile* is the same as that for pulling off a good *metaphor.* The term of comparison B should be recognizable but at the same time unusual.

Exercise 22

Take our trite examples — "Jane eats like a bird" and "Jack is as slow as molasses" — and try for more electrifying similes. *If you find yourself stuck, try coming up with a* simile *regarding your own daily life or surroundings.*

In recent years, so much has been made of the *metaphor* that literary folks tend to look down on the *simile* as a poor country cousin, but not so — not by a long shot. Note, for instance, how well *similes* serve this master, Herman Melville, in his incomparable novel *Moby Dick,* which is chock-full of such-like:

> Next morning the not-yet-subsided sea rolled in long slow billows of mighty bulk, and striving in the Pequod's gurgling track, pushed her on *like giants' palms outstretched.* The strong, unstaggering breeze abounded so, that *sky and air seemed vast outbellying sails;* the whole world boomed before the wind. Muffled in the full morning light, the invisible sun was only known by the spread intensity of his place, where his bayonet rays moved on in stacks.

> Emblazonings, as of crowned Babylonian kings and queens, reigned over everything. The sea was *as a crucible of molten gold, that bubblingly leaps with light and heat.* (*Italics mine.*)

Is this not absolutely stunning? How diminished this passage would be without those similes.

Exercise 23

See for yourself. Read the passage aloud as it is, and then read it again without the similes, running on "the strong unstaggering breeze abounded so" with "that the whole world boomed before the wind," and changing the last sentence to "The sea was bubbling with light and heat."

Like *metaphors* — for instance, those in Blake's "London" — *similes* can be strung together to create a powerful effect, indeed like beads on a string. One of the all-time famous examples of this occurs in the Song of Songs, which is a collection of ancient courtship and wedding songs. In these excerpts, first a man is singing, then a woman:

> BEHOLD, thou art fair, my love; behold, thou art fair; thou hast doves' eyes within thy locks: thy hair is as a flock of goats, that appear from mount Gilead.
>
> Thy teeth are like a flock of sheep that are even shorn, which came up from the washing; whereof every one bear twins, and none is barren among them.
>
> Thy lips are like a thread of scarlet, and thy speech is comely: thy temples are like a piece of pomegranate within thy locks.
>
> Thy neck is like the tower of David builded for an armoury, whereon there hang a thousand bucklers, all shields of mighty men.
>
> Thy two breasts are like two young roes that are twins, which feed among the lilies. . . .
>
> My beloved is white and ruddy, the chiefest among ten thousand.

> His head is as the most fine gold, his locks are bushy, and black as a raven.
>
> His eyes are as the eyes of doves by the rivers of waters, washed with milk, and fitly set.
>
> His cheeks are as a bed of spices, as sweet flowers: his lips like lilies, dropping sweet smelling myrrh.
>
> His hands are as gold rings set with the beryl: his belly is as bright ivory overlaid with sapphires.
>
> His legs are as pillars of marble, set upon sockets of fine gold: his countenance is as Lebanon, excellent as the cedars.
>
> His mouth is most sweet: yea, he is altogether lovely. This is my beloved, and this is my friend, O daughters of Jerusalem.

By our standards today, the whole thing is clearly overdone. But the exaggerated terms of comparison do help to convey a general feeling of lushness and eroticism, which seems to have been the author's or authors' intention.

Exercise 24

Just for fun, think of someone you love or like just as a friend and make a list of his or her particularly appealing attributes and attach a simile to each. Not to worry if this turns into a comedy or a circus, yes?

As we saw with *metaphors*, an individual *simile* can be quite long and involved, and there are several different kinds of *extended similes*. One of them is the biblical *parable*, which was intended as a teaching device to a receptive, nonreading public. Its pattern is invariably the same: A is compared to B, and then B is elaborated upon with the idea that the listener will apply it to A. The Parable of the Mustard Seed, where it's understood that the birds of the air are us, humanity, will make this clearer:

> Another parable put he forth unto them, saying, The kingdom of heaven is like to a grain of mustard seed, which a man took, and sowed in his field:

> Which indeed is the least of all seeds: but when it is grown, it is the greatest among herbs, and becometh a tree, so that the birds of the air come and lodge in the branches thereof.

Exercise 25

Try your hand at composing a short parable. If you have trouble coming up with a subject, try using life *and begin it with something like "Life is like a flower garden."*

Another form of *extended simile* is the *epic simile*, which serves to clarify a specific event involving action and the emotion aroused by it. Homer employed it in his *Iliad* and *Odyssey*, then Virgil in his *Aeneid*, then later in the Renaissance, literary colossi like John Milton in his thoroughly Christian treatment of the Fall in *Paradise Lost*, and later yet Romantic poet William Wordsworth in his artistic autobiography *The Prelude*, which he cast as an *epic*.

Here's an example from *The Iliad.* The setting is the beach near the plain of Troy, where the Greek besiegers have their ships anchored. Hektor, leader of the Trojan army, has launched a counterattack against them. Among the Greeks is Telemonian Aias, who on the one hand is spoiling for a fight with Hektor, but on the other is worried about the danger to the fleet from him. So he views this enemy's approach both with longing and apprehension, and his state of mind is compared to that of a lion being kept at bay from some cattle by their owners:

He stood stunned, and swung the sevenfold ox-hide
 shield behind him
and drew back, throwing his eyes round the crowd of
 men, like a wild beast,
turning on his way, shifting knee past knee only a little;
as when the men who live in the wild and their dogs have driven
a tawny lion away from the mid-fenced ground of their oxen,
and will not let him tear out the fat of the oxen, watching
nightlong against him, and he in his hunger for meat closes in
but can get nothing of what he wants, for the raining javelins

> *thrown from the daring hands of the men beat ever against him,*
> *and the flaming torches, and these he balks at for all of his fury*
> *and with the daylight goes away, disappointed of desire;*
> so Aias, disappointed at heart, drew back from the Trojans
> much unwilling, but feared for the ships of the Achaians. . . .
> (*Italics mine.*)

Note how closely Milton followed the pattern in this celebrated passage in *Paradise Lost.* Newly descended to Hell, Satan is suffering much:

> Nathless he so endur'd, till on the Beach
> Of that inflamed Sea, he stood and call'd
> His Legions, Angel Forms, who lay intrans't
> *Thick as Autumnal Leaves that strow the Brooks*
> *In Vallombrosa, where th' Etrurian shades*
> *High overarch't imbow'r; or scatter'd sedge*
> *Afloat, when with fierce Winds Orion arm'd*
> *Hath vext the Red-Sea Coast, whose waves o'erthrew*
> *Busiris and his Memphian Chivalry,*
> *While with perfidious hatred they pursu'd*
> *The Sojourners of Goshen, who beheld*
> *From the safe shore thir floating Carcasses*
> *And broken Chariot Wheels;* so thick bestrown
> Abject and lost lay these, covering the Flood,
> Under amazement of thir hideous change.
> (*Italics mine.*)

Exercise 26

'Tisn't easy, that's for sure. Nathless — I mean, nevertheless — give the epic simile *a whirl too. If you're stuck for a subject, think of some event in sports like a baseball player stealing a base or a wide receiver grabbing for a ball while galloping toward his opponents' end zone.*

Before moving on, I'd like to impress one thing on both new and reconsidering poets: just as poems must come of themselves, so too must *metaphors* and *similes.* Never force a *metaphor* or *simile* into being; above all, the last thing in the world you ever want to say is, "My poem is too plain, I've got to add some *metaphors* and *similes* to it," which I've heard some not-so-inexperienced writers exclaim, so help me.

In this section will be found a bunch of tools that you may not be aware of, or it's possible that you're aware of them without realizing that they're old tricks of the trade with names. Ideally, you as a budding or redefining poet should consciously and conscientiously try out each of them for future serious use. But if you find that rough going, cease and desist. Above all, unless you have some reason to do so deliberately (e.g., parodying someone else), don't overuse any of the stuff, or you'll risk being accused of showing off your verbal gymnastic ability at the expense of meaning and depth. Needless to say, simply being familiar with the terms — all of them polysyllabic and of Greek origin — is useful only for showing off your pseudo-knowledge to dilettantes and for expertly doing crossword puzzles. Finally, note that there's no real order to what follows: I've simply thrown all the tools together, as one — or I anyway — would do with real ones in a real toolbox. Hint: there's a method to my madness, tich-tich.

Personification, Apostrophe, Etc.

Clinically speaking, psychologists would surely look askance at somcone's using personification (*prosopoeia*) — that is, investing something inanimate with human qualities — and if those human qualities turned out to be exclusively masculine in a positive sense, feminists would probably not be too friendly to the idea either. But giving something a human personality is such an ordinary thing for us all to do, and doing so in literature has such a long, distinguished history, that I had to include it here. In this passage from Thomas Gray's "Elegy Written in a Country Church-Yard," Ambition and Grandeur were given the abilities, respectively, to mock and hear:

> Let not ambition mock their useful toil,
> Their homely joys, and destiny obscure;
> Nor grandeur hear with a disdainful smile
> The short and simple annals of the poor.

Admittedly this is rather tame stuff. But take note of this passage from *The Prelude,* where William Wordsworth used a specialized form of personification called a *pathetic fallacy,* wherein a whole or a part of the great outdoors is humanized. Having just recounted how he stole a boat as a boy, the "I" goes on to say:

> . . . ;lustily
> I dipped my oars into the silent lake,
> And, as I rose upon the stroke, my boat
> Went heaving through the water like a swan;
> When, from behind that craggy steep till then
> The horizon's bound, a huge peak, black and huge,
> As if with voluntary power instinct
> Upreared its head. I struck and struck again,
> And growing still in stature the grim shape
> Towered up between me and the stars, and still,
> For so it seemed, with purpose of its own
> And measured motion like a living thing,
> Strode after me. . . .

And that strong presence, it seems, was enough to make him bring the boat back.

Exercise 27

Think of some mechanical device that has caused you a whole heap of trouble, and, if you haven't done so already, endow it with a name and a personality; your computer might be a good candidate. Write a letter to the manufacturer in which you describe your problems with said device as if it's a real person who has wronged you. That'll do it.

Closely related to personification is the *apostrophe*, an address to an absent being or abstract quality as if it were present. In Wordsworth's poem "Tintern Abbey," which was mentioned in the previous chapter, the "I" expatiated on the curative powers of Nature, including the river Wye, and then went on to say:

If this
Be but a vain belief, yet, oh! how oft—
In darkness and amid the many shapes
Of joyless daylight; when the fretful stir
Unprofitable, and the fever of the world,
Have hung upon the beatings of my heart—
How oft, in spirit, have I turned to thee,
O sylvan Wye! thou wanderer thro' the woods,
How often has my spirit turned to thee!

Exercise 28

Write a new letter of complaint, this time to your mechanical device itself, using the second person.

A cousin to the apostrophe is the rhetorical question (*erotema*), which is a question addressed to no one in particular whose answer is self-evident. A good example is the opening statement of the leader of the Chorus in Milton's *Samson Agonistes*, when he encounters Samson, a prisoner of the Philistines, blind and shorn:

. . . .Can this be hee,
That Heroic, that Renown'd,
Irresistible *Samson*? whom unarm'd
No strength of man, or fiercest wild beast could withstand;
Who tore the Lion, as the Lion tears the Kid,
Ran on embattled Armies clad in Iron,
And weaponless himself,
Made Arms ridiculous, useless the forgery
Of brazen shield and spear, the hammer'd Cuirass,
Chalybean temper'd steel, and frock of mail
Adamantean Proof;. . .

Exercise 29

Standing before it, ask the air why your mechanical device does some of the dumb things it does.

Purposeful Omissions

At times, instead of rephrasing, you may want to deliberately omit a word or two from a passage for emphasis (*ellipsis*). We often do this without realizing it, as for example when we say, "When in doubt, leave out" instead of "When you are in doubt, leave it out." This form of omission should be used sparingly, lest a passage you're working on begin to look like a telegram.

Exercise 30

Strike out some words in your rhetorical question of Exercise 29 to make it more emphatic. If this doesn't work for some reason, try it on a text from some previous exercise.

Again, to be emphatic, you may want to leave out the conjunctions between a series of related clauses (*asyndeton*). A good example is Caesar's famous explanation of what happened in Gaul: "I came, I saw, I conquered."

Exercise 31

Return to the piece of action writing you worked up in Exercise 15 and create some new effects by deleting some of the conjunctions.

Colorful Synonym Substitution

If you don't want to repeat the same old garden-variety noun in a given passage and don't care to use a pronoun, there are any number of ways of handling the situation with style. You can substitute a part for the whole of something (*synecdoche*) — for example, "guns" for "weapons," "meat" for "entree," "hands" for "employees," "silver" for "change." You can use an attributive or suggestive word (*metonymy*) instead of your subject — like the "homeless" for "people who are destitute." Also possible is your dreaming up a descriptive word or phrase or a proper name for a quality associated with your subject (*periphrasis*) — "slave driver" for "employer," "Sleeping Beauty" for a "sleepy-head."

Exercise 32

Get hold of a to-do list or a shopping list, and where you can, substitute colorful synonyms.

Truth Distortion

It's often said that good liars make good writers (and vice versa), so while telling lies in real life may get you into trouble, doing so on paper can often pay off. Two modes of truth distortion are exaggeration (*hyperbole*), as in the description of beautiful Helen of Troy as "the face that launched a thousand ships," and understatement (*litotes*), as in *crime of passion* for *brutal murder*.

Exercise 33

Take your original list of Exercise 32 and write a short account of how you attended to your to-do's or bought the items you needed using hyperbole throughout. Then revise your account, understating all of your exaggerations.

Another truth-distorting device is the *euphemism*, a benign or neutral-sounding synonym that one uses in place of something unpleasant, for example, "pass away" for "die" and, in wartime, "collateral damages" for "civilian casualties." Recently there's been a wave of new coinages in this mode in socially conscious circles, for example, "physically challenged," "learning disabled," "at risk," and so on.

Exercise 34

Try inventing a few new euphemisms for unmentionables around the house, beginning with the toilet.

Yet one more truth-distorting device is the *non sequitur*, an inference that doesn't follow from the premises. T. S. Eliot showed himself to be a master of this device in his celebrated poem "The Love Song of J. Alfred Prufrock," as this one of many passages shows:

> For I have known them all already, known them all:—
> Have known the evenings, mornings, afternoons,
> *I have measured out my life with coffee spoons; (Italics mine.)*

Exercise 35

> *Be a master of the* non sequitur *too, or try. Begin by writing a simple statement, like "I'm going to the store," follow it with another, like "I have to buy thus and such," and then follow that one with a third statement that has absolutely no relation to it, like "Whatever happened to the next-to-last Samurai?" That's all there is to it.*

A final truth-distorting device is *irony*, the conveying of a meaning opposite to the one a person intends. An excellent example is that slogan-like refrain in Antony's funeral oration in *Julius Caesar*, where he refers again and again to Brutus, leader of the conspirators, as an honorable man.

Exercise 36

> *Who has never waxed ironical? Write an ironical comment on the effect your letter of complaint of Exercise 27 is likely to have on the head of the company that manufactured your malfunctioning device.*

Wordplay and playing with words

Another way of spicing things up verbally is with *puns*. But for this you really have to use your head, so if yours is tucked away somewhere, get it out and dust it off. Did you know that there are three kinds of *puns*? Like most of our other tools, they've all got ghastly names, like diseases, but not to bother your head with them (anymore than with the others). It's important to note only what they stand for, which is fairly straightforward:

paranomasia: using two or more words that sound alike. Example: The "prophets" prophesied by Baal and walked after the things that do not "profit."

antanaclasis: using the same word or a phrase in two or more senses. Example: There are three "ways" to "waylay" someone.

syllepsis: using the same word literally and figuratively. Example: The jilted girl "ate" her sandwich and her heart out.

Did you happen to notice the *antanaclasis*-like *pun* on Brutus's name in Antony's speech "Oh judgment! Thou art fled to brutish beasts"? Fancy that, yes?

Exercise 37

Try your hand at each of the puns — or try doing all three together in one blast, I dare you. If you need a context, put them in a letter to a friend — you know, show off.

A closely related device is *antihimera,* using one part of speech for another — as in "The rejected suitor dogged her footsteps" (noun "dog" as verb), "the catch of the day" (verb "catch" as noun), "She is a very-soon type of person" (adverbs "very" and "soon" combined to make an adjective), and "Chew it up good" (adjective "good" as adverb).

Exercise 38

Turn a noun into a verb and a verb and a noun into a verb, and use each of your new creations in a sentence — that should do it. If you want to mess English grammar up a little in the process, as the folks on Madison Avenue did with their ad for Winston cigarettes once upon a time — to wit, "Winston tastes good like a cigarette should" — be my guest.

Yet another kind of wordplay involves transposing the initial letters of words that go together, usually an adjective-noun combination — for example, making "crushing blow" into "blushing crow." In English, we call this sort of thing a *spoonerism* after Dr. Spooner, an Anglican minister who reputedly invented it. Susan Walker, my editor, has advised me that *spoonerisms* can happily involve other parts of speech as well. For instance, Dr. Spooner is said to have replied to a parishioner who remarked, "What a chutiful burch you have here" with "Many thinkle peep so, may I sew you to a sheet?" She has also heard of someone on the radio turning "Get the best in bread" into "Get the breast in bed." Once, as a child, when she was setting the table for dinner, she asked her mother quite innocently if she should lay out both sporks and foons.

A similar kind of wordplay, called *Schüttelreim*, exists in German, and my publisher, Arnold Greissle-Schönberg, has imported it into English. His creations run from the simple — "The cat is running, but the rat is cunning " and "Take a shower, shake a tower" — to the delightfully complex — "See the flight, flee the site, sight the flea, flight to sea" and "Lunatic, tuna lick, tick a loon, lick a tune." To these, he's added a father's admonition — "If you're hot in the shed, you'll get a shot in the head" — and this little ditty he composed on the road — "You're driving a little fast. So what if you fiddle last. If you are the last to fiddle, you'll just have to fast a little."

Exercise 39

> *One spoonerism of your own creation will do here. If you feel particularly ambitious, try to top Arnold with a Schüttelreim of your own. But do yourself a favor and don't go and fall overly in love with this stuff.*

Besides playing with words, one can also diddle with their spelling. That is, you can add syllables to the front (*prosthesis*), middle (*epenthesis*), or end (*proparalepsis*) of a word as in the following: "besmirched" for "smirched," "orientating" for "orienting," "embrasure" for "embrace." You can shrink words down in the same way (*aphaereis, syncope, apocope*) — as in "'kay" for "okay," "o'er" for "over," and "shrink" for "head shrinker."

You can also transpose letters of words (*metathesis*), that is, use "traispe" for "traipse" and "pisghetti" for "spaghetti," as small children are known to do. And then, alas, there's the verb "ask." Before 1066 A.D. it was "axe," and now, through usage, it seems to be on its way to becoming "axe" again, just as "nuclear" may be in danger of turning into "nucular" (tich-tich).

I guess I should also mention here that you can, if you should so desire it, change the very sounds of words (*antisthecon*) — make "dreary" into "duh-reary" and "hermaphrodite" into "morphydye."

Exercise 40

Have a ball with all this fiddle-faddle — but do yourself and others a favor and keep it clean, puh-lease!

If you wish to know more about these matters, there's a list of works under Books about Prosody and Related Matters in my Bibliography. The places to start would seem to be Harmon and Holman's *A Handbook to Literature* and Corbett and Connors's *Classical Rhetoric for the Modern Student.* Also of interest is William Packard's *Poet's Dictionary*, where *double, triple, multiple, negative, past-tense, tentative,* and *juxtaposed metaphors* are explored.

The following alternate meanings of common words, found by a friend on the Internet, has to be the ultimate in wordplay such as the Greeks surely never dreamt of:

> Coffee (n.): "the individual upon whom one coughs."
>
> Flabbergasted (adj.): "appalled over how much weight you have gained."
>
> Abdicate (v.): "to give up all hope of ever having a flat stomach."
>
> Esplanade (v.): "to attempt to give an explanation while drunk."
>
> Willy-nilly (adj.): "impotent."
>
> Negligent (adj.): " a condition in which you absent-mindedly answer the door in your nightgown."

Lymph (v.): "to walk with a lisp."

Gargoyle (n.): "olive-flavored mouthwash."

Flatulence (n.): "emergency vehicle that picks you up after you are run over by a steamroller."

Testicle (n.): "a rather humorous question on an exam."

Rectitude (n.): "the formal, dignified bearing adopted by certain proctologists."

Pokemon (n): "a Rastafarian proctologist."

Oyster (n.): "a person who sprinkles his conversation with Yiddishisms."

Circumvent (n.): "an opening in the front of boxer shorts worn by Jewish men."

Rhymes

— aka Sound Correspondences —

Sound, meaning how something strikes your ear and, ultimately, affects your sensibility, plays an important role in all forms of human communication, including poetry — indeed, especially poetry. When a similar sound is repeated in a poem, it's generally called rhyme; that is, one word is said to rhyme with another. I prefer the term *sound-correspondence*, but I'm not about to launch a crusade in favor of it, so in this book, you'll find me using the two terms interchangeably, along with the word *echo* both as a noun and a verb. Better that you should learn the intriguing intricacies of sound and sound-repetition, and leave terminology to eternal test takers and indefatigable crossword puzzle enthusiasts.

Rhyming can be very boring and silly in the hands of a dullard, but when practiced by a master, it can be superb. Whether working with traditional or free verse, the poet offers his or her audience a sound and then an *echo* of it, and before that *echo* dies away, the poet puts forth another sound and *echo*, and then another, and so on, or perhaps he or she plays with a few sounds, going back and forth from one to the other — until the poem is simply alive with it all. Besides their ornamental function, the echoes are — indeed they should be — intricately bound up with the meaning of a poem, though in the case of free verse, this can be so subtle as not to be fully appreciated and can be even totally overlooked by some readers.

A question may arise as to when all this *echoing* began. Since all civilized societies have poetic traditions, the answer has to be way back to that distant point in preliterate time after man had become a distinct species. What the various forms of verse were like in those early days, to say nothing of the languages, is anybody's guess. I like to think that we can get some inkling by going back to our own individual preliterate beginnings. In other words, since the "phylogenetic" way is blocked, I'm suggesting that we take an excursion up the "ontogenetic" highway. If this turns out to be all "Greek" to you, not to worry your head over it. Just let Her rave on and do your thing, okay?

So-o-o, let's wax a little primitive, shall we?

Exercise 1

Here's a list of baby words: "ba-ba," "bu-bu," "boo-hoo," "bow-wow," "da-da," "doe-doe," "doggy," "ga-ga," "gu-gu," "ha-ha," "ka-ka," "ma-ma," "mi-mi," "pa-pa," "pee-pee," "poo-poo," "rah-rah," "ta-ta," "wee-wee." Add others if you wish and chant them out loud, making sure to get your body involved. If you have this urge to beat on a desk or chair-back with a pen while doing so, by all means beat away, but do concentrate on the echoes and don't be overly concerned with the rhythms, which we'll be covering in the next chapter. Needless to say, the idea is to enjoy yourself with this, but if things don't pan out, it's no big deal. Just blame it all on me for suggesting it and carry on. Nobody's perfect <sniff>.

Be that as it may, lets go one step further in our pseudo-return to our verbal roots.

Exercise 2

Remember your pet words from chapter two? Well, get them out again — or if you didn't happen to do that exercise or lost your list, make one up now. Yes, take up your pen and a sheet of paper and put some fun-words down, whatever comes into your head that sounds flaky. And when you're done, do you know what you're going to have? Word salad. The next thing to do is — you guessed it — to read your salad aloud, making sure, of course, to get your body involved.

Poems whose outstanding feature is their rhyme are usually cute and clever, and run the gamut from greeting card verse of the "Roses are red, / Violets are blue" variety to short, snappy witticisms such as those of Ogden Nash and Dorothy Parker, as for instance:

Nash is brash
But Parker is darker

While still in the cutesy vein, some longer poems that rely mainly on rhyme for their effect can come with profound messages. Consider this charming one, "Uppon a Deedmans Hed" by John Skelton (1460?-1529). And don't be turned off by the weird look of the words; that's part of its ongoing charm:

Youre ugly tokyn
My mynd hath brokyn
From worldly lust;
For I have dyscust
We ar but dust,
And dy we must.
   It is generall
To be mortall:
I have well espyde
No man may hym hyde
From deth holow-eyed,
With synnews wyderyd, *withered*
With bonys shyderyd, *shattered*
With hys worme-etyn maw

And hys gastly jaw
Gaspyng asyde,
Nakyd of hyde,
Neyther flesh nor fell. *skin*
  Then by my councell,
Loke that ye spell *study*
Well thys gospell:
For wherso we dwell,
Deth wyll us quell
And with us mell. *mix*
  For all oure pamperde paunchys,
There may no fraunchys *franchise*
Nor worldly blys
Redeme us from this:
Oure days be datyd
To be chekmatyd,
With drawttys of deth *drafts*
Stoppyng oure breth;
Oure eyen synkyng,
Oure bodys stynkyng,
Oure gummys grynnyng,
Oure soulys brynnyng! *burning*
To whom then shall we sew
For to have rescew,
But to swete Jesu
On us then for to rew?
  O goodly chyld
Of Mary mylde,
Then be oure shylde!
That we be not exylyd
To the dyne dale *dun*
Of boteles bale, *bootless / sorrow*
Nor to the lake
Of fendys blake. *fiends / black*
  But graunt us grace
To se thy face,
And to purchace
Thyne hevenly place
And thy palace,
Full of solace,

Above the sky,
That is so hy,
Eternally
To beholde and se
The Trynyte!
Amen.

Somehow this poem has a curiously modern ring to it, doesn't it? Like, doesn't it remind you a bit of something today? Like rap? Not only in its crazy single-rhyming strategy but also in its intent to shake the reader up? It reminds one of a kid gorging him- or herself on ice cream.

Exercise 3

Write a short poem with political or social overtones in which you imitate Skelton's mode of multiple end-rhymes, or just go for rap (which you'll find ain't as easy as it looks, turning out a good one, I mean.)

Playtime is over, it is time to get very serious now. Well — not quite yet. Before moving on to the nitty-gritty, let me pass by you this utterly charming work by Robert Herrick (1591-1674), which is quaintly entitled "Anacrontick Verse." In it, Herrick deftly used the same rhyme at the ends of all eight of its lines and additionally created a slightly varied repeating line (or refrain) that each time emotionally mirrors what's happening on the preceding line:

Brisk methinks I am, and fine,
When I drinke my capring wine:
Then to love I do encline;
When I drinke my wanton wine:
And I wish all maidens mine,
When I drinke my sprightly wine:
Well I sup, and well I dine,
When I drinke my frolick wine:
But I languish, lowre, and Pine,
When I want my fragrant wine.

We'll be covering refrains a little later on in this chapter, after — after —

Exercise 4

What do you say to writing a response to Herrick in which you pay him back in his own coin?

Conventional Rhyming

Rhymes can be either complete, meaning with an exact duplication of one or more syllables — for example, "sky" and "high" in Skelton's poem — or they can be partial, where there's only a hint of a similarity between syllables. One normally associates rhymes with the ends of poetic lines, but as we shall see, they can occur anywhere in them.

As I mentioned earlier, in the first decades of the twentieth century, a number of leading poets turned their backs on form, including and especially conventional rhyme, and for a good long time just about no one of note was using it. "The Red Wheelbarrow" by William Carlos Williams, which functions with very subtle sound-correspondences, is a good example of what I mean:

> so much depends
> upon
> a red wheel
> barrow
>
> glazed with rain
> water
>
> beside the white
> chickens

We'll be taking a good long look at this poem in chapter eight. Let me simply point out here that nowadays the same thing holds as true for rhyming as for your choices of words: any kind of *sound-correspondence* is permissible as long as it works, meaning — and it bears repeating — as long as it's appropriate to what you're saying.

This isn't a new concept, by the way. It was first enunciated — not dreamt up, mind you — by Alexander Pope (1688-1744) in his famous *Essay on Criticism:*

> True Ease in Writing comes from Art, not Chance,
> As those move easiest who have learn'd to dance.
> 'Tis not enough no Harshness gives Offence,
> *The Sound must seem an Eccho to the Sense.*
>
> (*Italics mine.*)

Complete Rhyme

Before the second decade of the nineteenth century, only the following were acceptable as complete rhymes in genteel poetic circles: identically sounding single-syllable words, like "love" and "dove"; a single-syllable word and an identical initial or final syllable of a two-syllable word, like "glee" and "plenty" and "rain" and "stainless"; and identical first or second syllables of two-syllable words, like "crafty" and "drafted" and "dissent" and "prevent." Rhymes involving two or more syllables — for example, "recent" and "decent" and "garage" and barrage" — were called feminine rhymes (gimme a break!) and considered the province of light and trivial verse; indeed, some critics of Wordsworth's day took him severely to task for rhyming "shocked her" with "doctor" in his mock-epic "The Idiot Boy." *Sound-correspondences* involving different syllables of polysyllabic words — for instance, "entice" and "decent"— were absolutely not to be thought of and relegated to the inept .

To rhyme single-syllable words can be elemental and direct — it's like painting straight out of the tube, so to speak — and can produce striking effects in the right hands. A good example is this short poem by Wordsworth titled "A Slumber Did My Spirit Seal," which was his reaction to the death of a girl named Lucy:

A Slumber did my spirit seal;
  I had no human fears:
She seemed a thing that could not feel
  The touch of earthly years.

No motion has she now, no force;
  She neither hears nor sees;
Rolled round in earth's diurnal course,
  With rocks, and stones, and trees.

Note how the *r*-sound of "rolled round" is reinforced by those in the end rhymes "fears" and "years" and "force" and "course," and the related *l*-sound in "seal" and "feel." The end-rhyme "sees" and "trees" in the second stanza extends the *ee*-sounds of the first stanza and thus adds to the rolling round motif (as does the repetition of "and" in the final line). One could go on and speak of how the internal *r*'s, *s*'s, *l*'s, and *e*'s reinforce the end-rhymes and further add to the rolling, but I'm sure you get the point.

A great poem, like chicken in the hands of an inferior cook, is hard to ruin.

Exercise 5

Forget the meaning of "A Slumber Did My Spirit Seal" for the moment, and maintaining the same rhyming pattern, substitute other single-syllable words on the end-lines of the two stanzas or, alternatively, retain all of the end-words and substitute nonsense statements for the rest of each line. Read the original poem aloud, then your nonsense version, and then the original again.

With the appearance of Lord Byron (1788-1824) on the literary scene, things began loosening up where complete rhyme was concerned. In his magnificent satiric epic *Don Juan*, Byron thumbed his nose at the rules, not only managing to eke out a rhyme with "new one" and "true one," for instance, but to top it off with "Juan" (pronounced "jew-on"):

I want a hero: an uncommon want,
  When every year and month sends forth a new one,
Till, after cloying the gazettes with cant,
  The age discovers he is not the true one:
Of such as these I should not care to vaunt,
  I'll therefore take our ancient friend Don Juan —
We all have seen him, in the pantomime,
Sent to the Devil somewhat ere his time.

And he went on to yet greater glory in that same work by rhyming "hen peck'd you all" with "intellectual":

'T is pity learned virgins ever wed
  With persons of no sort of education,
Or gentlemen, who, though well born and bred,
  Grow tired of scientific conversation;
I don't choose to say much upon this head,
  I'm a plain man, and in a single station,
But — Oh! ye lords of ladies intellectual,
Inform us truly, have they not hen-peck'd you all?

Exercise 6

Take the words "love" and "rain" and see how many single-syllable and polysyllabic words you can come up with to rhyme with each. Normally I'd say feel free to use a rhyming dictionary, but in this case it would be counterproductive, no? Substitute your words for those ending the lines of one or the other of Byron's stanzas. Read the original aloud, then your nonsense stanza aloud, and then the original again.

Nowadays, thanks to Byron and the poets who came after him, the fine distinctions as to what syllables can and cannot be rhymed have gone by the wayside, and today anything goes and indeed should go, where complete rhyme is concerned.

A word remains to be said here about the occasional use of complete rhymes in unrhymed poems. Milton showed himself to be the master of this stratagem, particularly in his final largely unrhymed work *Samson Agonistes*, where *sound-repetition* serves as a kind of highlighter. Note the *ight*–rhymes in this passage as an example of the kind of thing I mean:

Which shall I first bewail,
Thy Bondage or lost *Sight,*
Prison within Prison
Inseparably dark?
Thou art become (O worst imprisonment!)
The Dungeon of thyself; thy Soul
(Which Men enjoying *sight* oft without cause complain)
Imprison'd now indeed,
In real darkness of the body dwells,
Shut up from outward *light*
To incorporate with gloomy *night;*
For inward *light,* alas,
Puts forth no visual beam. *(Italics mine.)*

Partial Rhymes

Believe it or not, there are at least five different types of *partial rhyme:*

— *Near rhyme,* in which the consonants following the vowels in a given pair of syllables are related but not identical — Example: "grunt" and "trundle. "

— *Eye rhyme,* in which the rhyming syllables are spelled alike but pronounced differently — Example: "Come live with me and be my love, / And we shall all the pleasures prove," by Christopher Marlow (1564-1593).

— *Assonance,* a correspondence or near-correspondence of two or more vowels alone — Example: "neck" and "met."

— *Consonance,* a correspondence or near-correspondence of two or more consonants alone — Example: "fox" and "annex."

— *Alliteration,* where the initial consonants of words are the same, in other words a specialized form of *consonance* — Example: "Peter Piper picked a peck of pickled peppers." (We've already met with it in Anglo-Saxon poetry, which allowed for a correspondence of initial vowels as well.)

Exercise 7

Create one of each kind of your own, but take care not to make them so nonsensical as to obscure the aim of this exercise, which is most important.

Obviously, *partial rhymes* can only be spoken of with respect to rhymed poetry, where indeed they can be used to create subtle dissonant effects and lift one's poems out of the ordinary and mundane. The secret of doing this effectively is, as with other things, not to overuse partial rhymes. No better example of discretion in this respect can be found than in what looks like a very simple — almost simple-minded — poem by William Blake with the deceptively simple title of "Spring":

Sound the Flute!
Now it's mute.
Birds delight
Day and Night.
Nightingale
In the dale,
Lark in Sky
Merrily
Merrily Merrily to welcome in the Year

Little Boy
Full of joy.
Little Girl
Sweet and small,
Cock does crow

So do you.
Merry voice
Infant noise
Merrily Merrily to welcome in the Year.

Little Lamb
Here I am,
Come and lick
My white neck.
Let me pull
Your soft Wool.
Let me kiss
Your soft face.
Merrily Merrily we welcome in the Year.

In the first stanza, the rhymes are all complete; however, there is a hint of things to come in the *alliteration* of the *d*'s in "delight," "day," and "dale" and of the *n*'s in "now," "night," and "nightingale," and in the *eye rhyme* of "sky" and "merrily." In the second stanza, Blake became more openly daring with the *consonance* of "girl" and "small," *assonance* of "voice" and "noise," and *near rhyme* of "crow" and "you." And in the third stanza he played with *consonance* — "lick" and "neck," "pull" and "Wool," and finally "kiss" and "face."

Notice further how careful he was to begin each venture into *dissonance*, let's call it, with a pure rhyme – "Boy" and "Joy"; "Lamb" and "am." This is the way of great classical music — of Mozart and Beethoven! The use of "Merrily Merrily, to welcome in the Year" at the end of the first two stanzas and its variant with "we" to conclude the final stanza comes almost as a kind of taunt — "Look what I can do! Let's see you do better!"

In "Sailing to Byzantium," which is in the same stanza that Byron used and indeed made famous in his *Don Juan*, the poet William Butler Yeats (1865-1939) established, by a very low-keyed use of partial rhyme, that he was after other "game" and not in competition with Byron:

That is no country for old men. The *young*
In one another's arms, birds in the trees,
— Those dying generations — at their *song*,
The salmon-falls, the mackerel-crowded *seas*,
Fish, flesh, or fowl, commend all summer long
Whatever is begotten, born, and *dies*.
Caught in that sensual music all neglect
Monuments of unageing intellect. (*Italics mine.*)

Yeats's restraint in his use of partial rhyme continues in the next two stanzas and then disappears in the final one, once he's made it crystal-clear that he was operating in a different continuum from Byron's. The stanza becomes whole — healed, if you will:

An aged man is but a paltry thing,
A tattered coat upon a stick, unless
Soul clap its hands and sing, and louder sing
For every tatter in its mortal *dress*,
Nor is there singing school but studying
Monuments of its own *magnificence;*
And therefore I have sailed the seas and come
To the holy city of Byzantium.

O sages standing in God's holy fire
As in the gold mosaic of a *wall*,
Come from the holy fire, perne in a gyre,
And be the singing-masters of my *soul.*
Consume my heart away; sick with desire
And fastened to a dying *animal*
It knows not what it is; and gather me
Into the artifice of eternity.

Once out of nature I shall never take
My bodily form from any natural thing,
But such a form as Grecian goldsmiths make
Of hammered gold and gold enameling
To keep a drowsy Emperor awake;
Or set upon a golden bough to sing
To lords and ladies of Byzantium
Of what is past, or passing, or to come. (*Italics mine.*)

Exercise 8

Mess up the last stanza of Yeats's poem above by substituting nonsense words that partially rhyme on three alternately rhymed lines. As before, read the original aloud, then your nonsense stanza, and then the original again.

As I said earlier, rhymes can occur anywhere on a line. When at the ends, they're known as *end-rhymes;* when in the midst of a line, they're referred to as *internal rhymes.*

END-RHYMES

Line-ends can rhyme consecutively or in alternation or in an envelope arrangement. When a pair of *end-rhymes* occurs consecutively, the two lines are called a *couplet,* and they're referred to by a pair of small letters (*aa*). A paragraph consisting of *couplets* would thus be designated *aabbccdd,* etc. The following excerpt from Yeats's "Sailing to Byzantium" is a *couplet,* and indeed so too are all the terminal pairs of lines in the selections by Byron as well as Yeats above:

> And therefore I have sailed the seas and come
> To the holy city of Byzantium.

When a *couplet* can stand on its own as a syntactic unit, as is the case with this one, it's called a *closed couplet;* when one is run on with the rest of a stanza, as are some of the other couplets in "Sailing to Byzantium," we refer to it as an *open couplet.*

Exercise 9

A single rhymed couplet is in order here. Whichever you prefer, sense or nonsense.

In lines where *end-rhymes* alternate with other *end-rhymes*, the arrangement is called *cross-rhyming*, and the rhymes are designated *abab*, etc. Wordsworth used *cross-rhymes* in the two stanzas of "A Slumber Did My Spirit Seal," and they're indicated as *abab cdcd*. Just so we're all marching to the same tune, go back to page 116 and take another look at this poem to see that what I say is so.

Exercise 10

While you're there, write an imitation of one of the stanzas of "A Slumber Did My Spirit Seal."

Occasionally poets arrange one *couplet* inside another to form, so to speak, an *envelope* (*abba*), which is what Keats gave us in the opening to "On First Looking into Chapman's Homer":

> Much have I travell'd in the realms of gold,
> And many goodly states and kingdoms seen;
> Round many western islands have I been
> Which bards in fealty to Apollo hold.

Exercise 11

Let's see what you can do with the envelope arrangement.

We shall have occasion to refer to these different arrangements of end-rhymes again when we come to deal with individual stanza and verse forms in the chapters that follow.

Internal Rhymes

Sound-correspondences can also occur between words in the interior and at the end of a line. My favorites are the two master strokes that Blake achieved in the last two lines of "The Garden of Love." If you recall, the poem is about an "I" going to seek out an old love who has turned away from life and become religious. In the two final lines, Blake rhymed mid-line words "gowns" and "briars" with end-line words "rounds" and "desires" to give the woman's conversion and the end of the relationship a sense of finality:

> And I saw it was filled with graves,
> And tomb-stones where flowers should be:
> And Priests in black gowns, were walking their rounds,
> And binding with briars, my joys & desires.

The partial rhyme of "gowns" and "rounds" conjures up a crack in a bell, and the association of Jesus's crown of thorns with the binding of joys and desires provides an added note of irony. I could go on to talk about how the *alliteration* of the *b*'s and related *v* and *f's* in key words in the stanza, to say nothing of how the circularity of "walking their rounds" and "binding" contributes to it all, but I'm sure you get the picture by now.

Exercise 12

Take the following pairs of rhyming words and create one-liners with them: "cowers" and "towers"; "deal" and "meal"; "rush" and "brush." Make 'em sing.

Remember, we'll have occasion to deal vigorously with extra-subtle internal *sound-correspondences* when we zero in on *free verse* in chapter eight. Meanwhile, note what my friend Ilsa Gilbert does with external and internal rhymes, both full and partial, in "Zoo International, Basel, Switzerland":

> I so small
> and you so tall
> From a distance
> I spot that you are spotted.
> Perhaps I am too,
>
> But no one can see that.
> Besotted with you,
> My white and brown beauty,

Just for one day
In the zoo in Basel,
I allow myself to fall for a Giraffe!

And though I'm not a Swiss miss
and chocolate will not do,
Over a wine carafe,
I wish we could kiss—

If we could cross
the boundaries
of species
and borders!

What I particularly like about this poem is that the giraffe's spots are echoed in it. Ooh, did you miss something? Read-read-read it again!

Word and Phrase Rhyming

When one thinks about it, *word-* and *phrase-repetition* are, after all, other forms of rhyming. Happily, both have as an added blessing a reinforcement of meaning.

I can't think of a better example of single word-repetition than Edgar Allan Poe's poem "The Bells," zany as it is, which starts off —

Hear the sledges with the bells —
Silver bells!
What a world of merriment their melody foretells!
How they tinkle, tinkle, tinkle,
In the icy air of night!
While the stars that oversprinkle
All the Heavens, seem to twinkle
With a crystalline delight;
Keeping time, time, time,
In a sort of Runic rhyme,
To the tintinnabulation that so musically wells
From the bells, bells, bells, bells,
Bells, bells, bells —
From the jingling and the tinkling of the bells.

There are four more stanzas. Would you care to peruse them? I didn't think so. Even so —

Exercise 13

Think of a particular sound that everyone is familiar with, like an alarm clock going off, and see if you can come up with an imitation of "The Bells." A parody's welcome.

Single *word-repetition* can work with truly extraordinary effectiveness in the hands of a master like Wordsworth. In the opening paragraph of "Tintern Abbey," which he composed on a walking tour with his younger sister Dorothy, he set the scene in the beginning with the eye-catching repetition of "five" in the first two lines, supported by the words "length" and "long." It only required a repetition of "this" and "these," backed up by "again" in the balance of the paragraph, to make the scene as palpable as any painting or photo, maybe more so:

> *Five* years have past; *five* summers, with the length
> Of *five* long winters! and *again* I hear
> *These* waters, rolling from their mountain-springs
> With a soft inland murmur. — Once *again*
> Do I behold *these* steep and lofty cliffs,
> That on a wild secluded scene impress
> Thoughts of more deep seclusion; and connect
> The landscape with the quiet of the sky.
> The day is come when I *again* repose
> Here, under *this* dark sycamore, and view
> *These* plots of cottage-ground, *these* orchard-tufts,
> Which at *this* season, with their unripe fruits,
> Are clad in one green hue, and lose themselves
> 'Mid groves and copses. Once *again* I see
> *These* hedge-rows, hardly hedge-rows, little lines
> Of sportive wood run wild: *these* pastoral farms,
> Green to the very door; and wreaths of smoke
> Sent up, in silence, from among the trees!
> With some uncertain notice, as might seem
> Of vagrant dwellers in the houseless woods,

> Or of some Hermit's cave, where by his fire
> The Hermit sits alone. (*Italics mine.*)

Could you do as well, I wonder? I'd settle for half or even a quarter. Care to try?

Exercise 14

> *Write a short description of a scene — in prose, yes? — in which you conjure up immediacy by using "this" and "these."*

One thing that you should always bear in mind when it comes to repeating words in something you've written is that your repetitions must be — and seem — purposeful. This means that poets — but especially novices — must go over and over their work and ruthlessly weed out any unintended repetitions.

Exercise 15

> *For the sake of practice and getting into the swing of things in the repetition arena, this is a good time to review your repetitions in your short description from Exercise 14.*

Besides those covered above, there are several other, specialized forms of *single word repetition* that you should be aware of, which you may find come in handy from time to time as your pen's moving along.

First, there's the use of the same word or group of words at the ends of successive phrases or clauses (*epistrophe*). St. Paul's famous statement in I Corinthians is a good example of this:

> When I was a *child*, I spake as a *child*, I understood as a *child*, I thought as a *child:* but when I became a man, I put away *childish* things. *(Italics mine)*

Repeating a word or group of words at the beginning of successive phrases or clauses (*anaphora*) is obviously a close cousin. In the opening section of the first chapter of Genesis, particularly effective use is made of this (together with *epistrophe*):

> In the beginning God created the heaven and the earth.
>
> *And* the earth was without form, and void; and darkness was upon the face of the deep. *And* the Spirit of God moved upon the face of the waters.
>
> *And* God said, Let there be *light:* and there was *light.*
>
> *And* God saw the light, that it was good: and God divided the light from the darkness.
>
> *And* God called the light Day, and the darkness he called Night. *And* the evening and the morning were the first day. (*Italics mine.*)

In Jeffrey Greene's poem "The Anatomy of Night," note how effective the repetition of "night" is at the beginnings of the lines, drawing our attention to it and making it a focal point. But he was careful not to overload the reader: the occurrence of "night" is spaced out, just as the alliteration of its *n* with the *n*'s in the place-names are. Also of importance, by placing the last instance of "night" within its line, he provided a summary statement for the poem and at the same time rid the word of its power. Nor should we overlook the *anaphora-couplet* he created there in the end with the repetition of "the" at the beginnings of the last two lines:

> *Night* comes before dark,
> dark on the horizon,
> *night* in our swimsuits and towels
> where they hang on a bush,
> *night* over the cottages
> that grow whiter before they darken,
> the yellow of their kitchens,
> *night* over Cross Mills Library
> lit blue with its Starlight movie,
> *night* over the white church
> and its one-room school
> and Rathbone's fishhouse
> with its dark crowded tanks,

> *night* over Fort *Ninigret,*
> two massive maples at its heart
> and one boulder for thanks
> to the *Niantic* and *Narragansett* Indians,
> *night* over the bluffs where King George's
> man-o'-war and two of his fireships
> slipped toward *New London,*
> *night* in the statuary
> where one stone reads,
> "I would not want to live always,"
> *the* body of *night* in our hands,
> *the* dreams we wake from a little sad. *(Italics mine.)*

Anaphora has long been the stock-in-trade of seasoned orators; remember how the Gettysburg Address opens: "*Four score* and *seven years* ago our *fathers* brought *forth,* upon this *continent,* a *new nation, conceived* in Liberty, and dedicated to the proposition that all men are *created* equal." (*Italics mine.*) But in the hands of newly fledged speechifiers, the results can be very amusing — alas, oftentimes unintentionally so. If you're given to using this sort of thing, do so with extreme care or you risk making a fool of yourself.

Exercise 16

Write a short statement outlining the shortcomings of a politician, employer, or some official at your school, of course, making effective use of anaphora and epistrophe.

Another specialized kind of *word-repetition* is the use of different forms of the same word or words that come from the same root (*polyptoton*). Shakespeare said it all in these lines from *Troilus and Cressida:*

> The Greeks are *strong* and *skillful* to their *strength,*
> *Fierce* to their *skill,* and to their *fierceness* valiant,...
> (*Italics mine.*)

Which brings us back almost to *puns,* doesn't it?

Exercise 17

Think of three nouns that have adjectives derived from them and use them with reference to a favorite poet or sports team or what you will in a short passage.

We call the repetition of a whole line or group of lines a *refrain*, and you'll recall that we've already met with it in "Merrily Merrily, to welcome in the Year" and its variants in Blake's "Spring" (pages 119-120) and in Marc Antony's incisive taunts of Brutus and the other conspirators in his Funeral Oration for Caesar (pages 53-54). I can't help but mention still one more: a truly extraordinary use of a refrain that occurs in "Anatomy of the World: The First Anniversary" by John Donne (1571-1631), where the line "She, she is dead, she's dead: when thou know'st this" followed by another, which varies, is repeated now and again. Here are two instances; are they not as fresh as the day they were written, I ask you:

She in whom virtue was so much refined,
That for allay unto so pure a mind
She took the weaker sex, she that could drive
The poisonous tincture, and the stain of Eve,
Out of her thoughts, and deeds; and purify
All, by a true religious alchemy;
She, she is dead; she's dead: when thou know'st this,
Thou know'st how poor a trifling thing man is. . . .
(*Italics mine.*)

She that was best, and first original
Of all fair copies; and the general
Steward to Fate; she whose rich eyes, and breast,
Gilt the West Indies, and perfumed the East;
Whose having breathed in this world, did bestow
Spice on those isles, and bade them still smell so,
And that rich Indy which doth gold inter,
Is but as single money, coined from her:
She to whom this world must itself refer,
As suburbs, or the microcosm of her,

She, she is dead; she's dead: when thou know'st this,
Thou know'st how lame a cripple this world is.
(*Italics mine.*)

Let Ruth Fainlight, our guest poet, have the last say in the matter of refrains with "The Point of It All," in which futility is mirrored in or buffered by a dream — or is it?

Duplications and perspectives, like mirrored
halls or corridors in tourist hotels.
Static-sparking nylon carpets. Walls
a paler version of the same exhausted
colour under neon-strip illumination.
Smoothly-swinging double doors, marked
'Anarchy Storeroom,' 'Betrayal Department.'
The usual anxiety dream
including it all.

This time, another actor on the scene:
someone I hoped might be the very ally
to help reduce the tension that oozed its poison
through weeping eyes and skin. Alone, I knew
how I would lose control at the worst moment
and foolishly encourage and confirm
the malice and pleasure of my tormentor
(now also present) — who had to be
the cause of it all.

Wearily, we quartered every corner,
exploring spaces musty as cupboards, huge
and drafty as shopping precincts — stumbled
across an empty office whose wide windows
opened on a sunset sky and showed how high
above the street we were. But it was always
the wrong place and time for easy answers.
The next part of the dream I forget:
the point of it all.

Does it hurt if the repetition of "all" makes us think of the conspiracy in *Julius Caesar:* "But Brutus is an honorable man, / So are they all honorable men"? Not one bit, wouldn't you say? In fact, it adds to the richness of Ruth's poem, doesn't it? And if one also calls to mind "Do I wake or sleep?" — that devastating last line of Milton's sonnet on his recently deceased wife that begins, "Methinks I see my departed saint"? The same.

Exercise 18

> *Take your nonsense imitation of Wordsworth's "A Slumber Did My Spirit Seal" in Exercise 5 and use the same line to end both stanzas. Voilà, you've got a refrain, quick and dirty.*

Before we leave this subject of verbal repetition, I should point out that there are any number of long works in which words and phrases are repeated over and over to effect, much as a leitmotif is in a Wagnerian opera or snatches of a theme song in a Broadway musical. Shakespeare was particularly adept at this sort of thing, often repeating words and phrases to keep reminding his audience of the real subject of a play lest they be distracted by digressions. *Julius Caesar,* where "honor" and its cousin "honest" as well as "noble" are sounded again and again throughout the five acts, is a good case in point. Even more important in it is the repetition of "all," beginning with the opening scene where a cobbler and a tribune bandy words over it and its homonym "awl," and continuing through Antony's Funeral Oration, when he indicates where Brutus's knife penetrated Caesar's mantle and cries out, "This was the most unkindest cut of all." The repetition of "all" here and there in the play to the bitter end, when justice catches up with the perpetrators, is for the sake of reminding audiences of that cut and that the whole of society, from the honorable men who tolerated the act to the ever-fickle rabble, shared the guilt in Caesar's assassination.

Shakespeare went even further in his handling of theme words in *Macbeth,* written later in his career. With their murder of the king, Macbeth is full of remorse, which Lady Macbeth tries to assuage by telling him, "What's done cannot be undone," and henceforth, throughout the play, not only are the words "done" and "do" repeated again and again but also oodles of words rhyming with them, like "won," "sun," "minion," "double," "bubble," "rump," "thumb," "come," "drum," "due," "duties," "dues," "undone," "dunnest," "masterdom," "trumpet-tongued," "ambition," "none," "undaunted," "summons," "unrule," "downy," "unbecoming," "anon," "scorpions," "down," "overcome," "summer's," "wonder," "son," "gone," "Acheron," "fool," "cool," "wren," and "run," not to mention the names of the murdered King and his family — Duncan, Malcolm, Donalbain. Indeed, the two syllables *un* and *oo* sound like drumbeats throughout the play — to the very last line, which features "one" and "Scone."

Below are several matters that seem to belong in this chapter — which is Her euphemistic way of saying that She didn't know what else to do with them.

Onomatopoeia or Verbal Sound Effects

When I was an undergraduate, the word *onomatopoeia* was much bandied about in connection with poetry, indeed to the point where it seemed as if that was what poetry was all about. Hopefully, those of my generation, besides myself, know better nowadays. So what is it already, in case you're not in the know and are wondering? Purely and simply, the use of a verbal expression to picture a sound, and actually, without consciously realizing it, we're constantly employing *onomatopoeia* in our daily lives, as our many short sound-picturing verbs like "hiss," "slam," "whirr," and "sizzle" testify.

In the hands of a poetic word-smith with a super-sensitive ear, *onomatopoeia* can be a formidable tool, and top honors surely go to Shakespeare for the Heath Scene in King Lear, where the harsh sounds of the words that old, mad Lear chokes out — like "crack," "rage," "cataracts," "hurricanoes," "spout," "drenched," "drowned," "cocks," and so on — echo the storm within him as well as that in the harsh human world around him:

> Blow, winds, and crack your cheeks! Rage, blow!
> You cataracts and hurricanoes, spout
> Till you have drench'd our steeples, drown'd the cocks!
> You sulph'rous and thought-executing fires,
> Vaunt-couriers of oak-cleaving thunderbolts,
> Singe my white head! And thou, all-shaking thunder,
> Strike flat the thick rotundity o' th' world!
> Crack nature's molds, all germains spill at once,
> That makes ingrateful man!

Poets can be far more subtle in their use of *onomatopoeia*, so much so that it can very nearly escape our attention. Note, for instance, the first stanza of Carl Sandburg's "Fog," where the consonance of *t*'s in "little cat feet" conveys the fog's stealthy, silent appearance.

More subtle yet is the use of the word "buzz" in "I Heard a Fly Buzz When I Died," by Emily Dickinson (1830-1886). Note what happens when you read the title without that word: "I Heard a Fly When I Died." But even more surprising is what happens if one eliminates "buzz" from the poem itself. Did you ever give any thought to that? Why not try it and see what I mean:

> I heard a Fly *buzz*–when I died–
> The Stillness–in the Room

Was like the Stillness in the Air
Between the Heaves of Storm–

The Eyes around–had wrung them dry–
And Breaths were gathering firm
For that last Onset–when the King
Be witnessed–in the Room–

I willed my Keepsakes–signed away
What portion of me be
Assignable–and then it was
There interposed a fly–

With Blue–uncertain–stumbling *Buzz*–
Between the light–and me–
And then the Windows failed–and then
I could not see to see–(*Italics mine.*)

Exercise 19

Do you remember that letter of complaint you wrote to a manufacturer about their product in Exercise 27 of chapter three? Well, dig it out and add some verbal sound effects to it to drive home your point.

More intriguing yet is a poet's suggesting something through a pacing of his or her words. Note how the poet Wallace Stevens (1879-1955) leads us to picture someone slowly and quietly beginning to improvise on a keyboard in the opening stanza of his "Peter Quince at the Clavier":

Just as my fingers on these keys
Make music, so the selfsame sounds
On my spirit make a music, too.

Music is feeling, then, not sound;
And thus it is that what I feel,
Here in this room, desiring you,

Thinking of your blue-shadowed silk,
Is music. . . .

Better known to you all, perhaps, is this speech by Prospero from Shakespeare's *The Tempest*, in which he, the king, resigns his role as magician. Note how the lilt and cadence of the verse, especially toward the end, are suggestive of the waving of a wand:

> Ye elves of hills, brooks, standing lakes, and groves,
> And ye that on the sands with printless foot
> Do chase the ebbing Neptune, and do fly him
> When he comes back; you demi-puppets that
> By moonshine do the green sour ringlets make,
> Whereof the ewe not bites; and you whose pastime
> Is to make midnight mushrooms, that rejoice
> To hear the solemn curfew; by whose aid,
> Weak masters though ye be, I have bedimm'd
> The noontide sun, call'd forth the mutinous winds,
> And 'twixt the green sea and the azur'd vault
> Set roaring war; to the dread rattling thunder
> Have I given fire, and rifted Jove's stout oak
> With his own bolt; the strong-bas'd promontory
> Have I made shake, and by the spurs pluck'd up
> The pine and cedar; graves at my command
> Have wak'd their sleepers, op'd, and let 'em forth
> By my so potent art. But this rough magic
> I here abjure, and, when I have requir'd
> Some heavenly music, which even now I do,
> To work mine end upon their senses that
> This airy charm is for, I'll break my staff,
> Bury it certain fathoms in the earth,
> And deeper than did ever plummet sound
> I'll drown my book.

Exercise 20

Can you picture something with a pacing of your words? Here are some possible subjects: "lifting a wineglass"; "taking a walk"; "getting out of bed in the morning."

It doesn't have to be great, does it? The important thing to remember is that you try to do it in a relaxed manner, just bearing in mind that it's only a flexercise. For now comes —

Thought Rhyming or Parallelism

Thoughts don't have any sound — or do they? If you carefully read through Hamlet, you'll see what I mean. Again and again, Shakespeare repeated the word "reason" and other words relating to sanity and madness. Hamlet's very grief over his father's death and mother's remarriage is close to madness.

Another mode of thought-echoing is to rephrase a statement using the same grammatical structure. Technically known as *parallelism*, this device was the mainstay of the authors of the Old Testament Psalms, where it occurred in three different forms:

> *synonymous* — where the sense of the first statement is repeated practically verbatim in the second — as in "At thy rebuke they fled; at the voice of thy thunder they hasted away."
>
> *synthetic* — where the second statement represents a progression from or consequence of the first – as in "They give drink to every beast of the field; the wild asses quench their thirst."
>
> *antithetical* — involving a second statement that contradicts or is antithetical to the first — as in "For the Lord knoweth the way of the righteous: but the way of the ungodly shall perish."

Exercise 21

Try creating a parallelism of each kind, using a recent event in the news of late as a departure point.

Some portions of the Old Testament, like the following attributed to Deutero-Isaiah, are notable for their climactic or stair-like building of parallel statements:

> He giveth power to the faint; and to them that have no might he increaseth strength.
>
> Even the youths shall faint and be weary, and the young men shall utterly fall:

> But they that wait upon the Lord shall renew their strength; they shall mount up with wings as eagles; they shall run, and not be weary; and they shall walk, and not faint.

The first two verses are examples of *synonymous parallelism;* the third verse (beginning with "But") is in opposition to them and so is in its entirety an example of the *antithetical* kind. Within the third verse, "they shall mount up with wings as eagles" is also *synonymous,* while the last two statements are consequences of the first two statements, hence examples of *synthetic parallelism.*

At least one of the psalms — the Twenty-third — is totally made up of smaller and greater parallel units:

> The Lord is my shepherd; I shall not want.
>
> He maketh me to lie down in green pastures: He leadeth me beside the still waters.
>
> He restoreth my soul: He leadeth me in the paths of righteousness for His name's sake.
>
> Yea, though I walk through the valley of the shadow of death, I will fear no evil: for thou art with me; thy rod and thy staff they comfort me.
>
> Thou preparest a table before me in the presence of mine enemies: thou anointest my head with oil; my cup runneth over.
>
> Surely goodness and mercy shall follow me all the days of my life: and I will dwell in the house of the Lord for ever.

Exercise 22

See if you can sort it out for yourself.

Parallelism can be highly effective in the hands of some of our relatively modern masters, like Alexander Pope in his at times devastating *Essay on Man.* I can't help getting chills when I read this. How about you?

> Know then thyself, presume not God to scan;
> The proper study of Mankind is Man.

Plac'd on this isthmus of a middle state,
A being darkly wise, and rudely great:
With too much knowledge for the Sceptic side,
With too much weakness for the Stoic's pride,
He hangs between; in doubt to act, or rest,
In doubt to deem himself a God, or beast;
In doubt his Mind or Body to prefer,
Born but to die, and reas'ning but to err;
Alike in ignorance, his reason such,
Whether he thinks too little, or too much:
Chaos of Thought and Passion, all confus'd;
Still by himself abus'd, or disabus'd;
Created half to rise, and half to fall;
Great lord of all things, yet a prey to all;
Sole judge of Truth, in endless Error hurl'd:
The glory, jest, and riddle of the world!

Clearly, Pope was familiar with every trick of the trade where *parallelism* is concerned, from line-to-line parallel phrasing ("With too much knowledge,.../With too much Weakness...") to the same within a line ("A being darkly wise, and rudely great"). And with those few basic tools, he knew how to build a whole passage to one grand climax.

While creating poetry of an entirely different texture, Thomas Gray (1716-1771) was also a master of *parallel statements*, as can be seen from the opening quatrain of his "Elegy Written in a Country Church-yard":

The curfew tolls the knell of parting day,
The lowing herd winds slowly o'er the lea,
The ploughman homeward plods his weary way,
And leaves the world to darkness and to me.

Everything is sleepy, languid, made so in part by the subject-verb pattern of the first three lines. The last line, with "ploughman" the understood subject of "leaves" provides a taste — but just a soupçon — of the same parallel structure, enough to create a subtle, nonjarring variation to that pattern.

In the opening of his sonnet "Nuns Fret Not at Their Convent's Narrow Room," Wordsworth began with a similar strategy, but as of the fourth line ("Maids, etc."), he gradually expanded his paralleling items for the sake of introducing variation:

> Nuns fret not at their convent's narrow room;
> And hermits are contented with their cells;
> And students with their pensive citadels;
> Maids at the wheel, the weaver at his loom,
> Sit blithe and happy; bees that soar for bloom,
> High as the highest Peak of Furness-fells,
> Will murmur by the hour in foxglove bells:

An extraordinary use of parallelism in our modern era occurs in "A Noiseless Patient Spider," by Walt Whitman (1819-1892), where in two stanzas of the same number of lines, an analogy is set forth between a spider weaving its web and the "I"'s soul:

> A noiseless patient spider,
> I mark'd where on a little promontory it stood isolated,
> Mark'd how to explore the vacant vast surrounding,
> It launch'd forth filament, filament, filament, out of itself,
> Ever unreeling them, ever tirelessly speeding them.
>
> And you O my soul where you stand,
> Surrounded, detached, in measureless oceans of space,
> Ceaselessly musing, venturing, throwing, seeking the
> spheres to connect them,
> Till the bridge you will need be form'd, till the ductile
> anchor hold,
> Till the gossamer thread you fling catch somewhere,
> O my soul.

Whitman was, perhaps, unique in his time, and is too in ours by and large, in looking upon the spider without fear and revulsion — indeed as a romantic hero much of a muchness with himself.

Exercise 23

> *Now that you see what's what with this most interesting tool, take your three parallel statements of Exercise 21 and revise them into a single one or start afresh, using one of them as a jumping-off point.*

Now that you've gotten your feet wet a little with sounds, what's your favorite tool? Me, I like "weird" *sound-correspondences,* by which I suppose I mean subtle ones, that is, those that are not easily recognizable.

A sort of graduation exercise is in order. Get out the ole writing implement and some paper and make some music, yes, just with sounds, yes, almost the way we began in this chapter. Make some sounds that appeal to you — and you alone. If it also makes sense, count yourself among the blessed — and congratulations.

But don't go banging on anything — not yet. It's coming up in the next chapter.

Rhythm and Meter

All types of communication among higher forms of life here on Earth — like four-footed animals and birds — have some kind of beat to them. That's rhythm. Just think of the sounds made by our household pets and common farm animals and you'll see what I mean.

Exercise 1

But don't just think about them, do it. Say them aloud in any old order, and do so again and again, making sure to get your body involved: "bow-wow," "wuff-wuff," "moo-oo-oo," "ba-a-a," "me-ow," "me-ew," "cheep-cheep," "pur-r-r-r," "arf-arf," "oink-oink," "neigh-eigh-eigh."

The beat of human languages is another story; even from their earliest days, such languages as existed had to be far more sophisticated. So-o-o — why don't we? — yes. And let's do this in two stages, okay?

Exercise 2

Remember how we tried to return to our distant past in the last chapter by creating a chant consisting of baby language?

> *Let's do it again, this time concentrating on its beat rather than the individual sounds, and again, swinging and swaying: "ba-ba," "boo-boo," "boo-hoo," "bow-wow," "da-da," "doe-doe," "doggy," "ga-ga," "goo-goo," "ha-ha," "ka-ka," "ma-ma," "mi-mi," "pa-pa," "pee-pee," "poo-poo," "rah-rah," "ta-ta," "wee-wee."*

What a racket, wouldn't you say? But you just wait, you ain't seen nuthin' yet!

Exercise 3

> *Gather together the following pieces of equipment: a small wooden cooking spoon or a pencil; a thin wine glass, preferably crystal; a Chinese rice bowl; a porcelain or ceramic plate; a stainless steel or aluminum pot; and a cast-iron skillet. I prefer a bathroom for this exercise because of the echoes, but suit yourself. Begin by banging on each item lightly with the spoon or pencil to note its distinctive sound. When you have them down pat — meaning, you can distinguish each in your head — repeat the baby sounds, of course accompanying yourself as you do so, as well as moving around.*

Voilá, the birth of rhythm — sort of.

There are two terms used by academic folks to describe two different rhythmic tendencies — falling and rising — but they're so fuzzy that I thought I'd warn you about them in advance. So why shouldn't we just ditch them? I truly wish we could, but alas, we can't-can't-can't, so you'll just have to grin and bear it, as I do.

As was stated earlier, the English language became a distinct entity sometime after the fifth century, when the Angles and Saxons broke away from their Germanic brethren and crossed over to that island that came to be called England (in other words, Angle Land). Their language is said to have had a falling rhythm, that is, in words of theirs consisting of two or more syllables, the accents were usually on the first syllables, indeed as is still the case with present-day German — for example, in *Bratwurst* (brát-wurst) and *Rostbraten* (róst-brat-en). To help you remember this rhythm, think of a bass drum beat (OOM-pa) and a waltz beat (OOM-pa-pa).

Exercise 4

> *Say the words "Bratwurst" and "Rostbraten" out loud, followed by their rhythms, OOM-pa and OOM-pa-pa, about ten times, and clap your hands and swing your hips if it helps.*

With the arrival of the Norman conquerors in 1066, there was, as previously noted, a wholesale importation of French words into English, but that wasn't all — the basic rhythm of English changed, to a rising one. Let the word "alone" (a-lóne) and the phrase "alone again" (a-lóne a-gáin) serve as examples, and cha-CHA and cha-cha-CHA serve as reminders.

Exercise 5

> *Needless to say, repeat the words "alone" and "alone again" out loud, followed by their rhythms, cha-CHA and cha-cha-CHA, about ten times, and needless to say, get your body involved if need be.*

Today, our spoken and written languages, regardless of whether they are formal, informal, or colloquial, are an interesting blend of the two traditions. We use rising rhythms (cha-CHA and cha-cha-CHA) for ordinary situations. This can be demonstrated quite simply with:

> The boy went to the store today.

There are four units in this sentence, which can be arranged as follows:

(1) The boy; (2) went to; (3) the store; (4) today

or

(1) The boy; (2) went;(3) to the store; (4) today.

Either way, we put our emphasis both in speech and reading on "boy," "went," "store," and the "day"-syllable of "today," meaning a majority of the units ("boy," "store," and -"day") are rising.

Exercise 6

Read it over aloud several times to see what I mean:

The bóy / wént to / the stóre / to-dáy.

or

The bóy / wént / to the stóre / to-dáy.

We use falling rhythms (OOM-pa and OOM-pa-pa) in situations that call for special emphasis, such as commands and instructions, beginnings of speeches, and curses, as can be seen in the following:

— Dróp it!

— Fríends, /Róm-ans / cóunt-ry-men, / lénd mé / yóur éars

— Dámn it!

However, it's important to realize that it's impossible to sustain a falling rhythm in modern everyday English, be it spoken or written, for very long.

Exercise 7

Try it, I dare you, but be fair, don't force things. There are folks who do that, as we shall presently see.

The Briefest of Histories

Needless to say, the rhythm of English verse followed that of the spoken and written language. With the accents invariably falling on the first syllable of polysyllabic words, Anglo-Saxon verse was altogether falling, indeed as one can see from the passage that we looked at in chapter two with respect to the development of our language, the Hymn by the seventh-century monk Caedmon:

Nū wē sculan herian   heofonrīces Weard
Metodes mihte   ond his mōdgeþonc
weorc Wuldorfæder,   swā hē wundra gehwæs
ēce Dryhten,   ord onstealde.
He ærest gescēop   eorðan bearnum
heofon tō hrōfe,   hālig Scyppend
ðā middongeard   moncynnes Weard
ēce Dryhten   æfter tēode
fīrum foldan   Frēa ælmihtig.

(Now we shall praise Heaven-kingdom's guardian,
God's power and His understanding,
work of the Glory-Father as He of each wonder,
the eternal Lord the foundation laid.
He first created for men's children
Heaven for a roof holy Creator;
the middle earth mankind's guardian,
the eternal Lord after made
for men, the earth Ruler almighty.)

Considering how wild and woolly the times were, the rules regarding this verse were very strict. Each line was a thing unto itself or, if you will, formed a unit, and there was a space in its midst that indicated a pause (in technical terms, a *caesura*). The first part of each line usually contained two accented or heavily stressed syllables and a variable number of unaccented or lightly stressed syllables; on the second part of each line, there was one accented or heavily stressed syllable and again a variable number of unaccented or lightly stressed syllables. For variety, there were only two accented or heavily stressed syllables on some lines, one before and one after the pause. To top it off, the initial letters of the accented syllables were alliterated. So all in all, not only did the language look and sound "foreign," so too did the verse.

Exercise 8

At the risk of belaboring, try reading this passage aloud, emphasizing the alliterations with your arms and torso. If you're in a group, it sometimes helps if one or more people read the first part of a line and one or more the second part. If you're alone, this is a good exercise to try before a mirror, marking the alliterations with shakes of your fist.

Of course, it's possible that you can't do this — you simply can't, in which case, here's a pair of nonsense lines in modern English that imitate the base line:

Tatter for our Tommy   tunnel up handy
Master over the maypole   Michael on ledger

Exercise 9

Cut your teeth on it instead of or in addition to "Caedmon's Hymn" above.

With the arrival of the Normans in England, native poets writing in English, especially those living in and around London, came under the influence of French verse, which by and large consisted of lines of ten syllables, and Latin verse, which had a regular pattern of alternating stressed and unstressed syllables as well as end-rhymes, so that by Chaucer's time (ca. 1343-1400), not only had the language changed, including its basic rhythm — from falling to rising — but also a new kind of English poetry was being written, whose basic rhythm followed suit (cha-CHA and cha-cha-CHA):

Whan that Aprill with his shoures soote *sweet*
The droghte of March hath perced to the roote,
And bathed every veyne in swich licour *such/liquid*
Of which vertu engendred is the flour;
Whan Zephirus eek with his sweete breeth *also*
Inspired hath in every holt and heeth *grove/field*
The tendre croppes, and the yonge sonne *shoots*
Hath in the Ram his halve cours yronne,
And smale foweles maken melodye,
That slepen al the nyght with open ye *eye*
(So priketh hem nature in hir corages): *them*
Thanne longen folk to goon on pilgrimages,
And palmeres for to seken straunge strondes,
To ferne halwes, kowthe in sondry londes: *known*
And specially from every shires ende
Of Engelond to Caunterbury they wende,
The hooly blisful martir for to seke,
That hem hath holpen whan that they were seeke. *helped/sick*

Exercise 10

To test this out, pronounce the third line–"Of which vertu engendred is the flour" — and follow it with cha-CHA, cha-CHA, cha-CHA, cha-CHA, cha-CHA.

It may prove a bit problematic to read the whole passage aloud because all of the syllables were to be pronounced. Nevertheless —

Exercise 11

Give it a whirl, just making sure that you do pronounce each and every one of them — for example, "londes" = "lónd-es;" "seke" = "séek-uh."

By the sixteenth century, Early Modern English with its heavy borrowings from Latin and Greek, and a further dropping of endings, had come into its own, as we've already noted. More to the point here, English verse with a rising rhythm was established as the norm. The opening stanza of "The Passionate Shepherd to His Love," by

Christopher Marlowe (1564-1593), says it all (cha-CHA, cha-CHA, cha-CHA, cha-CHA):

> Come live with me, and be my love,
> And we will all the pleasures prove
> That valleys, groves, hills, and fields,
> Woods, or steepy mountain yields.

Exercise 12

Fair's only fair: repeat these lines of Marlowe's aloud, too. Just bear in mind that the pronunciation would have been a little different from our own today, regardless of whether we speak Oxford English or Middle American. Think of its having a slight Irish lilt, and imitate it if you can, but if you can't, that's fine too as long as you bear it in mind.

And basically rising (cha-CHA and cha-cha-CHA) most verse in English has remained until today whether rhymed or unrhymed, traditional or free, no matter who claims what, because our ordinary everyday utterances, both spoken and written, are rising.

So what happened to the old (OOM-pa and OOM-pa-pa) style of verse? Did it die out? Not quite; it continued to be written in the backwaters of England, much modified by the changes in the language, of course. And now and then in the modern era, it reappeared in the oddest of places — or were they? Notable among these was the incantation that Shakespeare put in the mouths of the three witches in *Macbeth:*

> Double, double, toil and trouble;
> Fire burn and cauldron bubble.
> Scale of dragon, tooth of wolf,
> Witches' mummy, maw and gulf....

Fittingly, something similar issued from the mouth of Ariel, a spirit of the air, in his last play, *The Tempest:*

> Full fathom five thy father lies;
> Of his bones are coral made;

Those are pearls that were his eyes.
Nothing of him that doth fade
But doth suffer a sea-change
Into something rich and strange.

In both instances, it was as if he were harking back to some distant past in which another quite different order of things prevailed.

In the middle of the eighteenth century, Thomas Gray (1716-1771) made use of the same rhythm in "The Bard," in which he portrays the last Celtic bard prophesying before he dives off a cliff to his death:

Weave the warp, and weave the woof,
The winding-sheet of Edward's race.
Give ample room and verge enough
The characters of hell to trace.

Later in the same century, an echo of the beat appears in Blake's "Tyger":

Tyger tyger burning bright,
In the forest of the night;
What immortal hand or eye,
Could frame thy fearful symmetry.

And it also turns up at the end of Coleridge's curious "Vision in a Dream," which he titled "Kubla Khan":

Weave a circle round him thrice,
And close your eyes with holy dread,
For he on honey-dew hath fed,
And drunk the milk of Paradise.

Did you notice that all of the above examples, beginning with the two by Shakespeare, have something otherworldly, foreign, or primitive about them? Later on in this chapter we'll be looking at this type of verse in a little more detail. Suffice it to say here that it's very difficult to maintain that falling (OOM-pa) rhythm for very long. Sooner or later, the verse lapses into a rising (cha-CHA) rhythm, whether the poet likes it or not, as can be seen from this stanza later on in Blake's "Tyger":

> When the stars threw down their spears
> And water'd heaven with their tears:
> Did he smile his work to see?
> Did he who made the Lamb make thee?

After the first line, the falling (OOM-pa) rhythm becomes muddied, and by the last, we're clearly immersed in a rising rhythm: "Did he / who made / the Lamb / make thee?" or cha-CHA, cha-CHA, cha-CHA, cha-CHA.

Basic Rhythmic Units of Traditional English Verse

Before one can run, one must be able to walk, as the saying goes, and in the writing of poetry, that means one must have a firm grasp of what a syllable is so as to recognize one at will. As this matter may prove irritating to some folks, I have a relatively painless and rather fun way of dealing with it. We're going to cut our teeth on *haiku* at the same time. You don't know what it is or can't remember? Wait and see.

So. Let's all begin by dancing to the same tune: what is a syllable? A syllable is produced by a single impulse of one's speaking apparatus and thus can be a vowel or a diphthong by itself (for example, the "o" in "oval" or "eye" in "eyebrow") or else a vowel or diphthong flanked on either side or both sides by one or more consonants (the "bo" in "limbo," the "bor" in "labor," the "bort" in "abort"). All English words consist of syllables, and they are made up of one, two, three, four, five, six, seven, and probably more of them. There it is in a nutshell.

Now when a consonant comes between two vowels in a two-syllable word, there are two ways of dividing it into syllables, an American way and an English way. According to the American way, the consonant is part of the first syllable: "ven-om." The English would say that it's a part of the second syllable: "ve-nom." Since the majority of poetry in English has been written by people who were from Great Britain, we'll be using their system, which may take a bit of getting used to for some folks in the rest of the English-speaking world.

Exercise 13

Separate the following words into syllables and count them: "balance," "garbage," "fabricate," "articulate," "co-operation," "mispronunciation," "individuality," "prestidigitation."

Here are the answers:

ba-lance; gar-bage; fa-bri-cate; ar-ti-cu-late; co-op-e-ra-tion; mis-pro-nun-ci-a-tion; in-di-vid-u-al-i-ty; pres-ti-dig-i-ta-tion.

If you got too many wrong or experienced difficulty with this exercise, work on it some more with polysyllabic words from *The New York Times* or another periodical like it until you feel at ease doing it. If you got the hang of it, or once you do —

Exercise 14

Slowly and carefully pronounce each syllable of each of the words in Exercise 13 aloud.

Hold on to your hat, we're about to leave the world of sense again.

Exercise 15

Just for fun, choose individual syllables from the words and create some new words with them.

Enough of these childish games! Let's now get down to the nitty-gritty, shall we? Like some genuine poetry!

Exercise 16

Count up the syllables in the following excerpts and record the total on each line as well as in each word. Hints: in the third line of item (a) and the first line of item (e), the e's of "piled" and "rugged" are pronounced; the word "Pierian" in item (b) is pronounced péer-ee-an.

(a)
When I have fears that I may cease to be
Before my pen has glean'd my teeming brain,
Before high-piled books, in charactery,
Hold like rich garners the full ripen'd grain;

(b)
A *little Learning* is a dang'rous Thing;
Drink deep, or taste not the *Pierian* Spring:
There *shallow Draughts* intoxicate the Brain,
And drinking *largely* sobers us again.

(c)
I was thy neighbour once, thou rugged Pile!
Four summer weeks I dwelt in sight of thee:
I saw thee every day; and all the while
Thy Form was sleeping on a glassy sea.

(d)
The king sits in Dumferling town,
Drinking the blude-reid wine:
"O whar will I get a guid sailor,
To sail this ship of mine?"

Here are the answers per line:

a: 1 (10), 2 (10), 3 (10), 4 (10); b: 1 (10), 2 (10), 3 (10), 4 (10);
d: 1 (8), 2 (6), 3 (9), 4 (6).

The time has come the walrus said — did I say that before? Be that as it may, it's time to try our hand at composing a *haiku.* In case you really don't know or forgot, a *haiku* is a short Japanese poem with a history going back to antiquity. It was imported into English in the twentieth century and has enjoyed considerable popularity since then — that is, it was sort of imported because the Japanese language is so very different from our own.

So what is it already? It's a single stanza consisting of seventeen syllables, no more nor less, and these are to be arranged in three lines of five, seven, and five syllables, respectively. Ideally, the poet is supposed to depict nature as a whole via one small aspect, and somewhere on the three lines there should be a *kigo* or "season word" hinting at the time of year that's appropriate to the context — some symbol like our harvest moon, for instance. There are other features, but these, alas, tend to get lost in translation. Here's an example from one of the masters:

> Shaking his loose skin,
> A tired old horse scares away
> A white butterfly.
>
> Kobayashi Issa(1763-1827)

What do you say, shall we give it a whirl?

Exercise 17

A single one will do; be sure to have the correct number of syllables on each line — remember, five-seven-five.

Here's a lovely one, replete with mixed metaphor, by my editor, Susan Walker:

> Tears roll silently
> Down autumn's early plumage
> Mourning summer's death

If it turns out that you like this sort of thing, take a peek in the *Penguin Book of Japanese Verse* and then try your hand at some more, understanding that what you'd be engaged in doing is writing *pseudo-haiku.*

I should point out that at least one notable poet writing in English used syllables as the building blocks of her works. This was Marianne Moore (1887-1972), and here's one of her poems to chew on. Note how her use of the same number of syllables on the corresponding lines of each stanza tends to temper the "ringing" of the rhymes — to the point where they indeed seem to be "under water":

The Fish

wade
through black jade.
  Of the crow-blue mussel-shells, one keeps
  adjusting the ash heaps;
    opening and shutting itself like

an
injured fan.
  The barnacles, which encrust the side
  of the wave cannot hide
    there, for the submerged shafts of the

sun,
split like spun
  glass, move themselves with spotlight swiftness
  into the crevices —
    in and out, illuminating

the
turquoise sea
  of bodies. The water drives a wedge
  of iron through the iron edge
    of the cliff; whereupon the stars,

pink
rice-grains, ink-
  bespattered jellyfish, crabs like green
  lillies, and submarine
    toadstools slide each on the other.

All
external
  marks of abuse are present on this
  defiant edifice —
    all the physical features of

ac-
cident — lack
of cornice, dynamite grooves, burns, and
  hatchet strokes, these things stand
    out on it; the chasm side is

dead.
Repeated
  evidence has proved that it can live
  on what can not revive
    its youth. The sea grows old in it.

I used to think that there was something terribly artificial about this sort of thing, but in Ms. Moore's hands, it seems to work rather well, wouldn't you say? Clearly helping is the arrangement of her lines, which is identical in each stanza and which, to my way of thinking, suggests schools of fish swimming up and about.

There will be more, lots more, on line arrangement later on in chapter eight with respect to free verse. But for right now:

Exercise 18

How about it, would you like to try your hand at writing a syllabic poem of your own? It can be with as many syllables per line as you want, and with or without rhyme. If you're at sea where this is concerned, try writing a response to Marianne Moore, paying her back in her own coin.

Next case. As you couldn't help but note in my discussion of rhythms in our daily communications, one syllable in a word is pronounced with more emphasis than the other or others. For instance, in the word "believe," which consists of the syllables "be-" and "lieve," we give more emphasis to the second syllable when pronouncing it. But don't take my word for it —

Exercise 19

Pronounce "believe" several times, giving emphasis to the first syllable "be" and then to the second syllable "lieve."

Was I right or not?

It's essential that you be able to find the emphasized or, as we sometimes say, accented syllables in words of two syllables and more. The easiest way to do this is, of course, to look the words up in your dictionary, which will break them down into syllables, if it's a good one. But this can often turn out to be a long and tedious process, and your dictionary may not always be at hand, so best to learn to do this on your own. Let's begin very simply, shall we?

Exercise 20

> *Which syllable of the following two-syllable words do you give the weight to or accentuate in normal conversation: (a) "garbage"; (b) "decay"; (c) "lazy"; (d) "decade"; (e) "because"; (f) "murder." Suggestion: begin by dividing each word into its two syllables first and then reading each syllable over several times, giving emphasis now to the first one, now to the second — as we did with "believe" above in Exercise 19.*

Here are the answers:

(a) first; (b) second; (c) first; (d) first; (e) second; (f) first.

If it turns out that you got even one of these wrong, PLEASE don't go on to the next exercise! Practice some more with other two-syllable words you find here in this book — or anywhere! — until you can put your finger on the accented syllable in your sleep practically. And of course, be sure to check yourself out in your dictionary.

Next case — I mean, step.

Exercise 21

> *Find the accented syllable in each of the following words: (a) "hideous"; (b) "insanity"; (c) "bothersome"; (d) "ridiculous"; (e) "ruminate"; (f) "statistic"; (g) "harbinger." Don't get lazy here and try to do a quick-and-dirty: divide each word up into syllables first and then read each syllable over several times, varying the emphasis from one to the others.*

Check your answers:

(a) first, (b) second, (c) first, (d) second, (e) first, (f) second, (g) first.

And as before, if you got any wrong, keep working on these and other polysyllabic words until you're clear out of the proverbial woods.

Let me point out here as a footnote to this matter of accentuation that certain words with the same root seem to rearrange themselves in terms of emphasis with the addition of different suffixes. For instance, note what happens to the accentuation when we add "er" to the end of "photograph" to make "photographer" and what happens when we drop the "er" and add "ic" to change it to "photographic." Yes indeedee, English is not always a user-friendly language, as many foreigners have learned to their chagrin.

To go on, just as individual polysyllabic words carry accents, so too do phrases. For instance, take "so long," our alternate way of saying "goodbye." If, in speaking, you put the accent on "so" instead of on "long," people will look at you strangely, won't they?

Exercise 22

Mark the accents in each of the following, making sure to divide each word up into syllables first: (a) Supreme Being; (b) Happy Birthday; (c) aware again; (d) breakfast cereal.

For some folks, this turns out to be a piece of cake; for others, ooh-la-la. Check it out:

(a) second, first; (b) first, first; (c) second, second; (d) first, first.

And as before, don't even dream of going on until you have these down pat.

Now for the pièce de résistance.

Exercise 23

Below are our four excerpts again, this time with their polysyllabic words in italic. Divide each of those words up into its component syllables and mark the accented one:

(a)
When I have fears that I may cease to be
Before my pen has glean'd my *teeming* brain,
Before *high-piled* books, in charactery,
Hold like rich *garners* the *fullripen'd* grain;

(b)
A *little Learning* is a *dang'rous* Thing;
Drink deep, or taste not the *Pierian* Spring:
There shallow Draughts *intoxicate* the Brain,
And *drinking largely sobers* us *again.*

(c)
I was thy *neighbour* once, thou *rugged* Pile!
Four *summer* weeks I dwelt in sight of thee:
I saw thee every day; and all the while
Thy Form was *sleeping* on a *glassy* sea.

(d)
The king sits in *Dumferling* town,
Drinking the *blude-reid* wine:
"O whar will I get a guid *sailor,*
To sail this ship of mine?"

After all we've done before, this should have been as easy as pie. See for yourself:

be-fóre; teé-ming; high-píl-ed; char-ac-trý; gár-ners; full-ríp-ened; lít-tle; leár-ning; dán-g'rous; Piér-i-an; shál-low; in-tóx-i-cate; drín-king; lárge-ly; só-bers; a-gáin; néigh-bour; rúg-ged; súm-mer; slée-ping; glá-ssy; Dúm-fer-ling; Drín-king; blúde-reid; sái-lor.

So much for boring nitty-gritty. The time has come to get serious — but I mean really serious — about rhythm in English poetry. In the world of traditional English poetry, meaning poetry that was written from the time of Chaucer and his contemporaries on to today, the basic rhythmic unit of a poem is called a *foot,* and four different *feet* are recognized: the *iamb,* the *anapest,* the *trochee,* and the *dactyl.* However, do try to understand that there's no such thing as a poem consisting exclusively of *iambs, anapests, trochees,* or *dactyls.* If we speak of a piece of verse as being one or the other of these, we mean that it consists of one of them for the most part; in other words, it's predominantly, as opposed to exclusively, so.

An *iamb* consists of two syllables, a lightly stressed one (marked ˘), followed by a heavily stressed one (marked ´). Let the words "because" (˘´) and "alone"(˘´) serve as examples of single-word *iambs,* and as in our discussion of prose, let our old friend cha-CHA be the *iamb*'s rhythmic translation. To anticipate our adventures together in the next chapter, which is devoted exclusively to *iambic* verse, more traditional poetry has been written in *iambs* than in the three other feet combined.

An *anapest* is made up of a pair of lightly stressed syllables (marked ˘˘) followed by a heavily stressed syllable (marked ´). "In the still" (˘˘´) and "of the night" (˘˘´) are good examples of *anapests,* and they can be translated rhythmically as cha-cha-CHA.

A *trochee* is the opposite of an *iamb,* consisting of a heavily stressed syllable followed by a lightly stressed one (´ ˘). Let "recent" and "bedlam" serve as examples of single-word *trochees,* and OOM-pa as its rhythmic translation.

A *dactyl* is made up of a heavily stressed syllable followed by two lightly stressed syllables (´ ˘ ˘); translated OOM-pa-pa, it is thus the opposite of the *anapest.* "Holiday" and "fabricate" are good examples of single-word *dactyls.*

Do we need a review, do you think? I just lov-ov-ove reviews, don't you?

Exercise 24

Make up a kind of chant consisting of our four basic rhythms: cha-CHA, cha-cha-CHA, OOM-pa, and OOM-pa-pa, and do it — do it! If you so desire, beat out the CHA's and OOM's by tapping your foot or slapping your thigh, or even banging a ruler or pen on the edge of your desk.

Now let's take a closer look at the *iamb.* In the first line of Marlowe's "Passionate Shepherd to His Love," the feet, which are separated by slashes, are all *iambs* (cha-CHA):

Come live / with me, / and be / my love.

And so too are the feet in the rest of the stanza except for two single departures: "hills" and "woods" on the third and fourth lines:

> And we / will all/ the pleas/ ures prove
> That val / leys, groves, / hills, / and fields,
> Woods, /or steep/ y moun / tain yields.

Exercise 25

The following is an experiment, and like all such, it may end in dismal failure. But try it anyway, okay? Write out the four lines of Marlowe's poem as I have them above and underneath each foot, substitute cha-CHA or just cha or CHA where appropriate. Read your cha-CHA poem aloud.

Did that hurt? I don't know. Did it help? I don't know either. The question now is: is you is or is you isn't up to this next? How about it?

Exercise 26

The following are lines from three of the stanzas that we worked with in Exercise 23. Let me tell you in advance that they're all iambic. Analyze them as I did the stanza from "The Passionate Shepherd to His Love"— or as we say, scan them— marking off weak and strong stresses and separating the feet with slashes. You've already done some of the drudgery in dividing the polysyllabic words into separate syllables:

> *(a) Before my pen has glean'd my teeming brain*
>
> *(b) And drinking largely sobers us again*
>
> *(c) I saw thee every day; and all the while*

How did you make out? Well, I hope and trust. Let's see:

> *(a) Be-fóre / my pén/ has gléan'd/ my téem-/ing bráin*
> *(b) And drín-/ king lárge-/ ly só-/ bers ús/ a-gáin*
> *(c) I sáw/ thee év-/ (e)ry dáy;/ and áll/ the whíle*

Exercise 27

But if things didn't pan out, try substituting cha-CHA for the feet or simply beating out the time with something.

The big question now is, can you take it yet one step further, like one giant step?

Exercise 28

Create three lines of your own iambs, using those above as models, and scan them in the same way. Hint: if this seems a bit overwhelming or you plain run into trouble, simply use the lines as grids and substitute any old words so long as they are the same number of syllables, with the accents in the same places; for example, use "rather" for "drinking."

Hm, word salad again. Salad is good, but word salad? So much word salad? Hm. Well, let's assume you got your three lines, and they make some kind of sense.

Exercise 29

Create three lines of iambs without reference to your models.

Ooooh, what I said! My fingers are in my mouth, and my eyes are popping. How did you make out? Good, not good?. . .

Let's move on to *anapests*, *trochees*, and *dactyls*.

Exercise 30

Identify the following as an anapest, trochee, or dactyl: (a) "birdhouse"; (b) "in-between"; (c) "ramshackle"; (d) "as a rule"; (e) "in a fix."

How close did you come? If not too close, don't lose any sleep over it. Clap or tap it out:

(a) trochee, (b) dactyl, (c) trochee, (d) anapest, (e) anapest.

Exercise 31

Scan the following snippets and identify the predominant foot. Don't forget to divide the polysyllabic words into separate syllables first:

(a) Piping down the valleys wild

(b) When the voices of children are heard on the green

(c) After the pangs of a desperate lover

If you didn't realize it, note the extra syllable in item (a) and the odd fourth foot in (c):

(a) Pi-ping/ down the/ val-leys/ wild
(b) When the voi-/ ces of chil-/ dren are heard/on the green
(c) Af-ter the/ pangs of the/ des-per-ate/ lo-ver

Poems written in *anapests* are usually rhymed and for that reason may seem a little more artificial than those in *iambs,* which, as we will see in the next chapter, occur in both unrhymed as well as rhymed poems. *Anapestic* poems range in quality from the ridiculous to the sublime, from this long-time favorite by Clement Moore (1779-1863):

'Twas the night before Christmas, when all through the house
Not a creature was stirring, not even a mouse;
The stockings were hung by the chimney with care,
In hopes that St. Nicholas soon would be there;

to Blake's lovely and moving "Nurse's Song" from his *Songs of Innocence:*

When the voices of children are heard on the green
And laughing is heard on the hill,
My heart is at rest within my breast
And every thing else is still.

Then come home my children, the sun is gone down
And the dews of night arise
Come come leave off play, and let us away
Till the morning appears in the skies.

No no let us play, for it is yet day
And we cannot go to sleep
Besides in the sky, the little birds fly
And the hills are all cover'd with sheep.

Well well go & play till the light fades away
And then go home to bed
The little ones leaped & shouted & laugh'd
And all the hills ecchoed.

But — but — but — does it consist of pure *anapests*?

Exercise 32

Check it out by analyzing or, as we say, scanning it.

Oh what a tangled web we weave. . . .

Exercise 33

Try writing a short poem in anapests — oh, let's say, no more than ten lines. Consider a pastoral or rural setting for it, similar to Blake's.

Next is something very curious that I recently came upon. In his free verse poem "Thirteen Ways of Looking at a Blackbird," twentieth-century poet Wallace Stevens played around with the numbers 1 and 3, and one of his tricks was to include an anapest here and there, beginning with the phrase "Thirteen Ways" in the title. Get a load of this *(Italics mine)*:

I
Among twenty snowy mountains,
The only *moving thing*
Was the eye of the blackbird.

II
I was of three minds,
Like a tree
In which there are three blackbirds.

III
The blackbird whirled in the *autumn winds.*
It was a small part of the *pantomime.*

IV
A man and a woman
Are one.
A man and a woman and a blackbird
Are one.

V
I do not know which to prefer,
The beauty of inflections
Or the beauty of innuendoes,
The blackbird whistling
Or just after.

VI
Icicles filled the long window
With *barbaric glass.*
The shadow of the blackbird
Crossed it, *to and fro.*
The mood
Traced in the shadow
An indecipherable cause.

VII
O thin men of Haddam,
Why do you imagine *golden birds?*
Do you not see how the blackbird
Walks around the feet
Of the women about you?

VIII
I know noble accents
And lucid, inescapable rhythms;
But I know, too,
That the blackbird i*s involved*
In *what I know.*

IX
When the blackbird flew *out of sight,*
It *marked the edge*
Of one of many circles.

X
At the sight of blackbirds
Flying in a green light,
Even the bawds of *euphony*
Would cry out sharply.

XI
He rode over Connecticut
In a glass coach.
Once, a fear pierced him
In that he mistook
The shadow of his equipage
For blackbirds.

XII
The river is moving.
The blackbird must be flying.

XIII
It was evening all *afternoon.*
It was snowing
And it was going to snow.
The blackbird sat
In the *cedar-limbs.*

Am I imagining things or what?

Exercise 34

Why don't you take a whack at it: read the poem aloud, the whole thing, and do it naturally, as you would anything else.

Where *trochaic* verse is concerned, not to forget the examples that I cited earlier in this chapter (pages 150-151) as possibly being throwbacks or survivals of the old Anglo-Saxon type of verse. Of them, Blake's "Tyger," a stand-alone poem from his *Songs of Experience,* is obviously a *trochaic* masterpiece:

Tyger Tyger, burning bright,
In the forests of the night;
What immortal hand or eye,
Could frame thy fearful symmetry?

In what distant deeps or skies
Burnt the fire of thine eyes!
On what wings dare he aspire?
What the hand, dare seize the fire?

And what shoulder, & what art,
Could twist the sinews of thy heart?
And when thy heart began to beat,
What dread hand? & what dread feet?

What the hammer? what the chain,
In what furnace was thy brain?
What the anvil? what dread grasp,
Dare its deadly terrors clasp?

When the stars threw down their spears
And water'd heaven with their tears:
Did he smile his work to see?
Did he who made the Lamb make thee?

Tyger Tyger burning bright,
In the forests of the night:
What immortal hand or eye,
Dare frame thy fearful symmetry?

This needs a class-act treatment.

Exercise 35

Do it, scan it, and see how truly magical it is.

Question: does it detract or add to your pleasure to know that Blake lapsed into *iambs* at times?

Exercise 36

Try writing a poem — a short one is okay — in trochees yourself now. If you can, make it about some powerful natural force like a tiger.

Works written in *dactyls* are rare in English because it's devilishly difficult to sustain that OOM-pa-pa measure beyond a few lines. Even so, look at this really good try from "The Charge of the Light Brigade" by Alfred Lord Tennyson (1809-1892)

Half a league, half a league,
Half a league onward,
All in the valley of Death
  Rode the six hundred.
"'Forward the Light Brigade!
Charge for the Guns!" he said.
Into the valley of Death
  Rode the six hundred..

Exercise 37

Just how good is this, really?

Do I dare ask this of you?

Exercise 38

Yes, yes, just to say that you did, you tried, give the good old dactyl a whirl.

So much for rhythm; we come now to the final matter to be covered in this chapter, *meter,* which is easier to grasp. Purely and simply, *meter* has to do with the number of feet on a line or on a number of lines of a poem or in a whole poem, and one refers to it by the Greek words for the numbers (like *tetra* for *four*) plus the word *meter.* So a single line or several lines of verse or a whole block could consist of so many feet per line and be referred to as *monometer* (one), *dimeter* (two), *trimeter* (three), *tetrameter* (four), *pentameter* (five), *hexameter* (six), and so on. For instance, each of the lines of that stanza of Marlowe's "Passionate Shepherd" consists of four *iambs* or *iambic feet,* so we'd refer to them as being in *iambic tetrameter:*

Come live / with me, / and be / my love
And we / shall all / the plea-/ sures prove
That val- / leys, groves, / hills, / and fields,
Woods, /or steep- / y moun- / tain yields.

In poetic circles, it's customary to use a numeral and a letter of the alphabet, beginning with *a,* to indicate the meter and rhyme of a passage. Thus the full scheme of Marlowe's stanza above would be *4a4a4b4b.*

Exercise 39

Just for fun, go back to Exercise 23 and name the rhyme and meter for each of the stanzas there and give the shorthand.

Here we are:

(a) cross-rhymed iambic pentameter: 5a5b5a5b
(b) iambic pentameter couplets, 5a5a5b5b
(c) cross-rhymed iambic pentameter: 5a5b5a5b
(d) alternating unrhyming iambic tetrameter and rhyming iambic trimeter: 4a3b4c3b

That most of that poetry above is in *iambic pentameter* should not surprise anyone, for just as most traditional English verse has been written in *iambs*, a good deal of that *iambic* verse — as much as 75%, I've heard tell — is in *pentameter.* To look ahead, in the next chapter we'll be dealing exclusively with poems in *iambic pentameter*, both rhymed and unrhymed, and trying our hands at each. But for right now, by way of sneaking up on it all —

Exercise 40

Let's work on a full scansion of the two juicy morsels below and determine what meter and rhyme scheme each is in. Do-o-o remember to break up the polysyllabic words into separate syllables first:

(a)

She Dwelt Among the Untrodden Ways
by
William Wordsworth

She dwelt among the untrodden ways
Beside the springs of Dove,
A Maid whom there were none to praise
And very few to love:

A violet by a mossy stone
Half hidden from the eye!
— Fair as a star, when only one
Is shining in the sky.

She lived unknown, and few could know
When Lucy ceased to be;
But she is in her grave, and, oh,
The difference to me!

(b)

Ozymandias
by
Percy Bysshe Shelley

I met a traveler from an antique land
Who said: Two vast and trunkless legs of stone

Stand in the desert...Near them, on the sand,
Half sunk, a shattered visage lies, whose frown,
And wrinkled lip, and sneer of cold command,
Tell that its sculptor well those passions read
Which yet survive, stamped on these lifeless things,
The hand that mocked them, and the heart that fed:
And on the pedestal these words appear:
"My name is Ozymandias, king of kings:
Look on my works, ye Mighty, and despair!"
Nothing beside remains. Round the decay
Of that colossal wreck, boundless and bare
The lone and level sands stretch far away.

Don't peek, okay?

a. alternating iambic tetrameter and iambic trimeter: 4a3b4a3b,
4c3d4c3d, 4e3f4e3f
b. alternate rhymed iambic pentameter: 5a5b5a5b
5a5c5d5c5e5d5e5f5e5f

If you'd like more information on any of the material covered in this chapter, the best places to start are Paul Fussell's *Poetic Meter and Poetic Form* and Joseph Malof's *Manual of English Meters.*

Postscript

I began this chapter with the proposition that our daily language is generally in a rising rhythm or, if you will, *iambic* (cha-CHA) and *anapestic* (cha-cha-CHA), and that we reserve a falling rhythm, *trochaic* (OOM-pa) and *dactylic* (OOM-pa-pa), for situations that call for special emphasis, such as commands and instructions, and beginnings of speeches. And this goes for poetry as well, both of the traditional and nontraditional or *free-verse* varieties.

We'll be giving separate consideration to the latter later on in chapter eight. To anticipate, let's see what we find in *free verse* poems by two of our guests, beginning with Ruth Fainlight's "Prism":

Braided like those plaits of multi-
coloured threads my mother kept
in her workbox (beige, flesh, and fawn
for mending stockings, primary tones
to match our playclothes, grey and black
for Daddy's business suits), or Medusa-
coils of telephone wires, vivid
as internal organs exposed in their packed
logic under the pavement, nestling
in the gritty London clay,
associations fray into messages:

codes to unravel, cords to follow
out of prison, poems which make
no concession, but magnify
the truth of every note and colour,
indifferent whether they blind or deafen
or ravish or are ignored; the blueprint
of a shelter against the glare
— and the waterfall to build it near —
the perfect place to sit and hear
that choir of hymning voices, and watch
the prism of the rainbow spray.

There are eleven lines in each stanza and a soupçon of end-rhyme in "fawn" and "tones," "black" and "packed," and "glare," "near," and "hear." There's also a considerable amount of internal rhyme of different varieties, such as *alliteration, assonance,* and so on. More interesting yet, while the lines are not all uniformly of the same length, a surprisingly large number of them, like fifteen to be exact, consist of eight or nine syllables.

Let's look now at a *free verse* poem by Jeffrey Greene titled "Evening of the Whale":

What brings this whale tonight
through the outer
breakers of the harbor,
up the dredged

ship lanes and toward
the towering stacks
of United Illuminating
at the confluence of two poisonous rivers?
It should dream itself
out of here
the way it dreamed itself in,
but by now it is too late
in its inexplicable
steering and surfacing.
It comes because
we didn't think of it.
It comes from everywhere
we cannot go,
but grows in the mind.
It plows its way to the lights and stilts
of a fish and steak
restaurant by the water,
and we are its witnesses.
It comes to forgive us
because we are not thinking
of forgiveness.
It leaves behind its green palace
made of glass,
swimming here weightless
in its bulk.
All along
we are thinking only
that something destructible
is about to touch ground.

There are thirty-four lines in all and a fair number of end-rhymes in "outer" and "harbor," "dredged" and "toward," "stacks" and "rivers," "stilts" and "steak," and "water," "witnesses," "us," "forgiveness," "palace," "glass," and "weightless" as well as considerable internal rhyming, especially *anaphora* and *alliteration.* Again, one cannot help but notice the relative uniformity of line lengths: of the thirty-four lines of the poem, nine of the lines consist of six syllables and another seventeen of the lines of four, five, or seven syllables.

I hope and trust that by looking at the two poems above more closely, you can see the distinct differences in the approaches of the poets. Needless to say, this is a matter of vital importance.

A final word

I'm expecting that there'll be all kinds of flak from various professional linguistic folks regarding my views on the basic rhythms of English. To anticipate, let me add this: students should subsume it all under the rubric of Working Hypotheses and feel free to dump those views overboard as soon as they no longer serve any useful purpose.

Now who wants to fight?

"The river is moving..."

6

The Mighty iamb

Blank Verse to Sonnet

As I said in the previous chapter, most traditional English verse has been written in *iambs,* a unit of sound consisting of an unstressed followed by a stressed syllable (cha-CHA, which we indicate as ˘´). Also, because our everyday language, both spoken and written, is by and large in a rising rhythm, most so-called *free verse* is also essentially *iambic,* though it would hardly serve any useful purpose to demonstrate it, at least to go to any lengths to do so, wouldn't you say?

the Basics

Before we can run, we must be able to walk. Have I said that before? I should have. Let's begin by putting our *iambic* heads back on, shall we?

Exercise 1

> *Chant cha-CHA until you're out of breath or beat it out with a pencil or ruler or what you will until your hand gets tired. Do not make a pattern of your repetitions. It's important at this point that you hear cha-CHA.*

As I also said in the previous chapter, the most popular *iambic* pattern consists of five units or *feet*, and it is designated as *iambic pentameter;* we'd indicate it as ˘´/ ˘´ /˘´ /˘´/ ˘´ and chant it as cha-CHA, cha-CHA, cha-CHA, cha-CHA, cha-CHA. A good 75% of English verse that has the *iamb* as its base is written in *iambic pentameter*, and that includes among other things *The Canterbury Tales*, the better part of Shakespeare's plays, and Milton's *Paradise Lost.* So it behooves us, for starters, to get this pattern nailed down in our heads.

Exercise 2

> *Chant cha-CHA, cha-CHA, cha-CHA, cha-CHA, cha-CHA, and as you do so, clap your hands, stamp your foot, or beat it out with something. Do this again and again until you feel you can do it in your sleep.*

Needed next by you is a signature line. I like to use this first line from Keats's *sonnet*: "When I have fears that I may cease to be" (When I / have fears / that I / may cease / to be). But some folks prefer a nonsense line like "The black is blue when green is red goodbye" (The black / is blue / when green / is red / good-bye).

Exercise 3

> *Say your signature line, and say it again and again, as per usual clapping your hands, stamping your foot, or beating it out with something else.*

May I strongly recommend that you go back to Exercises 1, 2, and 3 from time to time while making your way through the rest of this chapter and repeat them again.

Here's a whole passage in *iambic pentameter*. Read it through several times, aloud if possible:

And yet therin, I pray you (my good priests)
Pray stil for me, and for my Glasse of steele
That it (nor I) do any minde offend,
Bycause we shew, all colours in their kinde.
And pray for me, that (since my hap is such
To see men so) I may perceive myselfe.
O worthy words, to ende my worthlesse verse,
Pray for me Priests, I pray you pray for me.

from *The Steel Glas* by George Gascoigne (1525-1577)

Boring, isn't it? But not to worry if you don't think so just now; you will in the end.

Exercise 4

Copy it out on a sheet of paper, leaving a goodly amount of space between each line, and do a full scansion of it.

Here's mine. Compare, but don't be overly concerned if we don't exactly agree; full scansions by different folks seldom do entirely:

And yet/ ther-in,/ I pray/ you (my/ good priests)
Pray stil/ for me, /and for/ my Glasse/ of steele
That it/ (nor I)/ do an-/ y minde/ of-fend,
By-cause/ we shew,/ all co-/ lours in/ their kinde.
And pray/ for me,/ that (since/ my hap/ is such
To see/ men so)/ I may/ per-ceive/ my-selfe.
O wor-/ thy words, /to ende/ my worth/lesse verse,
Pray for/ me Priests,/ I pray/ you pray/ for me.

Now for sure you should see how boring this passage is as verse. And the reason why should be readily apparent: it bumps up and down like a bouncing ball, repeating the same strategy again and again. It needs something, excitement of some kind — in a word, it needs some variety.

Here are the same number of lines from Antony's Funeral Oration, which are also in *iambic pentameter:*

Friends, Romans, countrymen, lend me your ears.
I come to bury Caesar, not to praise him.
The evil that men do lives after them;
The good is oft interred with their bones.
So let it be with Caesar. The noble Brutus
Hath told you Caesar was ambitious.
If it were so, it was a grievous fault,
And grievously hath Caesar answer'd it.

Even at a glance one can see that it's anything but boring. It's on fire! It's magnificent! But don't take my word for it or even Shakespeare's or the passage's reputation for it. Read it through several times, if possible aloud. And then try your hand at this —

Exercise 5

What else? Copy it out and do a full scansion of it as well.

Here's mine, and again, don't worry if we don't exactly agree:

Friends, Ro-mans, coun-try-men, lend me/ your ears.
I come/ to bu-/ry Cae-/ sar, not to/ praise him.
The ev-/ il that/ men do/ lives af-/ ter them;
The good/ is oft/ in-ter-/ red with/ their bones.
So/ let it be/ with Cae-/ sar. The no-/ ble Bru-/tus (enj.)
Hath told/ you Cae-/ sar was/ am-bi-/ tious.
If it/ were so, / it was / a grie-/ vous fault,
And grie-/ vou-sly/ hath Cae-/ sar answ-/ er'd it.

You really didn't have to do the scansion to figure out what makes it magnificent, did you? Variety is the answer, purely and simply that. With that "perfect" *iambic pentameter* line in mind, Shakespeare created variations on that pattern, and only now and then slipped one in to remind us of it or if you will, when it seemed "right" to him:

The good / is oft / in-ter-/ red with / their bones
If it / were so, / it was / a grie- / vous fault.

Exercise 6

Read the passage aloud again, substituting cha-CHA, cha-CHA, cha-CHA, cha-CHA, cha-CHA for those two lines.

Does this or does it not make sense in terms of the beat?

Exercise 7

Let's go one step further. Substitute cha-CHA, cha-cha-CHA, OOM-pa, OOM-pa-pa, DA-DA (for two strong stresses in a row) and dee-dee (for two weak stresses in a row) for your marks on the six "irregular" lines. Repeat one of your two "perfect" cha-CHA lines and follow it with your rendering of one of the six other lines. If you're in a group, go round the room in that fashion, a "perfect" line to one person, an "irregular" line to the next. If you're alone, try swingin' and swayin' before a mirror.

Hey, hey, we seem to have drifted away from meaning into pure sound, haven't we? Well, that's what the great English poets like Shakespeare were doing in part, making music with words. In fact, for the information of those who decry the fact that England never produced a composer on a par with Bach and Mozart — believe you me, those English poets were it!

General Considerations

Blank verse is the technical term for passages written in *unrhymed iambic pentameter* — that is, without complete end-rhymes — and we've already met with it in the passages by Gascoigne and Shakespeare above. Needless to say, there's good and bad *blank verse*, and this certainly applies to those two passages above. The question is, why is that by Shakespeare so extraordinary and that by Gascoigne utterly mediocre? Was the Bard privy to some insider info that the poetical dud was not? Did he perhaps have a set of rules that Gascoigne was not privy to? The answer is no; with the sole requirement in mind that his verse had to conform to speech, he simply let his extraordinary sensibility and ear guide him.

There are, however, rules — or, if you will, guidelines — for writing *blank verse,* that is, good *blank verse,* and for them we have scholars of a later date to thank, who extrapolated them from Shakespeare's practice and those of other great writers after him, like Milton and Wordsworth. Best to keep a copy of those first lines of Antony's Funeral Oration handy to refer to as you go through them:

1. The number of syllables per line, which are normally ten, can be varied to as few as nine, on rare occasions to eight when the sense warrants it, and to as many as twelve. In the Funeral Oration, line two ("I come") consists of eleven syllables, line five ("So let") of twelve syllables, and line six ("Hath told") of nine syllables.

2. In a given passage, *anapests, trochees,* and *dactyls* can be substituted for *iambs,* as can *spondees* (two strong stresses in a row) and *pyrrhics* (two weak ones in a row), but not in so wholesale a fashion as to obscure the passage's *iambic* texture. In the Funeral Oration, many of the *feet* are *iambic,* but often there's something else. For instance, in the seventh line, the second *foot* ("-vous ly") and possibly the last ("er'd it") are *pyrrhics,* and not to forget that magnificent first line, which starts off with a truncated *trochee* ("Friends,"), goes on to a full *trochee* ("Ro-mans"), then to a *dactyl* ("Count-ry-men"), and then to another *trochee* ("lend me"), and finally to an *iamb* ("your ears").

3. Instead of a pause at the end of a line, which is called an *end-stop,* one can run on or *enjamb* the sense or a syntac-

tical unit to the next line, never to the point, however, of destroying line-unity completely. Shakespeare *enjambed* the fifth and sixth lines: "The noble Brutus / Hath told you Caesar was ambitious." However, as we'll see below, his usual practice was to keep *enjambments* to a minimum for the sake of easy delivery by his actors and quick apprehension by his audience. It was left to writers of *blank verse* who came after him and wrote to be read, like Milton, to exploit the possibilities of *enjambments* more fully.

4. This final rule has to do with intra-line pauses or *caesuras* (indicated by // in a scansion), which we touched upon briefly in the last chapter with respect to Anglo-Saxon verse. Most "perfect" *blank verse* lines tend to have a pause like that after the second *foot* (or fourth syllable), even when there's no punctuation to indicate one; certainly one can hear a pause like that in our old friend, "When I have fears that I may cease to be," and such a pause is so marked on the seventh line of the Funeral Oration: "If it were so, it was a grievous fault." Indeed, scholars like Northrop Frye have gone so far as to claim that this "natural *caesura*" in the *blank verse* line is a hangover from that mid-line pause in Anglo-Saxon verse. Be that as it may, two rules regarding *caesuras* in good *blank verse* are that not every line has to have one and that where there is one, its place on a line can be varied. Poets from Shakespeare on tended to favor *caesuras* after the first or third *foot* as an alternative to those after the second, but on the second and fifth lines of the Funeral Oration, which are both very long, *caesuras* come in the fourth foot: "I come / to bu- / ry Cae- / sar, // not to / praise him" and "So / let it be / with Cae- / sar. // The no- / ble Bru- / tus." Another rule regarding *caesuras* is that there may be more than one per line, as happens in the opening line of Antony's speech: "Friends, // Ro-mans, // coun-try-men, // lend me // your ears."

Exercise 7

Let's return to our scansions of the passage from Gascoigne's "Stel Glas" and "Friends Romans" and put in the caesuras and note the enjambments.

After you're done, then and only then check yours against mine:

Friends, Ro-mans, coun-try-men, lend me/ your ears.
I come/ to bu-/ry Cae-/ sar, not to/ praise him.
The ev-/ il that/ men do/ lives af-/ ter them;
The good/ is oft/ in-ter-/ red with/ their bones.
So/ let it be/ with Cae-/ sar. The no-/ ble Bru-/tus (enj.)
Hath told/ you Cae-/ sar was/ am-bi-/ tious.
If it/ were so, / it was a grie-/ vous fault,
And grie-/ vou-sly/ hath Cae-/ sar answ-/ er'd it.

And yet/ ther-in, I pray/ you (my/ good priests)
Pray stil/ for me, and for/ my Glasse/ of steele
That it/ (nor I) do an-/ y minde/ of-fend,
By-cause/ we shew, all co-/ lours in/ their kinde.
And pray/ for me, that (since/ my hap/ is such (enj.)
To see/ men so) I may/ per-ceive/ my-selfe.
O wor-/ thy words, to ende/ my worth/lesse verse,
Pray for/ me Priests, I pray/ you pray/ for me.

Types of Blank Verse

During the English Renaissance, two distinctly different kinds of blank verse developed: *dramatic*, spearheaded by Christopher Marlow and perfected by Shakespeare; and *epic*, which was pretty much the province of John Milton. Later masters, like William Wordsworth in the nineteenth century, partook of both traditions and added something of their own.

Shakespeare's career spanned three decades; in that period of time, he authored thirty-odd plays, all largely in *blank verse.* While that *blank verse* underwent certain changes in conformity with changing public taste, there was a general consistency to it. Let's take a fresh look at it with Hamlet's famous soliloquy "To Be or Not to Be," which is representative of it at mid-career. Bear in mind that it was intended to be spoken and heard:

> To be, or not to be, that is the question:
> Whether 'tis nobler in the mind to suffer
> The slings and arrows of outrageous fortune,
> Or to take arms against a sea of troubles,
> And by opposing end them. To die, to sleep —
> No more — and by a sleep to say we end
> The heart-ache and the thousand natural shocks
> That flesh is heir to. 'Tis a consummation
> Devoutly to be wish'd. To die, to sleep;
> To sleep, perchance to dream. Ay, there's the rub,
> For in that sleep of death what dreams may come
> When we have shuffled off this mortal coil,
> Must give us pause. There's the respect
> That makes calamity of so long life.
> For who would bear the whips and scorns of time,
> Th' oppressor's wrong, the proud man's contumely,
> The pangs of despis'd love, the law's delay,
> The insolence of office, and the spurns
> That patient merit of th' unworthy takes,
> When he himself might his quietus make
> With a bare bodkin? Who would fardels bear,
> To grunt and sweat under a weary life,
> But that the dread of something after death,
> The undiscover'd country from whose bourn
> No traveler returns, puzzles the will,
> And makes us rather bear those ills we have
> Than fly to others that we know not of?
> Thus conscience does make cowards of us all;
> And thus the native hue of resolution
> Is sicklied o'er with the pale cast of thought,
> And enterprises of great pitch and moment
> With this regard their currents turn awry,
> And lose the name of action.

Exercise 9

Needless to say, this has to be read aloud. May I suggest that if a group is using this book, a new reader take over with each full stop, that is, after periods and question marks. If you're alone, try changing voices.

Hopefully you're not that new to Shakespeare and this passage, but if you are, don't proceed any further until you've done the reading, never for a moment forgetting that it was intended to be spoken aloud and heard.

Exercise 10

Copy out the first fourteen lines (up to "long life") and, leaving plenty of room between each line, do a complete scansion.

How many "perfect" lines did you find?

Four: "No more" etc.; "Devoutly" etc.; "To sleep" etc.; "That makes" etc.

How many other ten-syllables lines were there?

Two: "For in that sleep of death what dreams may come" and "When we have shuffled off this mortal coil."

How many with fewer than ten syllables?

One: "Must give us pause. There's the respect."

You should have noted as well the *caesura* after the second *foot* on line 13 ("Must give us pause."), the variations of *caesura* placement on lines 5 ("And by" etc.), 6 ("No more" etc.), 8 ("That flesh" etc.), and 9 ("Devoutly" etc.), and the multiple *caesuras* on lines 1 ("To be, or not to be,") and 10 (To sleep, perchance to dream. Aye,"), as well as the *enjambments* of line 2 with line 3 ("to suffer" with "The slings"), line 6 with line 7 ("we end" with "The heart-ache"), line 7 with line 8 ("natural shocks" with "That flesh"), and line 8 with line 9 ("consummation" with "devoutly").

And then there's a feature that's distinctive to Shakespeare's *blank verse* that I'm sure you couldn't help but notice: a line consisting of eleven syllables. In most, but not all cases, the extra syllable is a light beat that comes at the ends of lines that end with polysyllabic words: "question," "suffer," "fortune," "troubles," "consummation." To me, at least, they're reminiscent of the *uh*-sounds at the ends of many of Chaucer's lines (for instance, "Whan that April with his shoures soote," where the *es* of "shoures" and *e* of "soote" are pronounced). My guess is that besides being a distinctive kind of variation — Shakespeare's signature, so to speak — those extra terminal syllables of his had the function of allowing an actor to pause slightly and take a much-needed quick breath.

But there's more to the above piece of verse, prosodically speaking. And once you focus on it, what a wealth of *sound-correspondences* and *sound-devices* there are.

Exercise 11

Look at this passage for the sounds alone. Be sure to include not only partial end-rhyme and full and partial internal rhyme but also word rhymes and phrase rhymes, and onomatopoeia and parallelisms if any. To what extent do they contribute to the total effect of the passage?

We're now going to zero in on things, but I mean like really do it.

Exercise 12

In the space under each line of your scansion, substitute cha for each light stress and CHA for each heavy stress, and read it all aloud instead of the words.

I hope and trust this doesn't seem like sacrilege, or too much like it. Bear in mind that you're in the process of teaching yourself; remember also that like chicken in the hands of a new cook, Shakespeare is very hard to ruin.

Exercise 13

This may or may not work, but do give it a whirl, will you? Substitute nonsense words instead of the cha's and CHA's, making sure that your substitute words are of the same number of syllables and accented in the same place as those they're replacing. Read it all aloud. May I suggest that you do as you did when reading the original — that is, if you're in a group, have a new reader take over with each full stop, and if you're alone, try changing voices.

I'm a great fan of memorization, but to many people, it's a terrible bother. Nevertheless —

Exercise 14

Try, for your own dear sake, to commit the first fourteen lines to memory and recite them aloud — and put your heart and soul, to say nothing of body, into it.

I'm sure you've guessed what's coming next — but first, before that, take a look at this *blank verse* poem in the Shakespearian manner written by Ursula Melendi, a former student of mine:

The Anti-Neo-Nazi Protest

A sea of black umbrellas beckons me
To join with those who silently are gathered
On this cold and melancholy evening,
In solemn protest of the element,
Which, thriving and alive, has wormed its way
Into the branches of society,
Like deadly microbes of a dread disease.
Here, on this quiet, residential street
A gloomy and dilapidated house
Stands oddly isolated from the rest.
Its slightly cracked facade shows evidence
Of yesterday's attack with paint and tar;
The broken window panes have long been masked
With planks of sturdy and protective wood,
A feature which quite clearly makes this dwelling
The eye-sore of the well-kept neighborhood.
    In strict accordance with the City's rules,
No verbal outbursts, chants or slogans
Are uttered by the law-abiding crowd —
Yet whispers of disdain pervade the air.

As I peruse this silent rally,
Which seems grotesquely distant and unreal,
My thoughts can't help escaping to the past
And those who labored on this soil before.
Were they like us, staunch servants of the law,
Obeying orders and following rules?
They've gone and left us with a legacy
Of vengeance, guilt, immeasurable pain;
The image of a country once beloved,
Forever tarnished by the monstrous acts
Of one sadistic madman and his reign.
    The attic window opens to reveal
A modern monster with a well-known sneer.
I've seen that condescending smirk on Eichmann's face,
I know the eyes — so merciless and cold as steel —
The eyes of those convicted of the world's
Most barbarous and horrifying crimes.
My angry blood thuds wildly through my veins
As surges of revenge envelop me.
The crowd stands quietly, their voices still,
But my undaunting spirit whispers "Kill."
I want to see him writhe in his own blood
To make him pay for their atrocities,
Then watch him plead in pain and agony,
While echoes of my fits of laughter
Contemptuously quash his cries of woe.
But — would my anguish be assuaged
Or would his death redeem the millions lost?
Would I be kin to the assassins
Who freely shed the blood of innocence?
My heart is throbbing fiercely in my chest...
I cannot move, as I do not possess
The cruel and sadistic tendencies
Of those who gave us cause for this event;
Instead, I stand in solemn unity
With those who silently are gathered here.

So, now it's your turn, tra-la. But are you up to it, that is the question.

Exercise 15

> *Write a poem in Shakespearian-style blank verse at least ten lines long. You've got a choice: you can write a response to "To Be or Not to Be," adhering to it word for word and line for line, or you can simply write something, including a response, using Shakespeare's different stylistic features, including and especially that eleven-syllable line. If you're in need of a model, try spinning off "Friends, Romans" in some way, or if that doesn't appeal to you, why not pause here and get hold of a volume of his plays and read through the great tragedies at least —* **Hamlet, Othello, King Lear,** *and* **Macbeth** *— until you find a passage that really appeals to you.*

After you're done, check your passage against the rules on pages 182-183 to be sure that you've conformed to them, and if you haven't, take the time now to make the appropriate adjustments — with a smile, yes?

Exercise 16

> *Remembering that this is dramatic blank verse and therefore that it's all-important that it sound good and at the same time be readily apprehensible, read yours aloud.*

Don't be surprised if this results in your making additional changes. But what to do if you weren't able to write anything? Don't laugh, those of you who can and did turn out something — it can happen to the best of us. In that case, may I suggest that you return to your word-salad Shakespearian *blank verse* poem of Exercise 12 and try turning that into something meaningful.

Like many another young man in the generation following Shakespeare, John Milton (1608-1674) wanted to write for the stage more than anything else, and indeed he had two youthful successes in the boonies. However, in 1642, the London theaters were closed down, as it happens, by order of his own party, the Puritans, and when those theaters reopened in 1660 after the Restoration, they were to provide fare for an audience that he was utterly out of tune with. Added to that, Milton was blind by then and virtually under house arrest for his role in helping Cromwell. So what was there to do but write to be read, meaning epics like *Paradise Lost*, composed in a manner akin to that of Homer and Virgil, which was bound to result in a *blank verse* whose texture was a far cry from that of Shakespeare's. Consider the opening lines of his *Paradise Lost:*

> Of Man's First Disobedience, and the Fruit
> Of that Forbidden Tree, whose mortal taste
> Brought Death into the World, and all our woe,
> With loss of *Eden*, till one greater Man
> Restore us, and regain the blissful Seat,
> Sing Heav'nly Muse, that on the secret top
> Of *Oreb*, or of *Sinai*, didst inspire
> That Shepherd, who first taught the chosen Seed,
> In the Beginning how the Heav'ns and Earth
> Rose out of *Chaos:* Or if *Sion* Hill
> Delight thee more, and *Siloa's* Brook that flow'd
> Fast by the Oracle of God; I thence
> Invoke thy aid to my advent'rous Song,
> That with no middle flight intends to soar
> Above th' *Aonian Mount*, while it pursues
> Things unattempted yet in Prose or Rhyme.
> And chiefly Thou O Spirit, that dost prefer
> Before all Temples th' upright heart and pure,
> Instruct me, for Thou know'st; Thou from the first
> Wast present, and with mighty wings outspread
> Dove-like satst brooding on the vast Abyss
> And mad'st it pregnant: What in me is dark
> Illumine, what is low raise and support;
> That to the highth of this great Argument
> I may assert Eternal Providence,
> And justify the ways of God to men.

No question about it, this kind of *blank verse* was intended for close reading in an armchair, if for no other reason than those curious Latin-like syntactic features of placing a noun between two adjectives ("the upright heart and pure") and a verb between two subjects ("Or if *Sion* Hill / Delight thee more, and *Siloa's* brook"). When all is said and done, we have here what some people have described as Milton's magnificent "organ tones," by which was meant tones played on an instrument such as would have been built by his near-contemporary Johann Sebastian Bach. But needless to say — and once again — don't take my word for it.

Exercise 17

Read this passage aloud, and again may I suggest that if a group is using this book, a new reader take over with each full stop, and that if you're alone, you try changing voices.

The difference between Milton's approach and that of Shakespeare's should be readily apparent.

Exercise 18

Copy out the first sixteen lines (to "Rhyme") and, leaving plenty of room between each line, do a complete scansion.

How many "perfect" lines did you find?

Two: "Invoke thy aid to my adventrous Song" and "That with no middle flight intends to soar."

How many other ten-syllables lines were there?

Twelve.

How many with fewer than ten syllables?

None.

How many with more than ten syllables?

Two: "Of Man's First Disobedience and the Fruit" and "Delight thee more, and Siloa's Brook that flow'd."

How many *caesuras* after the second foot?

One: "Delight thee more, and Siloa's Brook that flow'd."

How many variations of single *caesura* placement?

Nine.

How many multiple *caesuras*?

One.

How many *enjambments*?

Eleven.

Exercise 19

As with "To be or not to be," look at this passage for the sounds alone. Be sure to include both end-rhymes and internal rhymes, and onomatopoeia and parallelisms, if any. To what extent do they contribute to the passage's total effect?

We're now going to home in on things again.

Exercise 20

As with "To be or not to be," substitute cha for each light stress and CHA for each heavy stress under each line of your scansion, and read them aloud instead of the words.

Once more, don't lose sight of the fact that you're in the process of teaching yourself, and remember that Milton, too, is very hard to ruin.

Exercise 21

Try substituting nonsense words instead of the cha's and CHA's, and when you're done, read it all aloud, having a new reader take over with each full stop as you did before, and changing voices if you're alone.

Again, I can't help stressing the importance of memorization. Try taking it from me on faith, pretty please —

Exercise 22

Commit the first sixteen lines to memory and repeat them over and over — until you've got it all in your head, much as serious pianists have a certain kind of music "in their fingers."

Now take a look at this blank verse poem in the manner of Milton by Lorraine Ghignone, another former student of mine:

Paradise Always

O wary of the serpent's legacy
That I remain in bondage to Earth's coarse

Vibrations — on this plane, so heavily
Entrapped. O weighty leaf! O pond'rous flake
Of snow. Fie, ignoble fruit upon strong
Verdant pillars. Paying your debt, boast flow'rs
Their wooden petals; and vexed oceans pound
Recrimination into stolid shores,
As clouds hang in obstreperous sentence —
Often weeping, but ne'er cleansing the world
Of its pernicious sin. But need this Shame
Be melded in our marrow? Need we kneel,
The humbled sinner? Nay, one's soul is pure
And filled with Spirit's light — mirroring
Its Artist. Eden, but once a place of yore,
Does not exist in this world's duality.
Perchance we are to serve a penance here,
To know each pleasure coupled with its pain —
To feel the velvet rose and prickly stem.
Still, this be not God's will for us, alone!
'Tis wasteful for the universe to thrive
Upon the flaws and crudeness of its parts.
'Tis, instead, more fruitful that created
Are all the contradictions of this world
For Soul to duly chafe itself against,
And from the friction, labor to refine
Itself — become so rarified that it
No longer needs this planet. Why remain
Where one no longer needs to be? Fly high!
Fly higher than the stars! No need to catch
The moon. Pass the moon! Leave the weight behind!
Soar into the finer universes!
The wingèd bird is stone unto the Soul
Who'st free, and, thus, begins to journey Home.

Exercise 23

Be not faint of heart. Remember that you've got all kinds of expedients to fall back on. But don't be overly ambitious, either: bear in mind that, as the old saying goes, a little bit — like ten lines — goes a long way. Be sure to include the major features of Miltonic blank verse that I've been at

> *pains to isolate, but take care when it comes to imitating his Latinate vocabulary and sentence-structure, which, like our attempts at imitating a formal style in chapter one, can degenerate into parody. If you're stuck for a topic, why not enlarge on one of your problems or handicaps as Milton did his blindness elsewhere in* ***Paradise Lost.***

Of course you may run into difficulties — but not to fret; simply take your word-salad poem of Exercise 21 and — well — you know.

After Milton, *blank verse* went into a kind of eclipse in English poetic circles and so remained until the late eighteenth century, when it experienced a revival in the hands of the Romantics. Wordsworth led the way, making it the vehicle of his ode "Tintern Abbey" and of his spiritual autobiography *The Prelude.* We've already looked at a passage from "Tintern Abbey" in chapter three; here's another, one of the high points of the poem:

> . . . —That time is past,
> And all its aching joys are now no more,
> And all its dizzy raptures. Not for this
> Faint I, nor mourn nor murmur; other gifts
> Have followed; for such loss, I would believe,
> Abundant recompense. For I have learned
> To look on nature, not as in the hour
> Of thoughtless youth; but hearing oftentimes
> The still, sad music of humanity,
> Nor harsh nor grating, though of ample power
> To chasten and subdue. And I have felt
> A presence that disturbs me with the joy
> Of elevated thoughts; a sense sublime
> Of something far more deeply interfused,
> Whose dwelling is the light of setting suns,
> And the round ocean and the living air,
> And the blue sky, and in the mind of man:
> A motion and a spirit, that impels
> All thinking things, all objects of all thought,
> And rolls through all things. Therefore am I still

A lover of the meadows and the woods,
And mountains; and of all that we behold
From this green earth; of all the mighty world
Of eye, and ear, — both what they half create,
And what perceive; well pleased to recognise
In nature and the language of the sense
The anchor of my purest thoughts, the nurse,
The guide, the guardian of my heart, and soul
Of all my moral being. . . .

Exercise 24

As with our samples from Shakespeare and Milton, read this passage aloud, and once again may I suggest that a new reader take over with each full stop if you're in a group or that you try changing voices if you're alone.

One thing should become apparent at once: Wordsworth seems easier to understand than Shakespeare and Milton. Can you guess why? Let's delve, shall we?

Exerciser 25

Copy out the first seventeen lines (to "man:") as you have with the passages from Shakespeare and Milton, and leaving plenty of room between each line, do a complete scansion.

How many "perfect" lines did you find?

Three: "And all its aching joys are now no more"; "Of something far more deeply interfused"; "Whose dwelling is the light of setting suns."

How many other ten-syllables lines were there?

Fourteen.

How many with fewer than ten syllables?

None.

How many with more than ten syllables?

None.

How many caesuras after the second foot?

One: "Of thoughtless youth; but hearing oftentimes."

How many variations of single caesura placement?

Seven.

How many multiple caesuras?

Two.

How many enjambments?

Nine.

Exercise 26

As before, look at this passage for the sounds alone. Be sure to include both end-rhymes and internal rhymes, and onomatopoeia and parallelisms, if any. To what extent do they contribute to the total effect of the passage?

Ready, set, go! Let's get closer.

Exercise 27

Substitute cha for each light stress and CHA for each heavy stress in the space under each line of your scansion, and read it all aloud instead of the words.

Once more, fret not, bearing in mind that the above and what follows are part of a learning experience.

Exercise 28

Replace the cha's and CHA's with nonsense words, and as before, read it all aloud, having a new reader take over with each full stop or changing voices if you're alone.

Now for the pièce de résistance or, in common parlance, a really cool trip.

Exercise 29

Memorize the first seventeen lines and recite them aloud.

By way of summarizing, how did Wordsworth, who was here at his best, resemble Shakespeare, how Milton, and in what way or ways was he uniquely himself? One of the pitfalls to be avoided is falling overly in love with Wordsworth because his stuff sounds more modern, and another is developing a fancy for Shakespeare and / or Milton because theirs has an old feel to it. Both attitudes are beside the point, yes? Beware!

In Victorian times, poets tended to fancy things up, including the old forms. For instance, in "Tears, Idle Tears" by Alfred Lord Tennyson (1809-1892), the poet ends each stanza with a variable *refrain*-line:

> Tears, idle tears, I know not what they mean,
> Tears from the depth of some divine despair
> Rise in the heart, and gather to the eyes,
> In looking on the happy Autumn-fields,
> And thinking of the days that are no more.
>
> Fresh as the first beam glittering on a sail,
> That brings our friends up from the underworld,
> Sad as the last which reddens over one
> That sinks with all we love below the verge;
> So sad, so fresh, the days that are no more.
>
> Ah, sad and stranger, as in dark summer dawns
> The earliest pipe of half-awaken'd birds
> To dying ears, when unto dying eyes
> The casement slowly grows a glimmering square;
> So sad, so strange, the days that are no more.
>
> Dear as remember'd kisses after death,
> And sweet as those by hopeless fancy feign'd
> On lips that are for others; deep as love,
> Deep as first love, and wild with all regret;
> O Death in Life, the days that are no more.

That *refrain*-line reminds me of a fashion-conscious woman trying to enhance a plain dress with a piece of flashy costume jewelry.

Exercise 30

Did Tennyson's fancying up of his blank verse give you any ideas of what you might do with your own? Do it!

Poets have continued writing in *blank verse* down to today. Significant among them is Wallace Stevens (1879-1955), notably in his "Sunday Morning," which consists of eight paragraphs, each fifteen lines in length. Here's how it begins:

Complacencies of the peignoir, and late
Coffee and oranges in a sunny chair,
And the green freedom of a cockatoo
Upon a rug mingle to dissipate
The holy hush of ancient sacrifice.
She dreams a little, and she feels the dark
Encroachment of that old catastrophe,
As a calm darkens among water-lights.
The pungent oranges and bright, green wings
Seem things in some procession of the dead,
Winding across wide water, without sound.
The day is like wide water, without sound,
Stilled for the passing of her dreaming feet
Over the seas, to silent Palestine,
Dominion of the blood and sepulchre.

These lines with their many polysyllabic words seem more Miltonic than Shakespearian, and I'm rather imagining that Stevens took his cue directly from the source, not via Wordsworth, for example.

So, what do you say, are you ready? Here, by way of encouragement, is a poem in *blank verse* that's uniquely his own by my former student Michael Toro:

Lovers within the Darkness

The city sleeps beneath a neon moon,
Glowing within: a dreamland entwining.
The two of us, she and I, imbued erotic;
Floods of night pour in through our window:
Reveal eyes that glimmer to glaring street lights,
From blood pulsating to motion in our loins;
In time to mouths compressed in nectars stirred within,
Our shadows cast a storm of torrid visions.
Profound embrace: our flesh ignites incessant flames —
Unites our spirits — tempestuous oceans;
Our bodies awash, ablaze, in waves enfolding,
Beads of sweat cascade in passion's rain;
The flow of city lights gleams and swirls upon us,
Our hearts beat as one in frenzied rhythm;

We merge transfigured through the chasms:
The brink begins to shine in the Eastern sky,
We thrust in rays of Mars and Venus soaring
Before the sun a wonder bursting a-glow,
As this night's embrace unwraps the dawn.

Exercise 31

Your turn now, yes? Finish what you started in Exercise 30, or begin afresh. Ten or so lines will do it.

Heroic Couplets

Chaucer made rhymed pairs of *iambic pentameter* lines as the basic units of his monumental *Canterbury Tales,* and we've already noted how contagiously catchy they are:

Whan that Aprill with his shoures soote — *sweet*
The droghte of March hath perced to the roote,
And bathed every veyne in swich licour — *such/liquid*
Of which vertu engendred is the flour;
Whan Zephirus eek with his sweete breeth — *also*
Inspired hath in every holt and heeth.... — *grove/field*

In the late seventeenth and early eighteenth centuries, John Dryden (1631-1700) and Alexander Pope (1688-1744) transformed those *couplets* into vehicles for their wit, as can be seen, for instance, in the opening to Dryden's *Absalom and Achitophel,* in which he used the biblical story to suggest how the Earl of Shaftsbury (alias Achitophel, one of King David's followers) was tempting Charles II's illegitimate son the young Duke of Monmouth (alias Absalom, a son of David) to rebel against his father:

In pious times, e're Priest-craft did begin,
Before *Polygamy* was made a sin;

When man, on many, multiply'd his kind,
E'r one to one, was cursedly, confind;
When Nature prompted, and no law deny'd
Promiscuous use of Concubine and Bride;
Then, *Israel*'s monarch, after Heaven's own heart,
His vigorous warmth did, variously, impart
To Wives and Slaves: And, wide as his Command,
Scatter'd his Maker's Image through the Land.
Michal, of Royal Blood, the Crown did wear,
A Soyl ungratefull to the Tiller's care:
Not so the rest; for several Mothers bore
To Godlike *David*, several Sons before.
But since like slaves his bed they did ascend,
No True Succession could their seed attend.
Of all this Numerous Progeny was none
So Beautifull, so brave as Absolon — :

The difference between the *couplets* in this passage and Chaucer's should be apparent at once: Dryden's tended to be self-contained units or, as we'd say, *closed*, whereas Chaucer's tended to be *run on*.

This form of the *couplet* came to be called the *heroic couplet* because Dryden and Pope first used them to set translations of parts of the *Aeneid* and *Iliad* in them, both *epics* or works featuring heroes. Of the two poets, Pope was clearly the master, a Shakespeare to Dryden's Marlowe, and he set the standard for a century of imitators down to Byron. Let this paragraph from Pope's *Essay on Criticism*, which you're already familiar with in part, serve as an example:

A *little Learning* is a dang'rous Thing;
Drink deep, or taste not the *Pierian* Spring:
There *shallow draughts* intoxicate the Brain,
And drinking *largely* sobers us again.
Fir'd at first sight with what the *Muse* imparts,
In *fearless Youth* we tempt the Heights of Arts,
While from the bounded *Level* of our Mind,
Short Views we take, nor see the *lengths behind*,

But *more advanc'd*, behold with strange surprize
New, distant Scenes of *endless* Science rise!
So pleas'd at first, the towring *Alps* we try,
Mount o'er the Vales, and seem to tread the Sky;
Th' Eternal Snows appear already past,
And the first *clouds* and *mountains* seem the last:
But *those attain'd*, we tremble to survey
The growing Labours of the lengthen'd Way,
Th' *increasing* prospect *tires* our wand'ring Eyes,
Hills peep o'er Hills, and *Alps* on *Alps* arise!

One tends to be dazzled by how cute these lines are and fail to notice their utter brilliance. For instance, did anyone notice that absolutely awesome pun, "New, distant Scenes of endless Science rise"? If you did, whoever you are, go to the head of the class!

And now, here we go again. Yes, a-gai-ai-ain:

Exercise 32

Needless to say, our first step is to read this passage aloud. The obvious way to do this is to change voices with each couplet, but also possible is to change voices with each second (or answering) line of a couplet.

Cool stuff, wouldn't you agree? Now for some nitty-gritty, but do bear it firmly in mind that, *end-rhymes* or not, this is still *iambic pentameter*. As I'm sure you realized during your reading, what the rhymes do is reinforce the end-of-line punctuation.

Exercise 33

Copy out the passage, and leaving plenty of room between each line as in the previous samples, do a complete scansion.

How many "perfect" lines did you find?

Nine: "And drinking etc."; "In fearless youth etc." ; "While from the bounded etc."; "Short Views we take etc."; "But more advanc'd etc."; "So pleas'd at first etc."; "Mount o'er the Vales etc."; "Th'eternal Snows appear etc."; "The growing labours etc."

How many other ten-syllable lines were there?

Ten.

How many with fewer than ten syllables?

None.

How many with more than ten syllables?

None.

How many *caesuras* after the second foot?

Four: "Short Views we take, nor see the Lengths behind"; "But more advanc'd, behold with strange Surprize"; "Mount o'er the Vales, and seem to tread the Sky"; "Hills peep o'er Hills, and Alps on Alps arise."

How many variations of single *caesura* placement?

One.

How many multiple *caesuras*?

One.

How many *enjambments*?

Three.

In the end, I'm sure you'll agree that leaving the matter of *sound-correspondence* aside, Pope's strategies of expression, including his modes of variation, were not all that different from those of the writers of *blank verse.*

Exercise 34

As before, look at this passage for the sounds alone, meaning both end-rhyme and internal rhymes as well as other forms of sound-correspondence, if any. To what extent does each contribute to the total effect of the passage?

Here we go again, more zeroing in:

Exercise 35

Substitute cha for each light stress and CHA for each heavy stress in the space under each line of your scansion, and read it all aloud instead of the words.

Don't be surprised if you found this exercise more fun than the one with the different samples of *blank verse.* Why? Simple, because the verse is fun.

Exercise 36

Replace the cha's and CHA's with nonsense words, and as before, read it all aloud.

This next should also present less of a problem than it did with *blank verse*, since rhyme acts as an aid to the memory or, if you will, as a mnemonic device.

Exercise 37

Commit the passage to memory and recite it aloud.

One of the problems that Pope had to face was that no matter how clever he was, sooner or later readers were bound to find those long paragraphs of rhyming *couplets* monotonous. One way of achieving variety was to include a *triplet*, that is, three end-rhymed lines, here and there. Note how he managed it in the following passage, also from his *Essay on Criticism:*

> But most by *Numbers* judge a Poet's Song,
> And *smooth* or *rough*, with them is *right* or *wrong;*
> In the bright *Muse* tho' *thousand charms* conspire,
> Her *Voice* is all these tuneful Fools admire,
> Who haunt *Parnassus* but to please their ear,
> Not mend their Minds; as some to *Church* repair,
> Not for the *doctrine*, but the *music* there.

Note how the unity of the lines "In the bright *Muse* tho' *thousand charms* conspire, / Her *Voice* is all these tuneful Fools admire" is broken by a continuation of the sense of the passage to "Not mend their Minds" in the midst of the *triplet.* At the same time, note how the last five lines are bound together by the terminal *r*-sounds. And the upshot is that the disruption of "normal" unity together with a differently achieved unity goes hand-in-hand with the sense. No question about it: it took sheer genius to accomplish this.

Another device that Pope used to break up monotony and create variety was the six-foot or *hexameter* line, commonly called an *alexandrine,* and nowhere does he do this more successfully than in the lines that conclude the above verse-paragraph:

These *Equal Syllables* alone require,
Tho' oft the Ear the *open Vowels* tire,
While *Expletives* their feeble Aid *do* join,
And ten low Words oft creep in one dull Line,
While they ring round the same *unvary'd Chimes*,
With sure *Returns* of still expected *Rhymes.*
Where-e'er you find *the cooling Western Breeze,*
In the next Line, it *whispers thro' the Trees:*
If chrystal Streams *with pleasing Murmurs creep,*
The Reader's threaten'd (not in vain) with *Sleep.*
Then, at the *last,* an *only* Couplet fraught
With some *unmeaning* Thing they call a *Thought,*
A *needless Alexandrine* ends the Song,
That like a wounded Snake, drags its slow length along.

Notice how Pope anticipated that magnificent finale with his inclusion of "creep" five lines earlier, which he reinforced by rhyming it with "sleep" and (partially) with "needless." And notice how our picture of the crawling snake is bolstered acoustically by the phrase "drags its slow length" — four heavy beats in a row — underlined by the repetition of *s*'s and *l*'s, which are anticipated by those in "needless," "Alexandrine," "ends," and "song" on the previous line, and how his repetition of *l* in the final three words — "slow length along" — really makes that snake crawl painfully.

My publisher, Arnold Greissle-Schönberg, who happens to be one of my favorite students, brought forth the following:

Tell Me Where

The trashy city has us by the throat
As to the sky it lifts its smoggy coat:
Above, a mass of grey and lifeless cubes,
Below, a net of trains in dusty tubes.
Graffiti grace the city's crumbling walls,

And homeless shapes lie bundled up in balls —
To find escape from winter's icy bite,
From hunger, drugs, and rape in aimless flight.
We see these lives in hopeless misery spent
And ask ourselves — "Where is our government?"

Brenda Siegel, another former student of mine, also had a good one. Notice how she worked student sarcasm into the fabric of the verse and made it work:

Essay on Teaching Poetry in Junior High

When teaching students of this age and clime,
Of poetry, of free verse or of rhyme,
We introduce loved poets, old and new,
For their perusal and their point of view.
Walt Whitman, for example, was the first;
His lines so bravely practiced and rehearsed.
"O, he's conceited and puffed up — a bore;
"He 'celebrates himself,' — we'll say no more.
"He writes of armpits and his body's smells;
"On grass and work and singing songs he dwells."
With Dickinson we tried to make the grade,
And gain the would-be critics' ayes and accolades.
"At least her poems are short, or so they look!
"But isn't 'frigate' dirty? — What's a book?"
Then Langston Hughes and Robert Frost alike
Incurred eighth-grade's displeasure and dislike.
Try Shakespeare and the class — or you — will strike:
"If you the tastes of eighth-grade dare to frame,
"Then introduce a poet worth the name!"

Exercise 38

Your turn: ten or more lines. If you can manage to include a triplet (as Ms. Siegel indeed did) or a hexameter line or both, that would indeed be extra cute and clever. If you find yourself getting stuck, which sometimes happens, try borrowing someone else's rhymes or even rhyme-words and gradually building sense with them. Try for full rhymes here and elsewhere in this chapter and the next, but if you find yourself having to choose sound for the sake of sound, don't — go for a partial rhyme instead, okay?

The *heroic couplet* lent itself particularly to short, witty statements or *aphorisms*, which Pope's work especially abounds in. "A little learning," etc., is one such, the snake simile is another, and here are some more:

'Tis not enough no Harshness gives Offence,
The *Sound* must seem an *Eccho* to the *Sense*.

Good-Nature and *Good-Sense* must ever join; *pron. "jine"*
To Err is *Humane*, to Forgive, *Divine*.

Nay, fly to *Altars; there* they'll talk you dead;
For *Fools* rush in where *Angels* fear to tread.

Do I dare? Well, Jean Campana Conway, another of my former students, felt particularly at home with this sort of thing and created a poem consisting of such *aphorisms:*

Celebrating the Best

Whenever there are problems to be solved,
Remember, never to become involved.

Do not extend your open helpful hand.
The thanks you get add up to specks of sand.

Do not expect the taker's warm respect.
Look forward to rejection most direct.

False kudos, bravos, kisses on the cheek
Belong to the naive, deprived, and meek.

If you discover that you are entwined,
Speak up at once and stress you are not kind.

Give only to yourself, merci beaucoup!
Just celebrate the best — Narcisstic YOU.

Exercise 39

So how about you? Two aphorisms would be just fine, but I bet you'll do more once you get started.

With the death of Pope, the *heroic couplet* went into a kind of eclipse, to reappear in the hands of Lord Byron (1788-1824), whose best use of it was as clincher lines to his *ottava rima* stanzas in *Don Juan*, which we'll discuss in the next chapter. After that, the eclipse seemed to become complete with Robert Browning's (1812-1889) adoption and development of the form for sober and straightforward *dramatic monologues*, as can be seen in the opening to the most well-known of them, "My Last Duchess":

> That's my last Duchess painted on the wall,
> Looking as if she were alive; I call
> That piece a wonder, now: Frà Pandolf's hands
> Worked busily a day, and there she stands.
> Will't please you sit and look at her? I said
> "Frà Pandolf" by design, for never read
> Strangers like you that pictured countenance,
> The depth and passion of its earnest glance,
> But to myself they turned (since none puts by
> The curtain I have drawn for you, but I)...

Needless to say, this sort of thing is a far cry from Pope's witty repartee; it's as if the cork fell into the champagne bottle and the fizz went out of it — but not so. Clearly it has its charm and should be appreciated as such. By the way, in case you're interested, the conversational effect is achieved by *enjambments* and unusual line endings, like "I call," often coupled with *caesuras* after the fourth *foot*.

Exercise 40?
Like to take a shot at it, heh-heh?

I find a touch of the one-and-only Pope in Matthew Arnold (1822-1888), a contemporary of Browning, who used *iambic pentameter couplets* in the final stanza of "Dover Beach." My guess is that this was to give that moving poem a kind of finality after seemingly random rhyming in the previous stanzas. Note that the *couplets* fittingly have a kind of weak snap and crackle to them:

Ah, love, let us be true
To one another! For the world, which seems
To lie before us like a land of dreams,
So various, so beautiful, so new,
Hath really neither joy, nor love, nor light,
Nor certitude, nor peace, nor help for pain;
And we are here as on a darkling plain
Swept with confused alarms of struggle and flight,
Where ignorant armies clash by night.

T. S. Eliot made considerable use of rhyming *iambic pentameter couplets* in "The Love Song of J. Alfred Prufrock," and many of them, like these for instance, have a kind of Popean ring to them:

Let us go, through certain half-deserted streets,
The muttering retreats
Of restless nights in one-night cheap hotels
And sawdust restaurants with oyster-shells: . . . (*Italics mine.*)

*

I have seen them riding seaward on the waves
Combing the white hair of the waves blown back
When the wind blows the water white and black. (Italics mine)

Eliot's occasional variations on the form are nothing short of awesome, reminiscent of some of the great musical variations in the past, like Brahms's variations on a tune by Haydn:

I grow old…I grow old…
I shall wear the bottoms of my trousers rolled.

*

I should have been a pair of ragged claws
Scuttling across the floors of silent seas.

Eliot's unique contribution to the Popean *couplet* is the development of his *non-sequitur* line — remember it from chapter three? — which is nothing short of sheer unadulterated brilliance:

For I have known them all already, known them all: —
Have known the evenings, mornings, afternoons,
I have measured out my life with coffee spoons; (*Italics mine.*)

*

We have lingered in the chambers of the sea
By sea-girls wreathed with seaweed red and brown
Till human voices wake us, and we drown. (Italics mine.)

Elegiac Quatrain

This stanza was made famous by Thomas Gray (1716-1771) in his "Elegy Written in a Country Church-Yard." Although composed to express sorrow over the death of Richard West, who was probably Gray's lover, it became and remained for countless generations of readers a lament for the common man.

The opening stanzas, the first of which we've encountered before, tell the whole tale where the verse form is concerned:

The curfew tolls the knell of parting day,
The lowing herd winds slowly o'er the lea,
The plowman homeward plods his weary way,
And leaves the world to darkness and to me.

Now fades the glimmering landscape on the sight,
And all the air a solemn stillness holds,
Save where the beetle wheels his droning flight,
And drowsy tinklings lull the distant folds:

Save that from yonder ivy-mantled tow'r,
The moping owl does to the moon complain
Of such as, wand'ring near her secret bow'r,
Molest her ancient solitary reign.

Beneath those rugged elms, that yew-tree's shade,
Where heaves the turf in many a mold'ring heap,
Each in his narrow cell for ever laid,
The rude forefathers of the hamlet sleep.

The breezy call of incense-breathing morn,
The swallow twitt'ring from the straw-built shed,
The cock's shrill clarion, or the echoing horn,
No more shall rouse them from their lowly bed.

For them no more the blazing hearth shall burn,
Or busy housewife ply her evening care;
No children run to lisp their sire's return,
Or climb his knees the envied kiss to share.

Oft did the harvest to their sickle yield,
Their furrow oft the stubborn glebe has broke:
How jocund did they drive their team afield!
How bow'd the woods beneath their sturdy stroke!

Let not ambition mock their useful toil,
Their homely joys, and destiny obscure;
Nor grandeur hear with a disdainful smile
The short and simple annals of the poor.

The boast of heraldry, the pomp of pow'r,
And all that beauty, all that wealth e'er gave,
Awaits alike th' inevitable hour.
The paths of glory lead but to the grave.

Did you notice that the *quatrains* are almost all self-contained? But how different their texture is from Pope's vibrant *couplets:* the "Elegy" is a lazy river by comparison. One factor contributing to this "laziness" is that it has relatively few *caesuras* and *enjambments;* another, as we've already noted in chapter four, is its hefty use of *parallelism.* Also contributing is the generally placid tone that Gray achieved via his stately diction and his predilection for unvoiced consonants, especially *r* and *l.*

Exercise 41

If the above didn't strike you at once, read the excerpt from Pope's "Essay on Criticism" *aloud and follow it with the above from Gray's* "Elegy."

Who says that we're finished with Gray? No, not by a long shot are we.

Exercise 42

Copy out the first sixteen lines (to "sleep."), and leaving plenty of room between each line as in the previous samples, do a complete scansion.

How many "perfect" lines did you find?

Eight: "The curfew tolls the knell of parting day"; "The lowing herd wind slowly o'er the lea"; "The plowman homeward plods his weary way"; "And leaves the world to darkness and to me"; "And all the air a solemn stillness holds"; "And drowsy tinklings lull the distant folds"; "Molest her ancient solitary reign"; "Beneath those rugged elms, that yew tree's shade."

How many other ten-syllables lines were there?

Six.

How many with fewer than ten syllables?

None.

How many with more than ten syllables?

Two.

How many caesuras after the second foot?

None.

How many variations of single caesura placement?

Two.

How many multiple caesuras?

None.

How many enjambments?

Two.

Oh what a tangled web we weave.

Exercise 43

Look at the passage by Gray for the sounds alone, meaning both end-rhymes and internal rhymes, as well as other forms of sound-correspondence, if any. To what extent does each contribute to the total effect of the passage?

Would anyone care to dance?

Exercise 44

Substitute cha for each light stress and CHA for each heavy stress in the space under each line of your scansion, and read it all aloud instead of the words.

Somehow this exercise wasn't as much fun as the same one with the excerpt from Pope. How so? Because this is funereal? Anyway, not to fret; as I've said before, it's all in a good cause.

Exercise 45

Replace the cha's and CHA's with nonsense words, and as before, read it all aloud.

Like the excerpt from Pope, this next shouldn't present much of a problem because, as I've said, rhyme acts as a reminder.

Exercise 46

Commit the passage from Gray to memory and recite it aloud.

Here's what my former student Linda Marie Wallace did with the *elegaic quatrain* à la Gray, spinning off the first line of Keats's famous *sonnet:*

Free

When I have thoughts that I may soon be free,
My eyes become a twilight star above.
But then the darkness covers what I see,
And I become an orphan — no longer loved.

Betrayed by those who wished the life of me,
Where I was shattered with their screams so loud.
They — blinded by my hurt and crying tears,
For they could not rejoice because they're proud.

So I became an orphan of their tree,
Where blame and hurt was put upon my branch.
But as I grow, I know what I shall be —
A growing flower free upon a ranch.

Exercise 47

Write a poem on a sad subject consisting of at least three elegaic quatrains.

After Gray, the *cross-rhymed iambic pentameter quatrain* was always reserved as a medium for sad subjects, and as such, it enjoyed a long, distinguished history down almost until today. Notable among the poets using it was Wordsworth, whose "Elegaic Stanzas" were written in memory of his brother John, who died in a shipwreck. The poem's subtitle — "Suggested by a Picture of Peele Castle, in a Storm, painted by Sir George Beaumont" — tells the whole story. Its opening lines we already know from our scansion of them in chapter five:

I was thy neighbour once, thou rugged Pile!
Four summer weeks I dwelt in sight of thee:
I saw thee every day; and all the while
Thy Form was sleeping on a glassy sea.

The pronoun *I* is much in evidence in the poem, and its tone, though sad, is personal and discursive. The high point comes in the end, when with the painting of Peele Castle in a storm in mind, Wordsworth declared:

O 'tis a passionate Work! — yet wise and well,
Well chosen is thc spirit that is here;
That Hulk which labours in the deadly swell,
This rueful sky, this pageantry of fear!

And this huge Castle, standing here sublime,
I love to see the look with which it braves,
Cased in the unfeeling armour of old time,
The lightning, the fierce wind, and trampling waves.

Farewell, farewell the heart that lives alone,
Housed in a dream, at distance from the Kind! *mankind*
Such happiness, wherever it be known,
Is to be pitied; for 'tis surely blind.

But welcome fortitude, and patient cheer,
And frequent sights of what is to be borne!
Such sights, or worse, as are before me here. —
Not without hope we suffer and we mourn.

A melancholic tone with an exotic "foreign" twist pervades Edward Fitzgerald's "Rubáiyát of Omar Khayyám" (composed 1859-1879), in which a slightly different rhyme scheme was used:

The Moving Finger writes; and, having writ,
Moves on: nor all your Piety nor Wit
Shall lure it back to cancel half a Line,
Nor all your Tears wash out a Word of it.

While not everyone will agree, I see a final flowering of the *elegaic quatrain* in Hart Crane's celebrated "Proem: To Brooklyn Bridge" (1930):

How many dawns, chill from his rippling rest
The seagull's wings shall dip and pivot him,
Shedding white rings of tumult, building high
Over the chained bay waters Liberty —

Then, with inviolate curve, forsake our eyes
As apparitional as sails that cross
Some page of figures to be filed away; —
Till elevators drop us from our day . . .

I think of cinemas, panoramic sleights
With multitudes bent toward some flashing scene
Never disclosed, but hastened to again,
Foretold to other eyes on the same screen;

And Thee, across the harbor, silver-paced
As though the sun took step of thee, yet left

Some motion ever unspent in thy stride, —
Implicitly thy freedom staying thee!

Out of some subway scuttle, cell or loft
A bedlamite speeds to thy parapets,
Tilting there momently, shrill shirt ballooning,
A jest falls from the speechless caravan.

Down Wall, from girder into street noon leaks,
A rip-tooth of the sky's acetylene;
All afternoon the cloud-flown derricks turn . . .
Thy cables breathe the North Atlantic still.

And obscure as that heaven of the Jews,
Thy guerdon . . . Accolade thou dost bestow
Of anonymity time cannot raise:
Vibrant reprieve and pardon thou dost show.

O harp and altar, of the fury fused,
(How could mere toil align thy choiring strings!)
Terrific threshold of the prophet's pledge,
Prayer of pariah, and the lover's cry, —

Again the traffic lights that skim thy swift
Unfractioned idiom, immaculate sigh of stars,
Beading thy path — condense eternity:
And we have seen night lifted in thine arms.

Under thy shadow by the piers I waited;
Only in darkness is thy shadow clear.
The City's fiery parcels all undone,
Already snow submerges an iron year . . .

O Sleepless as the river under thee,
Vaulting the sea, the prairies' dreaming sod,
Unto us lowliest sometime sweep, descend
And of the curveship lend a myth to God.

Do take note of Crane's unself-conscious use of *cross-rhymes,* both of the full and partial varieties — for example, "sleights," "scene," "again," "screen" — and how he, in a ploy uniquely his own, varied this with *couplets* — "away" and "day." Fittingly, by way of contrast, there are some *quatrains* whose line-endings have no relationship to one another, where sound is concerned — for example, the lines ending in "fused," "strings," "pledge," and "cry." Gray's "Elegy" was popular grade-school fare when Crane was a child; my father, who was of the same generation, could recite quite a few of its *quatrains* from memory, even in his old age, and I suspect that the "Elegy" made as indelible an impression on Crane.

The word, like the form, comes from the Italian word *sonetto* and ultimately from the Latin *sonus*, both meaning "sound." There are two major versions of the *sonnet* in English, the *Italian* or *Petrarchan*, after the fourteenth-century Italian poet Petrarch, and the *Elizabethan* or *Shakespearian*. The *Petrarchan* version was introduced into the language by Sir Thomas Wyatt (1503-1542) following a trip to Italy. The *Elizabethan* developed from it, and Henry Howard, Earl of Surrey (1517-1547), is credited with writing the first *sonnet* of this type. We'll cover the latter first because it consists of two building blocks that we're already familiar with: the *cross-rhymed iambic pentameter quatrain* and the *iambic pentameter couplet.*

Elizabethan or Shakespearian *Sonnet*

I should point out that quite a few poets, like Sir Philip Sidney (1554-1586) and Edmund Spenser (1552-1599), had taken a whack at this form or something resembling it before Shakespeare did. In other words, as with *blank verse,* he was by no means a Columbus when it came to developing it but rather took what he found and carried it to new unheard-of heights, shaping it into a vehicle for the intellect par excellence.

Typically, this *Elizabethan* or *Shakespearian* version consists of three parallel statements in three *quatrains* and an ironic twist in the *couplet;* the third *quatrain* is generally a little different from the first two. Let his Number 73, one of his characteristic and best-known *sonnets,* serve as our example. It's about an I-and-Thou relationship:

> That time of year thou mayst in me behold
> When yellow leaves, or none, or few, do hang
> Upon those boughs which shake against the cold,
> Bare ruin'd choirs, where late the sweet birds sang.
> In me thou see'st the twilight of such day
> As after sunset fadeth in the west,
> Which by and by black night doth take away,
> Death's second self, that seals up all in rest.
> In me thou see'st the glowing of such fire
> That on the ashes of his youth doth lie,
> As the death-bed whereon it must expire,
> Consum'd with that which it was nourish'd by.
> This thou perceiv'st, which makes thy love more strong,
> To love that well which thou must leave ere long.

Note how in the *quatrains* the "I"'s aging and forthcoming death are looked at from the point of view of the "Thou," and how this is done by means of three *analogies* (or *metaphors* or *conceits*) in which, without its being stated in so many words, the temperature rises from very cold to hot, and the color yellow becomes intensified to orange and red. Further, how that greatest intensity of color and heat in the third *quatrain* is complemented by the same *eye*-sound at the ends of all four of its lines: in "Fire," "lie," "expire," and "by."

The point of view is continued in the *couplet*: the "I"'s growing older causes the "Thou" to love him the more. Then, like a bad joke, comes the height of irony: the "I"'s death is viewed as the "Thou"'s departure. And interestingly, complementing that irony is the *end-rhyme* of "strong" and "long," which jangles with the "hang" and "sang" *end-rhyme* of the first *quatrain.*

Exercise 48

Read this sonnet aloud, using three voices: the first two quatrains, the third quatrain, and the couplet.

This next should be a piece of cake after all we've been through together.

Exercise 49

Copy this sonnet out, making sure to leave plenty of room between each line, and then do a complete scansion.

How many "perfect" lines did you find?

Nine: "When yellow leaves, or none,etc."; "Upon those boughs etc."; "In me thou see'st etc."; "As after sunset fadeth etc."; "Which by and by black night etc."; "In me thou see'st etc."; "That on the ashes of his youth etc."; "Consum'd with that etc."; "To love that well etc."

How many other ten-syllables lines were there?

Five.

How many *caesuras* after the second foot?

Three.

How many variations of single *caesura* placement?

None.

How many multiple *caesuras*?

One.

How many *enjambments*?

Four:

Now was this or was it not enlightening?

Exercise 50

Look at this sonnet for the sounds alone, meaning both end-rhymes and internal rhymes as well as other forms of sound-correspondence, if any. To what extent does each contribute to the total effect of the passage?

Are you ready to wiggle? Hope so....

Exercise 51

Substitute cha for each light stress and CHA for each heavy stress in the space under each line of your scansion, and read it all aloud instead of the words.

By now you should know what's coming next, yes?

Exercise 52

Replace the cha's and CHA's with nonsense words, and once more, read it all aloud — with feeling.

As before, this next shouldn't present much of a problem because, as I've said a number of times already, rhyme acts as a reminder.

Exercise 53

Commit this sonnet to memory and recite it aloud.

Not all of Shakespeare's *sonnet*s follow the same strategy. In his Number 29, for instance, the first two *quatrains* are run on, and there are two resolutions — after the end of the third *quatrain* and with the *couplet* — the one reinforcing the other like *addios* in an Italian opera:

When, in disgrace with fortune and men's eyes,
I all alone beweep my outcast state,
And trouble deaf heaven with my bootless cries,
And look upon myself and curse my fate,
Wishing me like to one more rich in hope,
Featur'd like him, like him with friends possess'd,
Desiring this man's art and that man's scope,
With what I most enjoy contented least;
Yet in these thoughts myself almost despising,
Haply I think on thee, and then my state,
Like to the lark at break of day arising
From sullen earth, sings hymns at heaven's gate;
For thy sweet love rememb'red such wealth brings
That then I scorn to change my state with kings.

Exercise 54

There's no point in belaboring things, is there? Still, be sure to note the sounds that are repeated and parallel statements, and the part they play in unifying the whole.

From both of the forgoing *sonnets* by the Bard, it seems clear that this form has two pivotal places: at the end of the second *quatrain* and at the end of the third. The third *quatrain* thus plays a double role: as a quickener of the first two *quatrains* and as an anticipator of the *couplet.*

Coraggio and take note. Here's "A Fantasy to Beyond," which Michael Toro, one of my former students, came up with:

The world's eclipsed behind a veil of dreams,
Our eyes avoid the Sun's reality;
We live our lives in masques, escapist themes,
In shades immortal, we hide in fantasy.
Each day, Destiny beckons us as Its slaves,
To rise to glory, beauty, and jewels.
Each night, Destiny lullabies us to our graves,
With songs of poets, prophets, and fools.
Once I glanced beyond the painted scene,
To glimpse the Truth engraved upon the Sun.
The light was a brilliant, intellectual sheen,
My mind enlightened was forced to run —
To seek illusion beneath my mortal shrouds,
From wizards' sorcery to rainbows in clouds.

And lest you think that Mr. Toro proved the exception rather than the rule, here's what the late Gjertine Johansen, another former student, came up with:

Mortality

When I reflect on weary Winter's age,
When icy wind my wrinkled skin will pierce,
When frozen fingers can not turn the page,
When howling blizzard proves itself too fierce.
Such daunting fears of my mortality,

Gush forth like reddest blood from gaping wound,
And stain white snow of deathly fantasy,
And turn to red the cold and dreaded mound.
Thus Time holds us as prisoners in a cage,
And mocks our futile efforts to escape,
And turns deaf ear to cries — A silent Sage
Who slowly weaves the fabric of black crepe.
But when the sweet Spring sun does kiss my cheek,
The Weaver's work fades deep in Lethe's creek.

Exercise 55

So, now, it's your turn. P. S. Remembering that this version of the sonnet is a poem of the head, is it too much to ask you to include a set of analogies *or conceits like those in Number 73? Hm, maybe so.*

If you got stuck, try using the rhymes of Shakespeare's Number 73 and 29 above or even those of Mr. Toro or Ms. Johansen, or write fourteen lines of nonsense, organizing them as two related *quatrains* followed by one that is less related and then a *couplet.*

After Shakespeare, this version of the *sonnet* went into a kind of eclipse from which it never really recovered — with a single notable exception, this one by John Keats (1795-1821) some two centuries later. We considered it in chapter three in connection with describing states of mind; let's have another look now with respect to its form:

When I have fears that I may cease to be
Before my pen has glean'd my teeming brain,
Before high-piled books, in charactery,
Hold like rich garners the full-ripen'd grain;
When I behold, upon the night's starr'd face,
Huge cloudy symbols of a high romance,
And think that I may never live to trace
Their shadows, with the magic hand of chance;
And when I feel, fair creature of an hour,
That I shall never look upon thee more,

Never have relish in the faery power
Of unreflecting love; — then on the shore
Of the wide world I stand alone, and think
Till love and fame to nothingness do sink.

The resemblance in basic strategy to Shakespeare's Number 73 should be immediately apparent: three *parallel statements* in three *quatrains;* the repetition of the *r*-sound in "hour," "more," "power," and "shore" in the final one; the echo of the *n*-sound of "brain" and "grain" in "think" and "sink" of the *couplet.* But note how many *enjambments* there are in comparison with Number 73, especially in the middle of a *quatrain* and how the *enjambment* on the twelfth line undermines the final *quatrain.* Quite wonderful as this work by Keats is, it's almost as if we were watching the dissolution of this form of the *sonnet* before our very eyes.

Italian or Petrarchan *Sonnet*

The fourteenth-century Italian poet Petrarch composed a series of *sonnets* (or a *sonnet sequence,* as we'd say) to celebrate his love for a woman named Laura, and largely because of this, the English version of his type of *sonnet* came to be associated with love and with subjects that are charged with emotion. Also consisting of fourteen lines, it begins with an *octet* made up of two *quatrains* with the same *end-rhymes* in *envelope* fashion (*abbaabba*), and this is followed by a *sestet* that loosely employs two or three more *end-rhymes, cdcdcd, cdecde, cdeced,* and *cdcdee* being the most favored English schemes. In the *octet,* a problem is set forth; in the *sestet,* a solution is offered. The whole thing with its two units has been likened to inhaling and exhaling or to the contraction and release of muscles.

Because our language isn't rich in words with similar endings like Italian and the other Romance languages, this version of the *sonnet* was slow to catch on after Sir Thomas Wyatt composed the first ones in English.

It was left to Milton, another lover of things Italian, to pave the way a century later, but another century would have to pass before a true master of the form emerged in Wordsworth, who wrote over five hundred of them, at least a dozen of which are incomparable beyond belief. Interestingly, rather than be challenged by its strict requirements, Wordsworth claimed in "Nuns Fret Not at Their Convent's Narrow Walls" that he found solace from his personal troubles in his efforts to conform to them.

In "The World Is Too Much with Us," one of his best-known works in this genre, he registered a common complaint that's still with us: we've lost touch with our roots, natural and poetical. After stating the problem in the *octet,* he went on to offer a solution in the form of a wish partaking of fantasy in the *sestet:*

> The world is too much with us; late and soon,
> Getting and spending, we lay waste our powers:
> Little we see in Nature that is ours;
> We have given our hearts away, a sordid boon!
> This Sea that bares her bosom to the moon;
> The winds that will be howling at all hours,
> And are up-gathered now like sleeping flowers;
> For this, for everything, we are out of tune;
> It moves us not.—Great God! I'd rather be
> A Pagan suckled in a creed outworn;
> So might I, standing on this pleasant lea,
> Have glimpses that would make me less forlorn;
> Have sight of Proteus rising from the sea;
> Or hear old Triton blow his wreathed horn.

Note how the *octet* laps over into the *sestet,* "It moves us not" being the last in the series of *parallel statements* beginning with "we lay waste," "we have given," and "we are out of tune" — which was a trick of Milton's. Note also how "It moves us not" is out of tune with those statements by not beginning with "we" as they do, so its function is pivotal or transitional where the end of the *octet* and beginning of the *sestet* are concerned. The same kind of "dissonance" occurs in the *sestet,* where the parallel statements "have glimpses" and "have sight of" are followed by "hear." The *sestet* is also linked to the *octet* by the *r* and *n* in "outworn," "forlorn," and "horn," which refers us back to the "oon" and "owers" *end-rhymes* of the *octet.*

Exercise 56

Read this sonnet aloud, using different voices for the octet and sestet or breaking it up in some other meaningful way. In other words, don't just blab it out.

Once more with feeling, the last time — in this chapter anyway.

Exercise 57

Copy this sonnet out, making sure to leave plenty of room between each line, and then do a complete scansion.

How many "perfect" lines did you find?

Five: "This Sea that bares her bosom to the moon"; "The winds that will be howling at all hours"; "A Pagan suckled in a creed outworn"; "Have glimpses that would make me less forlorn"; "Or hear old Triton blow his wreathèd horn."

How many other ten-syllable lines were there?

Six.

How many with fewer than ten syllables?

None.

How many with more than ten syllables?

Three.

How many *caesuras* after the second foot?

One.

How many variations of single *caesura* placement?

Three.

How many multiple *caesuras*?

Two.

How many *enjambments*?

One.

I hope this was as enlightening for you as it was for my classroom students of many moons ago.

Exercise 58

Look at this sonnet for the sounds alone, meaning both end-rhymes and internal rhymes as well as other forms of sound-correspondence, if any. To what extent does each contribute to the total effect of the passage?

Have patience, we're getting there.

Exercise 59

Substitute cha for each light stress and CHA for each heavy stress in the space under each line of your scansion, and read it all aloud instead of the words.

And now, tra-la:

Exercise 60

Replace the cha's and CHA's with nonsense words and read it all aloud.

As before, this next shouldn't present much of a problem because, as I've said a number of times already, rhyme acts as a reminder.

Exercise 61

Commit this sonnet *to memory and recite it aloud.*

Interestingly, our guest poet Ruth Fainlight tried this form of the *sonnet* using *assonance* alone, and made it work:

The Japanese Bath

I feared my heart would stop: the depth and heat
of water in the wooden tub, the thought
that even if I called you would not hear
from where you sat, beyond the ante-room,
silk-kimono'd by the painted screen.
I stretched my legs out, saw my body small
as a court lady of Kyoto, green
as moss around a temple garden pool

carp-filled, and how the same droplets of steam
frosting my hair beaded the darkened walls.
The silent isolation made me feel:
to come this far and drown could be foredoomed.
Then I stood up, showered off the dream
and ghosts with cold water, calm now, and cleaned.

Despair not, the real thing, with all the bells and whistles, can and has been done by a fledgling poet, and here's proof by my former student Jody Lo Presto:

A Psychic Psyche's Vow to Cupid

As evening softly kills the light of day,
I wait in my chambers until you return.
With pounding heart and quickening pulse I learn
That I desire more of you—please stay!
Are you some monster, I've heard people say,
That your nocturnal visits cause concern.
Morning dawns, I come awake and turn,
To find myself alone—you've gone away.
Should I believe what they profess is true,
And put my left-brain logic to the test?
No! Intuition tells me I am right—
There is no evil lurking inside you.
My body, mind, and spirit know you best;
Six senses pay you homage through the night.

And here's more proof by my former student Brenda Siegel:

On First Reading Arnold's "Dover Beach"

When first I gazed at Arnold's "Dover Beach,"
And saw the white chalk cliffs and tranquil bay,
Heard the grating roar of pebbles — felt the spray,
Then knew the greatest heights my soul could reach,
Experienced a beauty beyond speech,
Of words whose cadence carried me away,
And wondered when I'd waken from the sway
Of dreams of lands I'd tried so hard to reach.

True, — Arnold saw the beauty in the lands;
But looked beyond the scene with jaundiced eyes;
Saw maggots 'neath the glorious rocks and sands:
No certitude, no peace, no help — just lies.
The beauty of his poem is truth for me:
My joy, my light, my help, my verity.

Exercise 62

I'll tell you: it's bigger than both of us! Go to it. P.S. Remembering that this version of the sonnet is a poem of the heart, do-o-o schmaltz it up if you wish.

If you get stuck, try using the rhymes of Wordsworth's "World Is Too Much with Us" or even those of Ms. Siegel or Ms. Presto, or write fourteen lines of nonsense, organizing them as an *octet* and a *sestet.*

Keats, who was an admirer of both Shakespeare and Milton as well as of his older contemporary Wordsworth, tried his hand once — magnificently — at this form of the *sonnet* in "On First Looking into Chapman's Homer." To fully understand what he was saying, it is necessary to know that Chapman was a Renaissance translator of Homer, the "realms of gold" are books, and traveling is an *analogy* or *conceit* for reading:

Much have I travell'd in the realms of gold,
And many goodly states and kingdoms seen;
Round many western islands have I been
Which bards in fealty to Apollo hold.
Oft of one wide expanse had I been told
That deep-brow'd Homer ruled as his demesne;
Yet did I never breathe its pure serene
Till I heard Chapman speak out loud and bold:
Then felt I like some watcher of the skies
When a new planet swims into his ken;
Or like stout Cortez when with eagle eyes
He star'd at the Pacific — and all his men
Look'd at each other with a wild surmise —
Silent, upon a peak in Darien.

Note the pointed array of "I have"-*parallel statements* in the *octet* — "Much have I travell'd," "Round many western islands have I been," "Oft of one wide expanse had I been told" — and the single *echo* of them in the *sestet*—"Then felt I." The statements "Yet did I never breathe" and "Till I heard" in the final lines of the *octet* act as bridges to the *sestet* and to that *echo.* Of particular importance is the reminder of the "een" *end-rhyme* of the *octet* in the all-important "en" *end-rhyme* of the *sestet.*

A discussion of this type of *sonnet* wouldn't be complete without a mention, at least, of the "Forty-Third Sonnet" by Elizabeth Barrett Browning (1806-1861) from her sequence *Sonnets from the Portuguese:*

> How do I love thee? Let me count the ways.
> I love thee to the depth and breadth and height
> My soul can reach, when feeling out of sight
> For the ends of Being and ideal Grace.
> I love thee to the level of everyday's
> Most quiet need, by sun and candlelight.
> I love thee freely, as men strive for Right;
> I love thee purely, as they turn from Praise.
> I love thee with the passion put to use
> In my old griefs, and with my childhood's faith.
> I love thee with a love I seemed to lose
> With my lost saints,—I love thee with the breath,
> Smiles, tears, of all my life!—and, if God choose,
> I shall but love thee better after death.

This work has always had intensely positive supporters and comparably negative critics. Which are you? Why? Before giving serious thought to that, you might want to take note of her rather extensive use of *partial rhyme* and, to me, tedious repetition of "love thee." Too much mention of "love" by someone has always made me uneasy — how about you?

Mention should also be made here of Gerard Manley Hopkins (1844-1889), who had some very curious notions about rhythm and *sonnets*, separately and together. Among others, he came out with this perfectly weird version of the *Petrarchan* called "The Windhover":

I CAUGHT this morning morning's minion, king-
    dom of daylight's dauphin, dapple-dawn-drawn Falcon,
        in his riding
    Of the rolling level underneath him steady air, and striding
High there, how he rung upon the rein of a wimpling wing
In his ecstasy! Then off, off forth on swing,
    As a skate's heel sweeps smooth on a bow-bend: the hurl
        and gliding
    Rebuffed the big wind. My heart in hiding
Stirred for a bird,—the achieve of, the mastery of the thing!

Brute beauty and valour and act, oh, air, pride, plume, here
    Buckle! AND the fire that breaks from thee then, a billion
Times told lovelier, more dangerous, O my chevalier!

    No wonder of it: shéer plód makes plough down sillion
Shine, and blue-beak embers, ah my dear,
    Fall, gall themselves, and gash gold-vermilion.

The wording is certainly unusual at times, leading one to guess at Hopkins's meaning; consider "shéer plód makes plow down sillion" with its accents to indicate stress. Both the crazy syntax and forced emphases contribute to that peculiarly nervous or agitated quality of this work and, in the end, to our perception of his subject. Because of its almost total departure from *iambic pentameter* and use of a single rhyme in the *octet* (reminiscent of our old friend John Skelton), this work might well be called an *anti-sonnet.*

Our guest poet Ruth Fainlight's experiments with the form are, quite frankly, more to my liking than those of Elizabeth Barret Browning and Hopkins. A good case in point is her "Four Pheasants," where she really excelled at making the *Petrarchan octet* and *sestet* work for her. To anticipate, only words, no camera, still or moving, could achieve the magical narrowing and sharpening of focus one finds there:

> Where the road curves sharp left, it dips,
> and after heavy rain, a glisten of wet —
> what might be the bed of an old stream or
> an overflowing spring — marks the surface.
> The water sinks into the dark earth
> deepened by centuries of rotting leaves
> and decomposing creatures, and the trees arch.
> Their top branches meet above the gap.
>
> When the leaves are russet and gold, the wet road,
> fitfully lit by weak sunlight filtered through
> interlaced twigs, seems to lead somewhere important.
> From a bank of bronze and copper bracken,
> dew-beaded, frost-softened, four pheasants
> emerge, one behind the next, and stalk across.

Through the years there have been some curious *sonnet hybrids* in English, and in particular one might mention Milton's grand conclusion to his epic drama *Samson Agonistes*, where he gave these farewell lines, mixing *Shakespearian* and *Petrarchan* strategies, to the Chorus:

> All is best, though we oft doubt,
> What th' unsearchable dispose
> Of highest wisdom brings about,
> And ever best found in the close.
> Oft he seems to hide his face,
> But unexpectedly returns
> And to his faithful Champion hath in place
> Born witness gloriously; whence Gaza mourn
> And all that band them to resist
> His uncontrollable intent;
> His servants he with new acquist
> Of true experience from this great event
> With peace and consolation hath dismist,
> And calm of mind, all passion spent.

We'll see examples of other *sonnet hybrids* in the next chapter, namely in Keats's great odes and Shelley's "Ode to the West Wind."

Some mention should be made here of Robert Lowell (1917-1977), who wrote rhymeless fourteen-line poems in the spirit of the *sonnet*, which some folks like to term *ghost-sonnets*. How much further can one go with the *sonnet*? Well, in classical music, at least, composers have been known to go quite a bit further. The twentieth-century American composer John Cage, for instance, wrote a work for piano that consisted of a person sitting at a keyboard in silence for four minutes and thirty-three seconds and then arising to take a bow. Is there, perhaps, something similar in store for us from some poet of the future?

Exercise 63

Mess about with one or both forms of the sonnet and have some fun — I dare you.

"A bedlamite speeds to thy parapets..."

7

A Potpourri of Other Traditional Forms

There are many more traditional English verse forms besides the worthies covered in the last chapter. Quite a few, like the *sonnet,* are imports from foreign traditions, and indeed the cornucopia of English verse is as open today to borrowings from near and far as it ever was. So there's always the promise of more to come.

Not everything could be included in this chapter. I tried to do the best I could given the limitations of space and time. So consider what you find here the majors of the minors, and if you're still lusting after more or don't find your very own favorite form by the end of this chapter, may I suggest that you go further afield to such works as Paul Fussell's *Poetic Meter and Poetic Form* and Lewis Turco's *Book of Forms* for starters.

To Sing or Not to Sing

Art Songs

Everyone knows what a song is — it's a set of words that you sing to a tune. But an *art song?* Well, it's the same sort of thing, only the set of words is a poem that's pleasing to the ear but simple and indeed known in a musical setting. So is every simple, pretty poem that's sung an *art son*g? In a literal sense, yes, but some *art songs* are better than others. Who says? History says: they survive from one generation to the next; they stand the test of time.

The Angles and Saxons had them, but the Renaissance was the *art song*'s first real heyday in terms of both quantity and quality. Shakespeare led the way with the many songs in his plays; indeed, what could be lovelier than "Who is Sylvia" from *The Two Gentlemen from Verona:*

Who is Sylvia? What is she,
  That all our swains commend her?
Holy, fair, and wise is she;
  The heaven such grace did lend her,
That she might admired be.

Is she kind as she is fair?
  For beauty lives with kindness.
Love doth to her eyes repair,
  To help him of his blindness,
And, being help'd, inhabits there.

Then to Sylvia let us sing,
  That Sylvia is excelling.
She excels each mortal thing
  Upon the dull earth dwelling.
To her let us garlands bring.

After Shakespeare, there were so many lovely *art songs* that it quite takes one's breath away, and I simply didn't know where to begin — so here is one of my favorites, "To Celia," by Ben Jonson (1572-1637):

Drinke to me onely, with thine eyes,
  And I will pledge with mine;
Or leaue a kisse but in the cup,

And Ile not looke for wine.
The thirst that from the soule doth rise,
Doth aske a drinke diuine:
But might I of Iove's Nectar sup,
I would not change for thine.
I sent thee, late, a rosie wreath,
Not so much honoring thee,
As giuing it a hope, that there
It could not withered bee.
But thou thereon did'st onely breath,
And sent'st it backe to mee;
Since when it growes and smells, I sweare,
Not of it selfe but thee.

But please do take a look at my second favorites from this time: "Go and Catch a Falling Star," by John Donne (1572-1631); "To the Virgins to Make Much Time," by Robert Herrick (1591-1674); and "Go Lovely Rose," by Edmund Waller (1607-1687).

After the Renaissance, *art songs* continued to be written and set to music and sung in English. One of my post-Renaissance favorites is "So We'll Go No More A-Roving," by Lord Byron (1788-1824):

I

So, we'll go no more a-roving
So late into the night,
Though the heart be still as loving,
And the moon be still as bright.

II

For the sword outwears its sheath,
And the soul wears out the breast,
And the heart must pause to breathe,
And love itself have rest.

III

Though the night was made for loving,
And the day returns too soon,
Yet we'll go no more a-roving
By the light of the moon.

Ethnics like Scotsman Robert Burns (1759-1796) also got into the act with “ditties” like “A Red, Red Rose”:

My Luv is like a red, red rose,
  That’s newly sprung in June:
O my luv’s like the melodie
  That’s sweetly played in tune.

As fair art thou, my bonie lass,
  So deep in luve am I;
And I will luve thee still, my Dear,
  Till a’ the seas gang dry.

Till a’ the seas gang dry, my Dear,
  And the rocks melt wi’ the sun;
And I will luve thee still, my Dear,
  While the sands o’ life shall run.

And fare-thee-well, my only Luve
  And fare-thee-well a while!
And I will come again, my Luve,
  Tho’ ’twere ten thousand mile!

Ireland’s own Thomas Moore (1779-1852) had some good ones as well, including “Believe Me, If All Those Endearing Young Charms”:

Believe me, if all those endearing young charms,
    Which I gaze on so fondly to-day,
Were to change by to-morrow, and fleet in my arms,
    Like fairy-gifts, fading away, —
Thou would’st still be ador’d, as this moment thou art,
    Let thy loveliness fade as it will;
And around the dear ruin each wish of my heart
    Would entwine itself verdantly still!…

Patriotism loomed very large in that era, with “The Star Spangled Banner,” by Francis Scott Key (1779-1843), and later love of country with “The Road to Mandalay,” by Rudyard Kipling (1865-1936), an Anglo-Indian, many of whose poetic and fictional works now have a curiously modern ring to them:

By the old Moulmein Pagoda, lookin' lazy at the sea,
There's a Burma girl a-settin', and I know she thinks
o' me;
For the wind is in the palm-trees, and the temple-bells
they say;
"Come you back, you British Soldier; come you back to
Mandalay!"
Come you back to Mandalay
Where the old Flotilla lay:
Can't you 'ear their paddles chunkin' from Rangoon
to Mandalay?
On the road to Mandalay,
Where the flyin'-fishes play,
An' the dawn comes up like thunder outer China
'crost the Bay!...

Religiosity also loomed large with stirring march-like works like "Onward Christian Soldiers," by Sabine Baring-Gould (1834-1924), and "Battle-Hymn of the Republic," by Julia Ward Howe (1819-1910):

Mine eyes have seen the glory of the coming of the
Lord:
He is trampling out the vintage where the grapes of
wrath are stored;
He hath loosed the fateful lightning of his terrible swift
sword:
His truth is marching on.

I have seen Him in the watch-fires of a hundred circling
camps;
They have builded Him an altar in the evening dews
and damps;
I can read His righteous sentence by the dim and flar-
ing lamps.
His day is marching on....

The incomparable W.S. Gilbert (1836-1911), having teamed with the irascible Sir Arthur Sullivan (1842-1900), treated all this pomp and circumstance with delightful irreverence, as for instance, in this well-known aria from their operetta *HMS Pinafore:*

I am the very model of a modern Major-General,
I've information vegetable, animal, and mineral,
I know the kings of England, and I quote the fights
historical,
From Marathon to Waterloo, in order categorical;
I'm very well acquainted too with matters mathematical,
I understand equations, both the simple and quadratical,
About binomial theorem I'm teeming with a lot o' news —
With many cheerful facts about the square of the hypote-
nuse....
I'm very good at integral and differential calculus,
I know the scientific names of beings animalculous;
In short, in matters vegetable, animal, and mineral,
I am the very model of a modern Major-General.

Here in America, Stephen Foster (1826-1864) brought tears to everyone's eyes with lovely songs like "Beautiful Dreamer," with lyrics by himself:

Beautiful dreamer, wake unto me,
Starlight and dewdrops are waiting for thee;
Sounds of the rude world, heard in the day,
Lull'd by the moonlight have all pass'd away!
Beautiful dreamer, queen of my song,
List while I woo thee with soft melody;
Gone are the cares of life's busy throng,
Beautiful dreamer, awake unto me!
Beautiful dreamer, awake unto me!

Beautiful dreamer, out on the sea
Mermaids are chanting the wild lorelie;
Over the streamlet vapors are borne,
Waiting to fade at the bright coming morn.
Beautiful dreamer, beam on my heart,
E'en as the morn on the streamlet and sea;
Then will all clouds of sorrow depart,
Beautiful dreamer, awake unto me!
Beautiful dreamer, awake unto me!

The English-speaking world would soon have something real to cry about — in the terrible battlefield carnage of World War I. As a child in school in the late thirties, as things were heating up for a second such time of senseless brutality, we used to sing this sad song by Joyce Kilmer (1886-1918), who died in that first war:

I think that I shall never see
A poem as lovely as a tree.

A tree whose hungry mouth is prest
Against the earth's sweet flowing breast;

A tree that looks at God all day,
And lifts her leafy arms to pray;

A tree that may in Summer wear
A nest of robins in her hair;

Upon whose bosom snow has lain;
Who intimately lives with rain.

Poems are made by fools like me,
But only God can make a tree.

In the 1920s, thanks to Broadway and its musicals, the *art song* exploded, and so it has continued to do down to today, thanks to the movies and television, and more recently, the digital revolution. There are so many songs and song writers of note that one doesn't know where to begin or where to end; to name but a few off the top of my head — George and Ira Gershwin, Irving Berlin, Cole Porter, Jerome Kern, Richard Rodgers and Oscar Hammerstein, the Beatles, Bob Dylan, Laurie Anderson, Leonard Cohen, Paul Simon of Simon and Garfunkel, Bruce Springsteen, Mick Jagger and Keith Richards of the Rolling Stones, and Greg Brown. My own favorite is Herman Hupfeld's "As Time Goes By," you know, the one Sam sings in the movie *Casablanca:* Da-da-da, da-da-da, da-da-da DA-A-A

Exercise 1

> *It's time for another party, wouldn't you say? Yes indeedee, get out the ole bottle of wine or buy a new one, stick a flower in a vase, and light the candle in the saucer. If someone in your group plays an instrument, like a guitar, fine; if not, fine too. Get hold of a can or something and bang on it. The idea is to sing an old song and then a recent one. You don't know the tunes to the old ones? Ha ha, here's the kicker: find an older person who does and invite him or her to join the party. And if it should come to "As Time Goes By," rent or buy the movie and sing along with Sam.*

Happily, one doesn't have to know how to sing nowadays. Anyone can do it any which way and does, so don't feel self-conscious.

Exercise 2

> *What do you say, care to write a song of your own? A love song would be nice. You don't have anyone to write one to? Well, there's always — a pet? — a tree? — a stone? — me-e-e?*

Odes

The word comes from the Greek noun *oide*, meaning "song." Traditionally there are two kinds of *odes:* the *Pindaric*, after the Ancient Greek poet Pindar, and the *Horatian*, after Horace, the Roman man of letters. Pindar's *odes* celebrated the victories of athletes at the various sports festivals; Horace's *odes* were in praise of goodies like friendship, economy, and the simple life. Pindar's style is grandiose and flashy; Horace's is dignified and rational. Pindar's *odes* consist of different stanzas called *strophe*, *antistrophe*, and *epode*, and they were meant to be sung by a chorus, which also danced. Horace used a single stanza-form, albeit with variations, and his *odes* were usually performed by a singer or a small group of singers who were accompanied by a single musical instrument.

With the coming of the Renaissance, poets throughout Western Europe, including England, began writing poems in imitation of both kinds of *odes*, but those works were always wide of the mark. Why? Because both Greek and Latin prosodies were vastly different from theirs; to put it in a nutshell, the Greek and Roman conceptions of *meter* were of duration, not of lightness or heaviness, so the second syllable of an *iamb*, for instance, was pronounced for a longer period of time than the first syllable. In other words, they would've rendered "in love" as "in love-ove-ove" rather than "ĭn lóve," as we'd do it.

With this understood, be forewarned that the history of the *Pindaric* and *Horatian odes* in English is extremely thorny and fraught with confusion, even for the professional scholar — and don't be surprised if you find the various books in my bibliography disagreeing about them. In all fairness, the confusion began with the English and European poets, who, regardless of what they thought they were doing, couldn't possibly do better than provide weak imitations of the originals.

"On the Morning of Christ's Nativity," Milton's first great poem — and an utterly charming one it is — is a good example of a *pseudo-Horatian ode* in English. It consists of twenty-seven stanzas, as follows: *3a3a5b3c3c5b4d6d*. Here are the first three of those stanzas:

It was the Winter wild,
While the Heav'n-born child,
    All meanly wrapt in the rude manger lies;
Nature in awe to him
Had doff't her gaudy trim,
    With her great Master so to sympathize:
It was no season then for her
To wanton with the Sun, her lusty Paramour.

Only with speeches fair
She woos the gentle Air
    To hide her guilty front with innocent Snow,

And on her naked shame,
Pollute with sinful blame,
  The Saintly Veil of Maiden white to throw,
Confounded, that her Maker's eyes,
Should look so near upon her foul deformities.

But he her fears to cease,
Sent down the meek-ey'd Peace;
  She crown'd with Olive green, came softly sliding
Down through the turning sphere,
His ready Harbinger,
  With Turtle wing the amorous clouds dividing,
And waving wide her myrtle wand,
She strikes a universal Peace through Sea and Land.

Who but a gifted, talented, brilliant twenty-one-year-old could conjure up such a charming sexy scene between Nature and the Sun!

In the eighteenth century, there was a considerable amount of experimentation with the *pseudo-Horatian ode* on the part of Gray and his contemporaries, using Milton's work as a model, but the laurels surely go to Wordsworth for his "Ode to Duty." Taking a cue from Gray and the others, he simplified the rhyming pattern while maintaining the contrast between the first seven lines and the final *alexandrine* by keeping those lines short (*4a4b4a4b4c4c4d6d*):

Stern Daughter of the Voice of God!
O Duty! If that name thou love
Who art a light to guide, a rod
To check the erring, and reprove;
Thou, who art victory and law
When empty terrors overawe;
From vain temptations dost set free;
And calm'st the weary strife of frail humanity!

There are who ask not if thine eye
Be on them; who, in love and truth,
Where no misgiving is, rely
Upon the genial sense of youth:

Glad Hearts! without reproach or blot;
Who do thy work, and know it not:
Oh! if through confidence misplaced
They fail, thy saving arms, dread Power! around them cast.

Serene will be our days and bright,
And happy will our nature be,
When love is an unerring light,
And joy its own security.
And they a blissful course may hold
Even now, who, not unwisely bold,
Live in the spirit of this creed;
Yet seek thy firm support, according to their need.

I, loving freedom, and untried;
No sport of every random gust,
Yet being to myself a guide,
Too blindly have reposed my trust:
And oft, when in my heart was heard
Thy timely mandate, I deferred
The task, in smoother walks to stray;
But thee I now would serve more strictly, if I may.

Through no disturbance of my soul,
Or strong compunction in me wrought,
I supplicate for thy control;
But in the quietness of thought:
Me this unchartered freedom tires;
I feel the weight of chance desires:
My hopes no more must change their name,
I long for a repose that ever is the same.

Stern Lawgiver! yet thou dost wear
The Godhead's most benignant grace;
Nor know we any thing so fair
As is the smile upon thy face:
Flowers laugh before thee on their beds
And fragrance in thy footing treads;
Thou dost preserve the stars from wrong;
And the most ancient heavens, through Thee, are fresh
and strong.

To humbler functions, awful Power!
I call thee: I myself commend
Unto thy guidance from this hour;
Oh, let my weakness have an end!
Give unto me, made lowly wise,
The spirit of self-sacrifice;
The confidence of reason give;
And in the light of truth thy Bondman let me live!

First things first.

Exercise 3

Read all of the above by Wordsworth, changing voices for each stanza and possibly for the alexandrines. If you were as charmed by the snippet of the "Nativity Ode" as I am, find it in one of your anthologies and read it instead, all twenty-seven stanzas, using the same strategy.

I can't emphasize to you enough the importance of engaging in this kind of reading, so I hope and trust you've done it conscientiously.

Exercise 4

Copy out the first stanza of the "Ode to Duty," and leaving plenty of room between each line, do a complete scansion of the first seven lines.

How many "perfect" eight-syllable lines did you find?

Quattro.

How many other eight-syllables lines were there?

Trois.

How many with fewer than eight syllables?

Zero.

How many with more than eight syllables?

Zero.

How many single *caesuras*?

Quattro.

Are any of the *caesuras* in the same place?

Nix.

How many multiple *caesuras*?

None.

How many *enjambments*?

Trois.

Hoping and trusting the contrast between the first seven lines and the *alexandrine* was made clear by this.

Exercise 5

As before, look at this passage for the sounds alone, meaning both end-rhymes and internal rhymes as well as other forms of sound-correspondence, if any. To what extent does each contribute to the total effect of the passage?

Let's cut to the chase.

Exercise 6

Substitute cha for each light stress and CHA for each heavy stress in the space under each line of your scansion, and read it all aloud instead of the words.

The contrast between those seven lines and the *alexandrine* should be even more apparent now.

Exercise 7

Replace the cha's and CHA's with nonsense words, and as before, read it all aloud.

As before, this next should present less of a problem because of the "memorable" rhymes:

Exercise 8

Commit the stanza to memory and recite it aloud.

Hopefully you did this in the spirit of the poem.

Exercise 9

Using Wordsworth's stanza as a model (or Milton's, if you will), try your hand at a pseudo-Horatian ode; two or three stanzas should do it. Feel free to use partial rhyme, but do choose a serious subject, yes?

In the English literary world, *Pindaric* meant freedom and wildness by comparison with *Horatian*, and indeed the so-called *Pindaric odes* of Abraham Cowley (1618-1667), one of the earliest poets to try his hand at same, were so irregular that, were it not for their *end-rhymes*, parts of them could pass for *free verse* today. Spinning off of him was John Dryden (1631-1700) with the *pseudo-Pindaric* "Alexander's Feast," among other works, which was intended to be set to music and indeed was, by the immortal Handel. It was left to Gray with "The Progress of Poesy" and "The Bard," both subtitled *Pindaric* but — take my word for it — rather tame, to set the stage for Wordsworth and his "Immortality Ode," which scholar Gilbert Highet has called the "greatest modern Pindaric poem," my humble self agreeing.

Certainly there's much that's unusual in this poem, prosodically speaking. No two of its eleven stanzas are identical in structure; only the first and second consist of the same number of lines, but neither their line lengths nor rhyming patterns correspond. The line lengths throughout the rest of the poem are quite varied, going from four to fourteen syllables, and there's at least one instance of just about every kind of rhyming imaginable: traditional single-syllable rhymes as well as two-syllable rhymes (like "splendid" and "attended"). And the rhymes occur as *couplets, triplets* (like "stage," "Age," and "equipage"), *cross-rhymes, envelope rhymes, delayed rhymes,* and *internal rhymes.* Indeed, there are even two instances of no rhyme at all ("go" in Stanza II and "death" in Stanza X)! In sum, it's a virtuoso performance and by no means to be missed.

Briefly, stanzas I through IV speak of the loss of something: "The things which I have seen I now can see no more"; "…there hath past away a glory from the earth"; "Whither is fled the visionary gleam? / Where is it now, the glory and the dream?" The thing lost can be seen as childhood, mystical experiences, or the poetic imagination, or any combination thereof, including all three of them.

The balance of the poem presents an answer in two parts: stanzas V through VIII, which explain how the loss came about; and stanzas IX through XI, in which a consolation for the loss is offered — our philosophic or, if you will, mature minds, which are still capable of hearkening back to our origins, delighting in Nature's creations, and seeing into the life of things:

I

There was a time when meadow, grove, and stream,
The earth, and every common sight,
        To me did seem
    Apparelled in celestial light,
The glory and the freshness of a dream.
It is not now as it hath been of yore; —
    Turn wheresoe'er I may,
        By night or day,
The things which I have seen I now can see no more.

II

    The Rainbow comes and goes,
    And lovely is the Rose,
    The Moon doth with delight
  Look round her when the heavens are bare,
    Waters on a starry night
    Are beautiful and fair;
  The sunshine is a glorious birth;
  But yet I know, where'er I go,
That there hath past away a glory from the earth.

III

Now, while the birds thus sing a joyous song,
  And while the young lambs bound
    As to the tabor's sound,
To me alone there came a thought of grief:
A timely utterance gave that thought relief,
    And I again am strong:
The cataracts blow their trumpets from the steep;
No more shall grief of mine the season wrong;
I hear the Echoes through the mountains throng,

The Winds come to me from the fields of sleep,
And all the earth is gay;
Land and sea
Give themselves up to jollity,
And with the heart of May
Doth every Beast keep holiday; —
Thou Child of Joy, Shout round me, let me hear
thy shouts, thou happy Shepherd-boy!

IV

Ye blessèd Creatures, I have heard the call
Ye to each other make; I see
The heavens laugh with you in your jubilee;
My heart is at your festival,
My head hath its coronal,
The fulness of your bliss, I feel — I feel it all.
Oh evil day! if I were sullen
While Earth herself is adorning,
This sweet May-morning,
And the Children are culling
On every side,
In a thousand valleys far and wide,
Fresh flowers; while the sun shines warm,
And the Babe leaps up on his Mother's arm: —
I hear, I hear, with joy I hear!
— But there's a Tree, of many, one,
A single Field which I have looked upon,
Both of them speak of something that is gone:
The Pansy at my feet
Doth the same tale repeat:
Whither is fled the visionary gleam?
Where is it now, the glory and the dream?

V

Our birth is but a sleep and a forgetting:
The Soul that rises with us, our life's Star,
Hath had elsewhere its setting,
And cometh from afar:
Not in entire forgetfulness,
And not in utter nakedness,

But trailing clouds of glory do we come
        From God, who is our home:
Heaven lies about us in our infancy!
Shades of the prison-house begin to close
        Upon the growing Boy
But He beholds the light, and whence it flows,
        He sees it in his joy;
The Youth, who daily farther from the east
        Must travel, still is Nature's Priest,
        And by the vision splendid
        Is on his way attended;
At length the Man perceives it die away,
And fade into the light of common day.

VI

Earth fills her lap with pleasures of her own;
Yearnings she hath in her own natural kind,
And, even with something of a Mother's mind,
        And no unworthy aim,
        The homely Nurse doth all she can
To make her Foster-child, her Inmate Man,
        Forget the glories he hath known,
And that imperial palace whence he came.

VII

Behold the Child among his new-born blisses,
A six years' Darling of a pigmy size!
See, where 'mid work of his own hand he lies,
Fretted by sallies of his mother's kisses,
With light upon him from his father's eyes!
See, at his feet, some little plan or chart,
Some fragment from his dream of human life,
Shaped by himself with newly-learned art;
        A wedding or a festival,
        A mourning or a funeral;
            And this hath now his heart,
        And unto this he frames his song:
            Then will he fit his tongue
To dialogues of business, love, or strife;
        But it will not be long

Ere this be thrown aside,
And with new joy and pride
The little Actor cons another part;
Filling from time to time his 'humorous stage'
With all the Persons, down to palsied Age,
That Life brings with her in her equipage;
As if his whole vocation
Were endless imitation.

VIII

Thou, whose exterior semblance doth belie
Thy Soul's immensity;
Thou best Philosopher, who yet dost keep
Thy heritage, thou Eye among the blind,
That, deaf and silent, read'st the eternal deep,
Haunted for ever by the eternal mind,—
Mighty Prophet! Seer blest!
On whom those truths do rest,
Which we are toiling all our lives to find,
In darkness lost, the darkness of the grave;
Thou, over whom thy Immortality
Broods like the Day, a Master o'er a Slave,
A Presence which is not to be put by;
Thou little Child, yet glorious in the might
Of heaven-born freedom on thy being's height,
Why with such earnest pains dost thou provoke
The years to bring the inevitable yoke,
Thus blindly with thy blessedness at strife?
Full soon thy Soul shall have her earthly freight,
And custom lie upon thee with a weight,
Heavy as frost, and deep almost as life!

IX

O joy! that in our embers
Is something that doth live,
That nature yet remembers
What was so fugitive!
The thought of our past years in me doth breed
Perpetual benediction: not indeed
For that which is most worthy to be blest;

Delight and liberty, the simple creed
Of Childhood, whether busy or at rest,
With new-fledged hope still fluttering in his breast:—
        Not for these I raise
        The song of thanks and praise;
    But for those obstinate questionings
    Of sense and outward things,
    Fallings from us, vanishings;
    Blank misgivings of a Creature
Moving about in worlds not realised,
High instincts before which our mortal Nature
Did tremble like a guilty Thing surprised:
        But for those first affections,
        Those shadowy recollections,
    Which, be they what they may,
Are yet the fountain-light of all our day,
Are yet a master-light of all our seeing;
    Uphold us, cherish, and have power to make
Our noisy years seem moments in the being
Of the eternal Silence: truths that wake,
        To perish never:
Which neither listlessness, nor mad endeavour,
        Nor Man nor Boy,
Nor all that is at enmity with joy,
Can utterly abolish or destroy!
    Hence in a season of calm weather
        Though inland far we be,
Our Souls have sight of that immortal sea
        Which brought us hither,
    Can in a moment travel thither,
And see the Children sport upon the shore,
And hear the mighty waters rolling evermore.

X

Then sing, ye Birds, sing, sing a joyous song!
        And let the young Lambs bound
        As to the tabor's sound!
We in thought will join your throng,
        Ye that pipe and ye that play,
        Ye that through your hearts today

Feel the gladness of the May!
What though the radiance which was once so bright
Be now for ever taken from my sight,
Though nothing can bring back the hour
Of splendour in the grass, of glory in the flower;
We will grieve not, rather find
Strength in what remains behind;
In the primal sympathy
Which having been must ever be;
In the soothing thoughts that spring
Out of human suffering;
In the faith that looks through death,
In years that bring the philosophic mind.

XI

And O, ye Fountains, Meadows, Hills, and Groves,
Forebode not any severing of our loves!
Yet in my heart of hearts I feel your might;
I only have relinquished one delight
To live beneath your more habitual sway.
I love the Brooks which down their channels fret,
Even more than when I tripped lightly as they;
The innocent brightness of a new-born Day
Is lovely yet;
The Clouds that gather round the setting sun
Do take a sober colouring from an eye
That hath kept watch o'er man's mortality;
Another race hath been, and other palms are won.
Thanks to the human heart by which we live,
Thanks to its tenderness, its joys, and fears,
To me the meanest flower that blows can give
Thoughts that do often lie too deep for tears.

I have to confess that there are things about this extraordinary work that have always distressed me, first and foremost the kutchy-koo attitude toward the child in the seventh stanza. But through the years I've found myself returning to it again and again, and more and more looking at the cup as almost full. If nothing else, listen with me for a moment to the waves coming in at the end of Stanza IX and you'll see what I mean:

> Hence in a season of calm weather
> Though inland far we be,
> Our Souls have sight of that immortal sea
> Which brought us hither,
> Can in a moment travel thither,
> And see the Children sport upon the shore,
> And hear the mighty waters rolling evermore.

Exercise 10

You have to read the whole thing aloud — you just have to!

And now, for a little nitty-gritty, as painless as possible, obviously:

Exercise 11

Copy out the first two stanzas — which are complementing, yes? — and leaving plenty of room between each line, do a complete scansion.

How many "perfect" *iambic pentameter* lines did you find in each stanza?

Eight and null.

How many other ten-syllable lines were there?

Uno and None.

How many with fewer than ten syllables?

Zero and seven.

How many with more than ten syllables?

One and two.

How many single *caesuras*?

One and two.

How many multiple *caesuras*?

Nix.

How many *enjambments*?

One and two.

So in spite of the fact that the two stanzas look and read like companions, they're quite different, aren't they?

Exercise 12

Look at the two stanzas for the sounds alone, meaning both end-rhymes and internal rhymes as well as other forms of sound-correspondence, if any. Can you draw any conclusions about them and how they work together from what you found?

If you can't at first, keep working at it — you will.

Exercise 13

Substitute cha for each light stress and CHA for each heavy stress in the space under each line of your scansion, and read it all aloud instead of the words.

The music of the verse should've emerged somewhat.

Exercise 14

Replace the cha's and CHA's with nonsense words, and as before, read it all aloud.

Again, the "memorable" rhymes should make this next exercise present less of a problem:

Exercise 15

Commit the two stanzas to memory and recite them aloud.

Trusting you did this with gusto — if not with yours, then with mine.

Exercise 16?

Do I dare ask this of you? Three stanzas? Of any length? As wild and way out as you like? About your own thoughts of immortality?

With the appearance of Keats and his *odes* in the next generation, the literary terms *Horatian* and *Pindaric* ceased to have any meaning. He called three of his works by that name — "Ode to a Nightingale," "Ode to a Grecian Urn," and "Ode on Melancholy" — and one more, "To Autumn," has the same structure as they. All were written in an annus mirabilis, that is, a single wonderful year, which happened to be the year before he died.

Rather than risk ruining your digestion or having you get good and fed up with me and my tortuous ways, let me tell you that his stanza consists of the *quatrain* of the Shakespearian sonnet — *5a5b5a5b* — followed by one of the *sestets* of the *Petrarchan sonnet* — *5c5d5e5c5d5e* — except for the "Ode to a Nightingale," whose eighth line is a *trimeter:* 3c. Indeed, as I hinted toward the end of chapter six, Milton had tried this sort of thing in the final chorus of *Samson Agonistes,* so it's possible, even though the texture of Keats's odes and of that passage are quite different, that Keats took his cue for his stanza from there. Be that as it may, behold magnificence:

Ode to a Nightingale

I

My heart aches, and a drowsy numbness pains
  My sense, as though of hemlock I had drunk,
Or emptied some dull opiate to the drains
  One minute past, and Lethe-wards had sunk:
'Tis not through envy of thy happy lot,
  But being too happy in thine happiness,—
    That thou, light-winged Dryad of the trees,
      In some melodious plot
Of beechen green, and shadows numberless,
  Singest of summer in full-throated ease.

II

O, for a draught of vintage! that hath been
  Cool'd a long age in the deep-delved earth,
Tasting of Flora and the country green,
  Dance, and Provençal song, and sunburnt mirth!
O for a beaker full of the warm South,
  Full of the true, the blushful Hippocrene,
    With beaded bubbles winking at the brim,
      And purple-stained mouth;

That I might drink, and leave the world unseen,
And with thee fade away into the forest dim:

III

Fade far away, dissolve, and quite forget
What thou among the leaves hast never known,
The weariness, the fever, and the fret
Here, where men sit and hear each other groan;
Where palsy shakes a few, sad, last gray hairs,
Where youth grows pale, and spectre-thin, and dies;
Where but to think is to be full of sorrow
And leaden-eyed despairs,
Where Beauty cannot keep her lustrous eyes,
Or new Love pine at them beyond to-morrow.

IV

Away! away! for I will fly to thee,
Not charioted by Bacchus and his pards,
But on the viewless wings of Poesy,
Though the dull brain perplexes and retards:
Already with thee! tender is the night,
And haply the Queen-Moon is on her throne,
Cluster'd around by all her starry Fays;
But here there is no light,
Save what from heaven is with the breezes blown
Through verdurous glooms and winding mossy ways.

V

I cannot see what flowers are at my feet,
Nor what soft incense hangs upon the boughs,
But, in embalmed darkness, guess each sweet
Wherewith the seasonable month endows
The grass, the thicket, and the fruit-tree wild;
White hawthorn, and the pastoral eglantine;
Fast fading violets cover'd up in leaves;
And mid-May's eldest child,
The coming musk-rose, full of dewy wine,
The murmurous haunt of flies on summer eves.

VI

Darkling I listen; and, for many a time
  I have been half in love with easeful Death,
Call'd him soft names in many a mused rhyme,
  To take into the air my quiet breath;
Now more than ever seems it rich to die,
  To cease upon the midnight with no pain,
    While thou art pouring forth thy soul abroad
      In such an ecstasy!
  Still wouldst thou sing, and I have ears in vain—
    To thy high requiem become a sod.

VII

Thou wast not born for death, immortal Bird!
  No hungry generations tread thee down;
The voice I hear this passing night was heard
  In ancient days by emperor and clown:
Perhaps the self-same song that found a path
  Through the sad heart of Ruth, when, sick for home,
    She stood in tears amid the alien corn;
      The same that oft-times hath
  Charm'd magic casements, opening on the foam
    Of perilous seas, in faery lands forlorn.

VIII

Forlorn! the very word is like a bell
  To toll me back from thee to my sole self!
  Adieu! the fancy cannot cheat so well
    As she is fam'd to do, deceiving elf.
  Adieu! adieu! thy plaintive anthem fades
    Past the near meadows, over the still stream,
      Up the hill-side; and now 'tis buried deep
        In the next valley-glades:
    Was it a vision, or a waking dream?
      Fled is that music:—Do I wake or sleep?

Exercise 17

This work certainly deserves reading aloud. Try for different effects with different voices.

I hope you picked up on the repetitions, like "forlorn" at the end of Stanza VII and the beginning of Stanza VIII, which should be quite different from one another when they are read.

Exercise 18?

Of course if you'd also like to — One stanza? On another bird?

Other Common Forms & Stanzas

Octosyllabic Couplets

This verse form, which goes back to Chaucer, was much in vogue in the sixteenth and seventeenth centuries. Because its line was short compared with that of the *iambic pentameter* line, it tended to be limited to subject-verb-object constructions with few adjectives and adverbs, and this made for a rather sparse texture. There are two versions: with the *couplets closed* or *open.*

When the *couplets* are *closed,* as in much of "To His Coy Mistress," by Andrew Marvel (1621-1678), the results tend to be aphoristic:

> Had we but World enough, and Time,
> This coyness Lady were no crime.
> We would sit down, and think which way
> To walk, and pass our long loves Day.
> Thou by the *Indian Ganges* side
> Should'st Rubies find: I by the tide
> Of *Humber* would complain. I would
> Love you ten years before the Flood:
> And you should if you please refuse
> Till the Conversion of the *Jews.*

My vegetable love should grow
Vaster than Empires, and more slow.
An hundred years should grow to praise
Thine Eyes, and on thy Forehead Gaze.
Two hundred to adore each Breast:
But thirty thousand to the rest.
An Age at least to every part,
And the last Age should show your Heart.
For Lady you deserve this State;
Now would I love at lower rate.
    But at my back I alwaies hear
Times winged Charriot hurrying near:
And yonder all before us lye
Desarts of vast Eternity.
Thy Beauty shall no more be found;
Nor, in thy marble Vault, shall sound
My ecchoing Song; then Worms shall try
That long preserv'd Virginity:
And your quaint Honour turns to dust;
And into ashes all my Lust.
The Grave's a fine and private place,
But none I think do there embrace.
Now therefore, while the youthful hew
Sits on thy skin like morning dew,
And while thy willing Soul transpires
At every pore with instant Fires,
Now let us sport us while we may;
And now, like am'rous birds of prey,
Rather at once our Time devour,
Than languish in his slow-chapt pow'r.
Let us roll all our Strength, and all
Our sweetness, up into a Ball:
And tear our Pleasures with rough strife,
Thorough the Iron gates of Life.
Thus, though we cannot make our Sun
Stand still, yet we will make him run. (*Italics mine.)*

When the *couplets* are *open,* as happens in this magnificent passage from Milton's youthful poem *Il Penseroso,* the *run-on lines* tend to suggest a darting quality:

And when the Sun begins to fling
His flaring beams, me Goddess bring
To arched walks of twilight groves,
And shadows brown that *Sylvan* loves
Of Pine or monumental Oak,
Where the rude Axe with heaved stroke
Was never heard the Nymphs to daunt,
Or fright them from their hallow'd haunt.
There in close covert by some Brook,
Where no profaner eye may look,
Hide me from Day's garish eye,
While the Bee with Honied thigh,
That at her flow'ry work doth sing,
And the Waters murmuring
With such consort as they keep,
Entice the dewy-feather'd Sleep;
And let some strange mysterious dream
Wave at his Wings in Airy stream,
Of lively portraiture display'd,
Softly on my eyelids laid.
And as I wake, sweet music breathe
Above, about, or underneath,
Sent by some spirit to mortals good,
Or th' unseen Genius of the Wood.
But let my due feet never fail
To walk the studious Cloister's pale,
And love the high embowed Roof,
With antic Pillars massy proof,
And storied Windows richly dight,
Casting a dim religious light.
There let the pealing Organ blow
To the full voic'd Choir below,
In Service high and Anthems clear,
As may with sweetness, through mine ear,
Dissolve me into ecstasies,
And bring all Heav'n before mine eyes.
And may at last my weary age
Find out the peaceful hermitage,
The Hairy Gown and Mossy Cell,
Where I may sit and rightly spell

Of every Star that Heav'n doth shew,
And every Herb that sips the dew;
Till old experience do attain
To something like Prophetic strain.
These pleasures *Melancholy* give,
And I with thee will choose to live.

Note how Milton managed to relieve monotony by including a seven-syllable line among the eight now and then — for example, "While the Bee with honied thigh." Another such ploy was put in a line ending with one or more unstressed syllables like "And the Waters murmuring," "Dissolve me into ecstasies," and "Find out the peaceful hermitage."

First things first, as I'm fond of saying.

Exercise 19

Read "To His Coy Mistress" and the passage from "Il Penseroso" aloud, and remember, as always, to try for different effects with different voices.

Now you have to make a decision: which form of the *octosyllabic couplet* do you like better, the *closed* and aphoristic, or the *open* and dartingly run-on?

Exercise 20

Go to it; need I say more? Well, fifteen or so lines, okay? Do be sure to enter into the spirit of Marvel or Milton — that is, be cute and clever, or write about, let's say, some physical activity like jogging along a country road.

Terza Rima

This is a stanza consisting of three lines with *linking rhymes* (aba, bcb, cdc, and so on), and as its name indicates, it's an import from Italy. Because Italian has an abundance of words with similar endings, this stanza works marvelously well in that language; indeed, Dante (1265-1321) used it as his staple form in his *Divine Comedy*. However, to write a poem in English in *terza rima* is another story, as translators of Dante's *Comedy* know only too well.

Clearly, the prize for making *terza rima* work — and indeed more than work — goes to Percy Bysshe Shelley (1792-1822) in the "Ode to the West Wind." The poem consists of five identical sections; addressing the wind, as he's been doing all along, the "I" concludes:

Make me thy lyre, even as the forest is:
What if my leaves are falling like its own!
The tumult of thy mighty harmonies

Will take from both a deep, autumnal tone,
Sweet though in sadness. Be thou, Spirit fierce,
My spirit! Be thou me, impetuous one!

Drive my dead thoughts over the universe
Like withered leaves to quicken a new birth!
And, by the incantation of this verse,

Scatter, as from an unextinguished hearth
Ashes and sparks, my words among mankind!
Be through my lips to unawakened earth

The trumpet of a prophecy! O, Wind,
If Winter comes, can Spring be far behind?

The final *couplet* was Shelley's touch, not Dante's, and crazily, the whole passage forms a kind of *sonnet*, as do each of the other sections of the poem. But perish the thought that you should take my word for it —

***Exercise* 21**
See fer yerself.

Personally, I find this a bit much, but you may have other ideas. At any event:

***Exercise* 22**
See what you can do with terza rima, in three stanzas at least. As a matter of fact, why not consider answering Shelley back in his own coin as the Wind?

A Bouquet of Quatrains

After the *elegiac quatrain,* the most important four-line stanza in English is that of the *ballad.* Various versions, which were sung to tunes, originated in the boonies in the early Middle Ages and made their way into the towns and taverns. So popular did they become that religious hymns were often written in the same measures and sung to the same tunes to try and lure frequenters of taverns back into the churches. This tradition continued into the modern era: the forms of the *traditional four-line ballad stanza* and many of the hymns of Isaac Watts and John and Charles Wesley, all three of the eighteenth century, are identical.

The stanza consists of alternating lines of *iambic tetrameter* and *trimeter;* possibly it was a dim echo of the old Anglo-Saxon line, which, you'll recall, had three or four strong stresses. The *traditional ballad* always told a story, usually with a tragic ending, and it often involved love. People and things were described with *stock epithets* (or clichés, as we'd say today); for instance, a maiden's cheeks are "red as roses," her brow "milk-white." As was the case with the *octosyllabic couplet,* short lines like that meant that only the barest details could be included in the poem and not many of them at that. This, together with sudden, dramatic transitions, often resulted in a terse manner of telling and with a dead-pan tone.

There are *end-rhymes* on each of the *trimeter lines,* which act as reinforcements of the punctuation. The *tetrameter line* and following *trimeter line* tend to form a syntactic and narrative unit. The lack of rhyme at the ends of the *tetrameter lines* is made up for by a heavy use of *alliteration* internally. Other *echoing* features include *refrains* and a form of *parallelism* known as *incremental repetition,* whereby a phrase or a whole line is repeated with a slight variation for the sake of moving the story forward.

Let "Sir Patrick Spens," which relates a subtle blood-and-thunder story, serve as an example. Note that in the light of the tragedy that's hinted at, the king's drinking wine that's "blood-reid" in the beginning, assumes rather sinister implications, so "blood-reid" is not as trite as one might take it to be at first:

The king sits in Dumferling town,
  Drinking the blude-reid wine:
"O whar will I get guid sailor,
  To sail this ship of mine?"

Up and spak an eldern knicht,
  Sat at the king's richt knee:
"Sir Patrick Spens is the best sailor
  That sails upon the sea."

The king has written a braid letter
  And signed it wi' his hand,
And sent it to Sir Patrick Spens,
  Was walking on the sand.

The first line that Sir Patrick read,
  A loud lauch lauched he;
The next line that Sir Patrick read,
  The tear blinded his ee.

"O wha is this has done this deed,
  This ill deed done to me,
To send me out this time o' the year,
  To sail upon the sea?

"Mak haste, mak haste, my mirry men all,
  Our guid ship sails the morn."
"O say na sae, my master dear,
  For I fear a deadly storm.

"Late, late yestre'en I saw the new moon
  Wi' the auld moon in hir arm,
And I fear, I fear, my dear master,
  That we will come to harm."

O our Scots nobles were richt laith"
  To weet their cork-heeled shoon,
But lang or a' the play were played
  Their hats they swam aboon.

O lang, lang may their ladies sit,
  Wi' their fans into their hand,
Or ere they see Sir Patrick Spens
  Come sailing to the land.

O lang, lang may the ladies stand
  Wi' their gold kems in their hair,
Waiting for their ain dear lords,
  For they'll see them na mair.

Half o'er, half o'er to Aberdour
  It's fifty fadom deep,
And there lies guid Sir Patrick Spens
  Wi' the Scots lords at his feet.

Exercise 23
Scan the first two stanzas of "Sir Patrick Spens" just to get a feel for the beat.

How did you make out? Simple, yes?

Exercise 24
Do an extensive analysis of the sound-echoes, great and small.

Comparisons are odorous, as my good old friend Mrs. Malaprop once said. Even so, here's what my former student Lorraine Ghignone did in the form of a *ballad:*

Ballad of a Fallen Angel

My love was standing on the shore;
An angel then was she;
Her cheeks were roses in the light,
For all the world to see.
The sun was bright, exquisite light
Shone upon us two.
It was a time for quiet love,
And playful romping too.

She said: "My dear, 'Tis true, I fear,
That I'll begin to brood,
For I feel starved." Hence, I commenced
My gallant search for food.

Majestic sun hung o'er her crown,
And followed at my back;
While searching for our repast hid,
The sky went quickly black.

Believing this a shower mere,
The day'd ne'er come to ruin,
My angel kind would seek and find
The shelter of a dune.

But, nay, alas! I stood aghast!
There came a mighty squall;
In Neptune's lair, my angel fair
Was suddenly enthralled.

I dashed with Hermes' winged feet,
But they were made of lead —
My senses dulled; rocks cracked her skull!
I gasped, but she was dead.

Now each and ev'ry ev'ning comes,
And I stand on the shore.
I wait and seek the rosy cheek,
That I will see no more.

Show-and-tell time, yes?

Exercise 25

Make up a sad story, but keep it simple — like, make it about a lost dog or something like that. When you've got the main outline in your head, write it down, separating it into scenes, then portion the scenes out into stanzas and begin setting it down in the basic pattern — 4a3b4c3b. Don't forget to include word and phrase as well as incremental repetition at appropriate junctures, and keep your focus solidly on the situation, much as a newspaper reporter would. P.S. To enter into the spirit fully, give it a folksy flavor, possibly telling it in a dialect — Brooklyn, southern, or what you will — or with a foreign accent.

In the mid-eighteenth century a certain Bishop Thomas Percy began collecting the old *ballads,* and his edition of them, *Reliques of Ancient English Poetry*, served as a kind of primer for new poets coming along. Wordsworth and Coleridge were particularly influenced by what they found in the *Reliques* and composed imitations of the *ballads*, which we today refer to as *literary ballads*.

Wordsworth's most significant works in this vein were the Lucy poems, in which the main character was a creature of his imagination. The *quatrains* of one of the poems in that series, "Strange Fits of Passion I Have Known," are reminiscent of those of "Sir Patrick Spens," and various other features, like the maiden's being "Fresh as a rose in June" and the use of *incremental repetition* respecting the forward movement of the horse, also look back to the old *ballads*. However, it's important to note that in this poem, the focus is not on what has happened to Lucy in her cottage but on the internal reaction of the "I":

> Strange fits of passion have I known:
> And I will dare to tell,
> But in the Lover's ear alone,
> What once to me befell.
>
> When she I loved looked every day
> Fresh as a rose in June,
> I to her cottage bent my way,
> Beneath an evening-moon.
>
> Upon the moon I fixed my eye,
> All over the wide lea;
> With quickening pace my horse drew nigh
> Those paths so dear to me.
>
> And now we reached the orchard-plot;
> And, as we climbed the hill,
> The sinking moon to Lucy's cot
> Came near, and nearer still.
>
> In one of those sweet dreams I slept,
> Kind Nature's gentlest boon!
> And all the while my eyes I kept
> On the descending moon.

My horse moved on; hoof after hoof
He raised, and never stopped:
When down behind the cottage roof,
At once, the bright moon dropped.

What fond and wayward thoughts will slide
Into a Lover's head!
"O mercy!" to myself I cried,
"If Lucy should be dead!"

Coleridge took the old-time *ballad* tradition with its conventions and mannerisms and went to considerable pains to tell a long tale of crime, punishment, and deliverance in the "The Rime of the Ancient Mariner," thus creating an *extended literary ballad.* Note how he managed to use just about every trick in the *ballad* repertoire in the opening episode:

It is an ancient Mariner,
And he stoppeth one of three.
"By thy long grey beard and glittering eye,
Now wherefore stopp'st thou me?

The Bridegroom's doors are opened wide,
And I am next of kin;
The guests are met, the feast is set:
May'st hear the merry din."

He holds him with his skinny hand,
"There was a ship," quoth he.
"Hold off! unhand me, grey-beard loon!"
Eftsoons his hand dropt he.

He holds him with his glittering eye —
The Wedding-Guest stood still,
And listens like a three years' child:
The Mariner hath his will.

The Wedding-Guest sat on a stone:
He cannot choose but hear;
And thus spake on that ancient man,
The bright-eyed Mariner.

"The ship was cheered, the harbour cleared,
Merrily did we drop
Below the kirk, below the hill,
Below the lighthouse top.

The Sun came up upon the left,
Out of the sea came he!
And he shone bright, and on the right
Went down into the sea.

Higher and higher every day,
Till over the mast at noon — "
The Wedding-Guest here beat his breast,
For he heard the loud bassoon.

The bride hath paced into the hall,
Red as a rose is she;
Nodding their heads before her goes
The merry minstrelsy.

The Wedding-Guest he beat his breast,
Yet he cannot choose but hear;
And thus spake on that ancient man,
The bright-eyed Mariner.

"And now the STORM-BLAST came, and he
Was tyrannous and strong:
He struck with his o'ertaking wings,
And chased us south along.

One of the problems that Coleridge had to face in so long a work was monotony. Even under the best of circumstances, the attention of readers was bound to stray after so many stanzas of the same length and of the same strategy. One way that he came up with to relieve it was to run the stanzas on, but that he could do only once in a while because self-containment was a feature of the old-time *ballad* and absolutely necessary for maintaining its terseness. Another of Coleridge's stratagems was to insert five- and six-line stanzas resembling that basic four-line one here and there, like the following, which came right after the passage above:

With sloping masts and dipping prow,
As who pursued with yell and blow
Still treads the shadow of his foe,
And forward bends his head,
The ship drove fast, loud roared the blast,
And southward aye we fled.

Interestingly, when matters finally return to "normal" at the end of the poem, so, too, does the four-line stanza.

Of the next generation of Romantic poets, Keats became particularly enamored of the *ballad* and came up with his own home-grown variation of the stanza to tell a story of betrayal and bewitchment in "La Belle Dame Sans Merci." Note how the very short fourth line, heavily emphasized by the rhyme, creates an impression of the "I"'s having a sob in his throat:

I

Oh, what can ail thee, knight-at-arms,
  Alone and palely loitering?
The sedge has wither'd from the lake,
  And no birds sing.

II

Oh what can ail thee, knight-at-arms,
  So haggard and so woe-begone?
The squirrel's granary is full,
  And the harvest's done.

III

I see a lily on thy brow,
  With anguish moist and fever-dew;
And on thy cheeks a fading rose
  Fast withereth too.

IV

I met a lady in the meads,
  Full beautiful — a faery's child,
Her hair was long, her foot was light,
  And her eyes were wild.

V

I made a garland for her head,
  And bracelets too, and fragrant zone;
She look'd at me as she did love,
  And made sweet moan.

VI

I set her on my pacing steed,
  And nothing else saw all day long;
For sidelong would she bend, and sing
  A faery's song.

VII

She found me roots of relish sweet,
  And honey wild, and manna dew,
And sure in language strange she said —
  "I love thee true."

VIII

She took me to her elfin grot,
  And there she wept and sigh'd full sore,
And there I shut her wild wild eyes
  With kisses four.

IX

And there she lulled me asleep
  And there I dream'd — Ah! woe betide!
The latest dream I ever dream'd
  On the cold hill side.

X

I saw pale kings and princes too,
  Pale warriors, death-pale were they all;
They cried — "La Belle Dame Sans Merci
  Hath thee in Thrall!"

XI

I saw their starved lips in the gloam,
  With horrid warning gaped wide,
And I awoke and found me here,
  On the cold hill's side.

XII

And this is why I sojourn here
   Alone and palely loitering,
Though the sedge has wither'd from the lake,
   And no birds sing.

It's time for a little self-titillation, ooh-la-la.

Exercise 26

Come up with your own variation of the traditional ballad stanza — three stanzas will be sufficient, as the English say. But of course you'll have to make up a story first, yes?

Alfred Lord Tennyson (1809-1892) chose an *iambic tetrameter quatrain* with his *end-rhymes* in an *envelope* arrangement *(abba)* for his long poem *In Memoriam*, in which he mourned the death of a close friend. The short lines tend toward sparseness and a certain sobriety, which, as it happens, is appropriate to the subject matter. Tennyson ran some of the stanzas on, which held the monotony somewhat in check. As it opens, so it goes:

I held it truth, with him who sings
   To one clear harp in divers tones,
   That men may rise on stepping-stones
Of their dead selves to higher things.

But who shall so forecast the years
   And find in loss a gain to match?
   Or reach a hand thro' time to catch
The far-off interest of tears?

Let Love clasp Grief lest both be drown'd,
   Let darkness keep her raven gloss.
   Ah, sweeter to be drunk with loss,
To dance with Death, to beat the ground,

Than that the victor Hours should scorn
   The long result of love, and boast,
   "Behold the man that loved and lost,
But all he was is overworn."

What we actually have in the above is a *couplet* within another *couplet*—for example, "tones" and "stones" within "sings" and "things" in the first stanza. The third line of the *quatrain* resultantly receives an extra punch because of the immediate repetition of the second rhyme. This really is important to note, that is, in a negative sense. You don't want your emphasis to fall on a throw-away line. So who writes throw-away lines? Oh well. . . .

In "An Unworthy Rhyme," my former student Eugene Rasmussen did a fine job with this *quatrain:*

The task outdoes my worthless art,
To explain her beauty in rhyme;
It dims the Gods in their high clime,
The joyous light that fills her heart.

And who can so recall the fears
That love's first steps do surely bring;
The heart is born its song to sing,
The feeling fills the eyes with tears.

So feebly will I try to write
A tribute to my one true love,
And with the help of those above,
Her charm and grace I will not slight.

Exercise 27

Think of some late public figure whom you admire in particular and try composing a poem of your own in three or so In Memoriam-type quatrains.

The Limerick and Another Five-Liner

Let's cut to the chase:

There was a young lady from Gaul
Who wore a newspaper dress to a ball.
Her dress caught on fire
And burnt her entire
Front page, sporting section, and all.

Exercise 28

Can you top this? Try . . . I dare you!

Five is not a particularly comfortable number of lines to write English verse in because it means that one must either resort to a *triplet* or to some variation thereof like the *limerick* or to an odd, unrhymed line. One notable example of a five-line poem employing the latter that works is Wordsworth's "Idiot Boy," which tells the story of slow-witted Johnny Foy's midnight ride at his mother's behest to fetch a doctor for an ailing neighbor. What makes the poem work is that the story is told, replete with simple diction, sort of from Johnny's point of view:

> — Why bustle thus about your door,
> What means this bustle, Betty Foy?
> Why are you in this mighty fret?
> And why on horseback have you set
> Him whom you love, your Idiot Boy?
>
> Scarcely a soul is out of bed;
> Good Betty, put him down again;
> His lips with joy they burr at you;
> But, Betty! What has he to do
> With stirrup, saddle, or with rein?

It's very simple, isn't it, *4a4b4c4c4b;* indeed, it's the *In Memoriam quatrain* with an extra odd line at the beginning. And if the truth be known, it harkens back to something called a *mad-song* stanza (*4a4b2c2c4b*), which was in vogue during the early Renaissance. Somehow the unrhymed first line wasn't then a problem and doesn't seem to be so now in this poem. Why?

Exercise 29?

It's not hard to be a little spacey when one's been around me for a while, so a stanza or two of this shouldn't be all THAT difficult. Just pretend you're ME in one of my spacey fits.

Rime Couée or Tail-Rhyme Stanza

This is a six-line stanza, with a metrical scheme as follows: *4a4a4a2b4a2b.* With its satiric possibilities, it became the stock in trade of Robert Burns, who probably found it in Chaucer's "Tale of Sir Thopas." Here's his most well-known poem in this form; the occasion was the destruction of a mouse's nest by a plough. Burns became uncontested master of the two short lines, called *bob-* or *tail-lines*, which allowed for sallies of wit and the like, but note that, in the end, the poem is a very sad one — about himself. Have a look-see:

To a Mouse

Wee, sleekit, cowrin, tim'rous beastie,
O, what a panic's in thy breastie!
Thou need na start awa sae hasty,
Wi' bickerin brattle!
I wad be laith to rin an' chase thee,
We' murderin' pattle!

I'm truly sorry man's dominion,
Has broken nature's social union,
An' justifies that ill opinion,
Which makes thee startle
At me, thy poor, earth-born companion,
An' fellow-mortal!

I doubt na, whiles, but thou may thieve;
What then? poor beastie, thou maun live!
A daimen icker in a thrave
'S a sma' request;
I'll get a blessin wi' the lave,
An' never miss't!

Thy wee bit housie, too, in ruin!
It's silly wa's the win's are strewin!
An' naething, now, to big a new ane,
O' foggage green!
An' bleak December's winds ensuin,
Baith snell an' keen!

Thou saw the fields laid bare an' waste,
An' weary winter comin' fast,

An' cozie here, beneath the blast,
            Thou thought to dwell–
Till crash! the cruel coulter past
            Out thro' thy cell.

That wee bit heap o' leaves an' stibble,
Has cost thee mony a weary nibble!
Now thou's turn'd out, for a' thy trouble,
            But house or hald,
To thole the winter's sleety dribble,
            An' cranreuch cauld!

But Mousie, thou art no thy lane,
In proving foresight may be vain;
The best-laid schemes o' mice an' men
            Gang aft agley,
An' lea'e us nought but grief an' pain,
            For promis'd joy!

Still thou art blest, compar'd wi' me!
The present only toucheth thee:
But och! I backward cast my e'e,
            On prospects drear!
An' forward, tho' I canna see,
            I guess an' fear!

Exercise 30

A poem of at least one stanza of this is in order. To get into the Burnsian swing of things, try addressing an animal or even a vegetable — but not a mouse; get your own critter! Do it in Brooklyneese or some other American dialect, if you can manage it. Hey-hey, consider that you got extra points if you pull off something witty with the "bobs."

Rime Royale

With a pattern of *5a5b5a5b5b5c6c*, this stanza tends to be self-contained because of its length, with the *b-couplet* right smack in the center and the final off-kilter *couplet* adding to the difficulties. It was successfully used in turn by Chaucer,

Shakespeare, and Milton, but as I see it, top honors go to Wordsworth for his "Resolution and Independence." It's a poet's poem; strolling along on a desolate moor one bright sunny day after a fearful storm the night before, the "I"'s thoughts sadly turn to the lot of poets, how at first everything seems to be going their way and then how quite suddenly things can take a spiraling downward turn. In the midst of this gloom, comes this very old man, a gatherer of leeches, to teach the "I" fortitude by the example of his own long-suffering life.

Note how masterfully Wordsworth began this poem, indeed delineating a whole scene in this first stanza:

> There was a roaring in the wind all night;
> The rain came heavily and fell in floods;
> But now the sun is rising calm and bright;
> The birds are singing in the distant woods;
> Over his own sweet voice the Stock-dove broods;
> The Jay makes answer as the Magpie chatters;
> And all the air is filled with pleasant noise of waters.

And how masterfully he knew how to achieve variety, for instance by setting off the final *couplet* from the rest of the stanza syntactically:

> While he was talking thus, the lonely place,
> The old Man's shape, and speech — all troubled me:
> In my mind's eye I seemed to see him pace
> About the weary moors continually,
> Wandering about alone and silently.
> While I these thoughts within myself pursued,
> He, having made a pause, the same discourse
> renewed.

Or else by making the fifth line a syntactic unit with the final *couplet:*

> At length, himself unsettling, he the pond
> Stirred with his staff, and fixedly did look

Upon the muddy water, which he conned,
As if he had been reading in a book:
And now a stranger's privilege I took;
And, drawing to his side, to him did say,
"This morning gives us promise of a glorious day."

But here's the master-stroke of all, an *epic simile* crossing over two stanzas:

As a huge stone is sometimes seen to lie
Couched on the bald top of an eminence;
Wonder to all who do the same espy,
By what means it could thither come, and whence;
So that it seems a thing endued with sense:
Like a sea-beast crawled forth, that on a shelf
Of rock or sand reposeth, there to sun itself;

Such seemed this Man, not all alive nor dead,
Nor all asleep — in his extreme old age:
His body was bent double, feet and head
Coming together in life's pilgrimage;
As if some dire constraint of pain, or rage
Of sickness felt by him in times long past,
A more than human weight upon his frame had cast.

Now I ask you: is this not fabulous?

Exercise 31

May I suggest the following modus op: copy out Wordsworth's text, leaving plenty of room of course, and retaining the end-words, write out nonsense lines to go with each. Then do the opposite: keep the internal text and substitute new end-words in the same rhyming pattern as the original. Next, think of a topic, like a particular morning that you yourself enjoyed, and make a list of relevant nouns, verbs, and adjectives, and then begin to compose, using the first stanza as a model.

Ottava Rima

This was the stanzaic form used by fourteenth-century Italian poets Ariosto and Tasso for their utterly monumental works *Orlando Furioso* and *Gerusalemme Liberata*, respectively. Consisting of an alternately rhyming *sestet* followed by a *couplet*, all of it in *iambic pentameter* (*5a5b5a5b5a5b5c5c*), the form allowed for a balanced narrative punctuated by a witty end-comment and thus proved to be a perfect vehicle for Byron in *Don Juan*, his volume-long *satiric epic*.

Needless to say, the *couplet* acted as a brake or reinforcement of punctuation for Byron, much as the *alexandrine* did at the end of the *rime royal stanza* for others, and as I pointed out before in chapter four, anything went as far as rhyme was concerned for Byron:

> 'Tis pity learned virgins ever wed
>   With persons of no sort of education,
> Or gentlemen, who, though well born and bred,
>   Grow tired of scientific conversation;
> I don't choose to say much upon this head,
>   I'm a plain man, and in a single station,
> But — Oh! ye lords of ladies intellectual,
> Inform us truly have they not hen-peck'd you all?

The stanzas are usually self-contained, but for the sake of variety and/or narrative continuity, he ran them on from time to time:

> Bob Southey! You're a poet — Poet-laureate,
>   And representative of all the race;
> Although 'tis true that you turn'd out a Tory at
>   Last, — yours has lately been a common case;
> And now, my Epic Renegade! What are ye at?
>   With all the Lakers, in and out of place?
> A nest of tuneful persons, to my eye
> Like "four and twenty Blackbirds in a pye";
>
> "Which pye being open'd they began to sing"
>   (This old song and new simile holds good),
> "A dainty dish to set before the King,"
>   Or Regent, who admires such kind of food; —
> And Coleridge, too, has lately taken wing,
>   But like a hawk encumber'd with his hood, —
> Explaining metaphysics to the nation–
> I wish he would explain his Explanation.

Here, to whet your appetite, is a cool poem in Byronic *ottava rima* stanzas by Silvana Fraser, another of my former students; the title, fittingly, is "Education":

When I think back upon my years of school,
So many things I learned, I still remember.
I wasn't called a nerd 'cause I was cool —
My favorite month was surely not September;
Yet knowledge was to me a form of fuel,
Ignited in me like a burning ember.
But kids are not so challenged nowadays,
For mediocrity is met with praise.

Today these kids go off to college dumb —
They fail at reading, writing, mathematics:
Their minds are just not challenged — they are numb;
If they receive a "D," they are ecstatic!
How worthless works of Shakespeare have become,
'Cause liberal minds think working hard's traumatic!
If shaping children's minds is education,
They must be teaching kids to hate this nation.

Exercise 32

How about it, just one little stanza. Only bear in mind: for a true Byronic flavor, the crazier the rhymes are and the more complex, the better. Go about it in the same way that I suggested for the rime royale in Exercise 31. Again, it's important that you have a topic and a list of relevant words by category — even if you don't use too many of them. And of course, if you really can't hack it, do settle for the nonsense, maybe go back to it some other time. Either way, not to forget multi-syllable rhyming words here, which are part of the fun.

The Spenserian

This nine-line stanza, which consists of eight lines of *iambic pentameter* in back-to-back *cross-rhymed quatrains* that are topped off by an *alexandrine end-rhyming* with the eighth line, in other words *5a5b5a5b5b5c5b5c6c*, is in essence the sine qua non of complex stanzas in English — as one used to say in Brooklyn, I wouldn't wish it on a dawg. It was devised by Sir Edmund Spenser (1552-1599) for his *Faerie Queen*, an allegorical work occupying many hundreds of pages in which Elizabeth I is glorified along with virtue, that is, as the folks of his day understood that concept. Here's a sample:

Redoubted knights, and honorable Dames,
 To whom I leuell all my labours end,
 Right sore I feare, least with vnworthy blames
 This odious argument my rimes should shend,
 Or ought your goodly patience offend,
 Whiles of a wanton Lady I do write,
 Which with her loose incontinence doth blend
 The shyning glory of your soueraigne light,
And knighthood fowle defaced by a faithlesse knight.

And here in a nutshell is what makes it tick: the *b-rhyme* ("end," "shend," "offend," and "blend") dominates the stanza until it intermingles with the *c-rhyme* ("write") and becomes lost in the *end-line echoes* of the *couplet* ("light" and "knight"). As with the *alexandrine* ending the *rime royal* stanza and the terminal *couplet* of the *ottava rima* stanza, the *alexandrine* closing this one, reinforced by the rhyme, acts as a brake, making the stanza self-contained.

In spite of the complexity of the *Spenserian* — or perhaps because of it — Wordsworth and others before and after him tried their hands at it, but truly the masterpiece in this stanzaic form is Keats's "Eve of St Agnes," in which he more or less retold the story of Romeo and Juliet. The opening of this poem is, in the words of Coleridge, a "miracle of rare device," combining coldness with relative silences:

St Agnes Eve — Ah, bitter chill it was!
The owl, for all his feathers, was a-cold;
The hare limp'd trembling through the frozen grass,
And silent was the flock in woolly fold:
Numb were the beadsman's fingers, while he told

His rosary, and while his frosted breath,
Like pious incense from a censer old,
Seem'd taking flight for heaven, without a death,
Past the sweet Virgin's picture, while his prayer he saith.

Note that the Beadsman's long prayer begins on line six with "while his frosted breath" and continues through the long last line, where it's metaphorically stretched. Keats picked up on this at the beginning of the next stanza — "His prayer, he saith, this patient, holy man" — and then, with it finished, the Beadsman begins to walk, and so begins the story of the separated young lovers, Porphyro and Madeleine.

Unlike Romeo and Juliet, Keats gave his story of thwarted young love a happy ending — that is, if you call the two of them running away together into a terrible gale happy. The poem ends as it began: with the Beadsman falling asleep after finishing his prayers and everything, like wisps of smoke, drifting back to cold and silence:

And they are gone: ay, ages long ago
These lovers fled away into the storm.
That night the Baron dreamt of many a woe,
And all his warrior-guests, with shade and form
Of witch, and demon, and large coffin-worm,
Were long be-nightmar'd. Angela the old
Died palsy-twitch'd, with meagre face deform;
The Beadsman, after thousand aves told,
For aye unsought for slept among his ashes cold.

It's no wonder that Shelley wrote "Adonais," his memorial to Keats, in *Spenserians.*

Exercise 33

What the hay, give it a whirl, what've you got to lose? One stanza will be sufficient. Go about it the same way I recommended you do with rime royale and ottava rima. If you wish, set it vaguely in the Middle Ages as a gesture in Keats's direction. And again, it's essential to have a topic firmly nailed, as well as word lists, before you even think of beginning. Also, once more, if you can't-can't-can't, no tears, please. Metrical nonsense is just fine.

Refrain Poems & Relatives

There are a whole lot of poems in English that depend upon *refrains* and/or intricate rhyme schemes for their effects. These are largely imports from medieval France or variations of same, and their names and forms are legion: *ballade, ballade supreme, double ballade, double ballade supreme, double refrain ballade, chant royale, rondeau, rondeau redoubled, rondel, rondel supreme, rondine, roundel, roundelay, triolet, sestina, villanelle.* Have I missed any? It wouldn't surprise me, and not to yell if you're a fan of this sort of thing. Just mosey on over to Lewis Turco's tome, where you'll find an exhausting list of same with descriptions.

Poems of this type were much beloved by Victorians like Algernon Charles Swinburne and Austin Dobson, and periodically they've become all the rage among a flock of young poets. As for me, I can well do without, which doubtless you can tell from my tone. Why? Except for rare instances, poems of this sort, indeed charming though they can be, call for prosodic gymnastics in the form of ingenuity and cleverness at the expense of deep feeling and profound thought, both to me essential ingredients of meaningful poetry. In short, I look upon them as good clean fun that's not to be taken too seriously. Consider, if you will, my lack of appreciation a failing on my part, but that's the way it is <sniff>.

Be that as it may, fair's fair, and here we go. The *ballade,* which isn't to be confused with the English *ballad,* consists of three *octets* rhyming *ababbcbc,* followed by an *envoi,* or farewell, in the form of a *cross-rhyming quatrain;* the last line of each stanza, including that of the *envoi,* is the same. The most famous *ballade* ever written is "The Ballade of Dead Ladies," by François Villon (ca. 1431-1463), which, happily, Victorian poet Dante Gabriel Rossetti made a masterly translation of:

Tell me now in what hidden way is
  Lady Flora the lovely Roman?
Where's Hipparchia, and where's Thais,
  Neither of them the fairer woman?
  Where is Echo, beheld of no man,
Only heard on river and mere, —
  She whose beauty was more than human?...
But where are the snows of yester-year?

Where's Héloise, the learned nun,
  For whose sake Abeillard, I ween,
Lost manhood and put priesthood on?
  (From Love he won such dule and teen!)
  And where, I pray you, is the Queen
Who willed that Buridan should steer
  Sewed in a sack's mouth down the Seine?...
But where are the snows of yester-year?

White Queen Blanche, like a queen of lilies,
  With a voice like any mermaiden —
Bertha Broadfoot, Beatrice, Alice,
  And Emermengarde the lady of Maine, —
  And that good Joan whom Englishmen
At Rouen doomed and burned her there, —
  Mother of God, where are they then?...
But where are the snows of yester-year?

Nay, never ask this week, fair lord,
  Where they are gone, nor yet this year,
Except with this for an overword, —
  But where are the snows of yester-year?

Exercise 34

You should by all means take a whack at this one if for no other reason than it's so seminal (hoo-hah). Here's a really cool topic: Ballade of the Dead Gents.

Among the shorter forms is the *roundel,* which is made up of three stanzas of four, three, and four lines, with two rhymes throughout plus a *refrain line* that occurs at the beginning and end of the first stanza and at the end of the third. In this *roundel* by Swinburne, so titled, note his use of round objects — "ring," "sphere," "pearl," "tear," etc. — as well as the many *r*'s to suggest "rounding":

A roundel is wrought as a ring or a starbright sphere,
With craft of delight and with cunning of sound unsought,
That the heart of the hearer may smile if to pleasure his ear
A roundel is wrought.

Its jewel of music is carven of all or of aught —
Love, laughter, or mourning — remembrance of rapture or fear —
That fancy may fashion to hang in the ear of thought.

As a bird's quick song runs round, and the hearts in us hear
Pause answers to pause, and again the same strain caught,
So moves the device whence, round as a pearl or tear,
A roundel is wrought.

Closely related to this one is the *rondeau,* which also employs two rhymes plus a *refrain.* It consists of three stanzas with its *refrain* at the beginning of the first stanza and at the ends of the other two — in other words, it really rounds them out. This *rondeau,* titled "In Flanders Fields," was written by John McCrae (1872-1918), a Canadian soldier killed in the carnage of World War I, and it's one of the few in this genre that really gets to a person, at least to me. The grimness of the reality of battlefield carnage contrasts boldly with the silly prettiness of the verse form:

In Flanders fields the poppies blow
Between the crosses, row on row,
That mark our place; and in the sky
The larks, still bravely singing, fly
Scarce heard amid the guns below.

We are the Dead. Short days ago
We lived, felt dawn, saw sunset glow,
    Loved and were loved, and now we lie,
        In Flanders fields.

Take up our quarrel with the foe:
To you from failing hands we throw
    The torch; be yours to hold it high.
    If ye break faith with us who die
We shall not sleep, though poppies grow
        In Flanders fields.

From the sublime to the ridiculous. The *triolet* consists of a single stanza eight lines in length that in addition to two rhymes, employs two *refrains: abaaabab.* Consider "Kiss" by Austin Dobson — honestly, could anything be sillier:

Rose kissed me to-day,
    Will she kiss me tomorrow?
Let it be as it may,
Rose kissed me to-day.
But the pleasure gives way
    To a savour of sorrow; —
Rose kissed me to-day, —
    Will she kiss me tomorrow?

Exercise 35

This is a kind of warm-up for what's coming next. Show what you can do with one of these: the roundel, the rondeau, or the triolet. Suggested topic: a parody of the latter with a dog or cat occupying center stage.

Now matters are about to become more complicated. In the *villanelle,* two rhymes and two *refrains* are employed over the course of five *tercets* (that is, three-line stanzas) and a *quatrain,* and obviously, top honors go to Dylan Thomas (1914-1953) for this now well-known poem:

Do not go gentle into that good night,
Old age should burn and rave at close of day;
Rage, rage against the dying light.

Though wise men at their end know dark is right,
Because their words had forked no lightning they
Do not go gentle into that good night.

Good men, the last wave by, crying how bright
Their frail deeds might have danced in a green bay,
Rage, rage against the dying of the light.

Wild men who caught and sang the sun in flight,
And learn, too late, they grieved it on its way,
Do not go gentle into that good night.

Grave men, near death, who see with blinding sight
Blind eyes could blaze like meteors and be gay,
Rage, rage against the dying of the light.

And you, my father, there on the sad height,
Curse, bless, me now with your fierce tears, I pray.
Do not go gentle into that good night.
Rage, rage against the dying of the light.

Villanelles need not be on such serious subjects and indeed can be great fun. Here, delightfully, is what my former student, Ursula Melendi, did with it:

Baker's Villanelle

I beg you leave the sugar in the cake
And do not waste the chocolate on the spoon;
You can't postpone the weeping at your wake.

Some cooks may know a hundred ways to bake
But keep their sweeteners hidden from the moon;
I beg you leave the sugar in the cake.

Although you know there is a lot at stake,
Indulge in truffles, tarts and macaroons;
You can't postpone the weeping at your wake.

Those wishing to shed ounces will forsake
Sweet chocolate taste for diet tea at noon;
I beg you leave the sugar in the cake.

Nutrition-conscious experts hit the brake
And stay away from fudge that makes me swoon;
You can't postpone the weeping at your wake.

So toss your diet cookies in the lake
And join this culinary picaroon;
I beg you leave the sugar in the cake —
You can't postpone the weeping at your wake.

Exercise 36

As the old song goes, so how about you? Make it as serious or silly as you wish, including a response either to Dylan Thomas or Ursula Melendi.

Oy, the *sestina.* In English, it's usually rendered in *iambic pentameter* and consists of six stanzas of six lines each plus a three-line *envoi.* The rules are formidable:

1. The last words of the first stanza are repeated as the last words of all the other stanzas, each time in a different order.

2. The very last word of each stanza is repeated as the last word of the first line of the stanza following.

3. Each line of the *envoi* must contain two of the last words.

Here's Swinburne's "I Saw My Soul," which I'm using because it most clearly demonstrates the form:

I saw my soul at rest upon a day
  As a bird sleeping in the nest of night,
Among soft leaves that give the starlight way
  To touch its wings but not its eyes with light;
So that it knew as one in visions may,
  And knew not as men waking, of delight.

This was the measure of my soul's delight;
  It had no power of joy to fly by day,
Nor part in the large lordship of the light;
  But in a secret moon-beholden way
Had all its will of dreams and pleasant night,
  And all the love and life that sleepers may.

But such life's triumph as men waking may
  It might not have to feed its faint delight
Between the stars by night and sun by day,

Shut up with green leaves and a little light;
Because its way was as a lost star's way,
A world's not wholly known of day or night.

All loves and dreams and sounds and gleams of night
Made it all music that such minstrels may,
And all they had they gave it of delight;
But in the full face of the fire of day
What place shall be for any starry light,
What part of heaven in all the wide sun's way?

Yet the soul woke not, sleeping by the way,
Watched as a nursling of the large-eyed night,
And sought no strength nor knowledge of the day,
Nor closer touch conclusive of delight,
Nor mightier joy nor truer than dreamers may,
Nor more of song than they, nor more of light.

For who sleeps once and sees the secret light
Whereby sleep shows the soul a fairer way
Between the rise and rest of day and night,
Shall care no more to fare as all men may,
But be his place of pain or of delight,
There shall he dwell, beholding night as day.

Song, have thy day and take thy fill of light
Before the night be fallen across thy way;
Sing while he may, man hath no long delight.

I was about to remark that I myself couldn't think of anything more deadening to the poetic self than a form like the *sestina* when — eureka! — it turned out that Ruth, our guest poet, has a fine *sestina* that works in terms of itself, so I take it all back, and here it is:

Blossom and Technology

I wasn't sure what to expect,
after flying for eighteen hours
over the Pole. Japan
was contradictory images:
stone and technology,
crowds and cherry blossom.

I came too late for the blossom,
the one sight I did expect,
as if technology
could slow seasons and hours
till certain images
confirmed: this is Japan.

Some things were strange in Japan:
not the imitation blossom,
but those plastic images
of meals you might expect
in restaurants. The hours
to make them, the technology!

An older technology
had created another Japan
where no count was taken of hours
spent training flowers to blossom
in a place you wouldn't expect,
or painting a screen with their images.

I wanted to keep those images.
My camera — technology
of the sort I came to expect
from anything bought in Japan —
was aimed at every blossom
and stone as it changed with the hours.

I stood and watched for hours
near the temple images
people's faces blossom:
prayer's technology
must be what fuels Japan,
which is not what you'd expect,

nor expect that so few hours
in Japan could reconcile images
of blossom and technology.

What I like about this is that there's nothing artificial or "fishy" about this; Ruth has managed to maintain her unique poetic identity in it. Brava!

Exercise 37

If it turns out you can't hack a sestina, why not devise your own refrain poem?

Look, for instance, at how my friend Rosalie Calabrese delightfully played around with two *refrain* lines:

On Thursday

Tomorrow will be Friday
No matter what:
Even if the world
Comes to an end
It will be Friday —
That's my guess —
If I should say
No more, that's it, finis,
It will be Friday
Nonetheless;
Like it or not,
Friday will be tomorrow
No matter what.

Fun & Games?

You'll forgive me, dear Readers, if now, after so long a travail, I indulge myself. I'd like to share with you, as space permits, some of my favorite poems, or tunes if you will. As there are quite a number of same, I decided to rein myself in to two, and even then I had to make compromises, as you'll now see.

One of my long-time favorites is Coleridge's "Kubla Khan," which we've met with before in passing a number of times. To remind you, Coleridge claimed that much more than was published came to him in a dream and that he was torn from writing it all down by the sudden appearance of a visitor, hence his sub-title "A Vision in a Dream. A Fragment." And to further remind you, I'm inclined to think this was a crock. My guess is that, perhaps thanks to opium, to which he was addicted, he'd ventured into the Absurd — indeed, way before his time — and didn't have the foggiest idea how else to explain things. Have a looksee; what do you think?

In Xanadu did Kubla Khan
A stately pleasure-dome decree:
Where Alph, the sacred river, ran
Through caverns measureless to man
Down to a sunless sea.
So twice five miles of fertile ground
With walls and towers were girdled round:
And there were gardens bright with sinuous rills,
Where blossomed many an incense-bearing tree;
And here were forests ancient as the hills,
Enfolding sunny spots of greenery.

But oh! that deep romantic chasm which slanted
Down the green hill athwart a cedarn cover!
A savage place! as holy and enchanted
As e'er beneath a waning moon was haunted
By woman wailing for her demon-lover!
And from this chasm, with ceaseless turmoil seething,
As if this earth in fast thick pants were breathing,
A mighty fountain momently was forced:
Amid whose swift half-intermitted burst
Huge fragments vaulted like rebounding hail,
Or chaffy grain beneath the thresher's flail:
And 'mid these dancing rocks at once and ever
It flung up momently the sacred river.
Five miles meandering with a mazy motion
Through wood and dale the sacred river ran,
Then reached the caverns measureless to man,
And sank in tumult to a lifeless ocean:
And 'mid this tumult Kubla heard from far
Ancestral voices prophesying war!

> The shadow of the dome of pleasure
> Floated midway on the waves;
> Where was heard the mingled measure
> From the fountain and the caves.
> It was a miracle of rare device,
> A sunny pleasure-dome with caves of ice!
>
> A damsel with a dulcimer
> In a vision once I saw:
> It was an Abyssinian maid,
> And on her dulcimer she played,
> Singing of Mount Abora.
> Could I revive within me
> Her symphony and song,
> To such a deep delight 'twould win me,
> That with music loud and long,
> I would build that dome in air,
> That sunny dome! those caves of ice!
> And all who heard should see them there,
> And all should cry, Beware! Beware!
> His flashing eyes, his floating hair!
> Weave a circle round him thrice,
> And close your eyes with holy dread,
> For he on honey-dew hath fed,
> And drunk the milk of Paradise.

Without a doubt, the whole thing is of one piece, one tissue, so to speak. The second verse paragraph ("But oh") is *synthetically parallel* with the first, and the third verse paragraph ("A damsel") is *antithetically parallel* to the first two paragraphs together. Also, in the first verse paragraph, Coleridge seemed to be painting a picture of the eighteenth-century ideal of the Beautiful, while in the last two verse paragraphs, he seemed to be doing the same with its opposite, the Sublime (or fearful).

What does the poem, crock or not, mean to me? Well, let's say, to me it's a microcosm of or a paradigm for our inexplicable universe, including and especially ourselves, the greatest puzzle of all, ever ongoing.

Exercise 38

> *Try a sort of a response to "Kubla Khan" — that is, see how much more absurd you can become in your own terms, bearing in mind that everything has to make some sort of sense.*

Another favorite of mine is Milton's "Lycidas." Published in 1638, it's a memorial poem with, let's call them, "shepherd-conceits," in which he mourned the death of Edward King, a college friend who was drowned at sea in 1637, to whom he gave the pastoral name Lycidas. It is interesting to note that Milton's mother died in the same year, and while his relationship with her couldn't have been all hearts and flowers, because those he had with women in his adulthood were rather stormy, still even under the worst of circumstances, a mother is a mother, and it's hard for me to believe that some heaviness of heart for her didn't figure in this poem between the lines.

Be that as it may, in the end it really doesn't much matter for whom Milton was personally grieving, whether it was a recently deceased friend whom he perhaps hadn't been in touch with since leaving college in 1632 or the shadowy figure of his late mother. It's the expression of grief in "Lycidas" that counts. And when I read it here in this day and age, I always look beyond Milton's personal concerns and view it as our shared grief over the slow — or, perhaps in the light of the current world situation, not-so-slow — passing of our way of life. Here's how it begins:

> Yet once more, O ye Laurels, and once more
> Ye Myrtles brown, with Ivy never sere,
> I come to pluck your Berries harsh and crude,
> And with forc'd fingers rude,
> Shatter your leaves before the mellowing year.
> Bitter constraint, and sad occasion dear,
> Compels me to disturb your season due:
> For *Lycidas* is dead, dead ere his prime,

Young *Lycidas*, and hath not left his peer:
Who would not sing for *Lycidas*? he knew
Himself to sing, and build the lofty rhyme.
He must not float upon his wat'ry bier
Unwept, and welter to the parching wind,
Without the meed of some melodious tear.

And now let's be done with it; here's the conclusion:

Weep no more, woeful Shepherds weep no more,
For *Lycidas* your sorrow is not dead,
Sunk though he be beneath the wat'ry floor,
So sinks the day-star in the Ocean bed,
And yet anon repairs his drooping head,
And tricks his beams, and with new-spangled Ore,
Flames in the forehead of the morning sky:
So *Lycidas*, sunk low, but mounted high,
Through the dear might of him that walk'd the waves,
Where other groves, and other streams along,
With Nectar pure his oozy Locks he laves,
And hears the unexpressive nuptial Song,
In the blest Kingdoms meek of joy and love.
There entertain him all the Saints above,
In solemn troops, and sweet Societies
That sing, and singing in their glory move,
And wipe the tears for ever from his eyes.
Now *Lycidas*, the Shepherds weep no more;
Henceforth thou art the Genius of the shore,
In thy large recompense, and shalt be good
To all that wander in that perilous flood.
  Thus sang the uncouth Swain to th 'Oaks and rills,
While the still morn went out with Sandals gray;
He touch't the tender stops of various Quills,
With eager thought warbling his Doric lay:
And now the Sun had stretch't out all the hills,
And now was dropt into the Western bay;
At last he rose, and twitch't his Mantle blue:
Tomorrow to fresh Woods, and Pastures new.

Once one gets over the hurdles of Milton's curious Latinate constructions and classical references, this work seems as fresh today as the day he wrote it — like Blake's "London," with its mixed metaphors.

Exercise 39

Do yourself a favor: find the whole thing in an anthology and read it, joining hands with me over the thought waves as you do so.

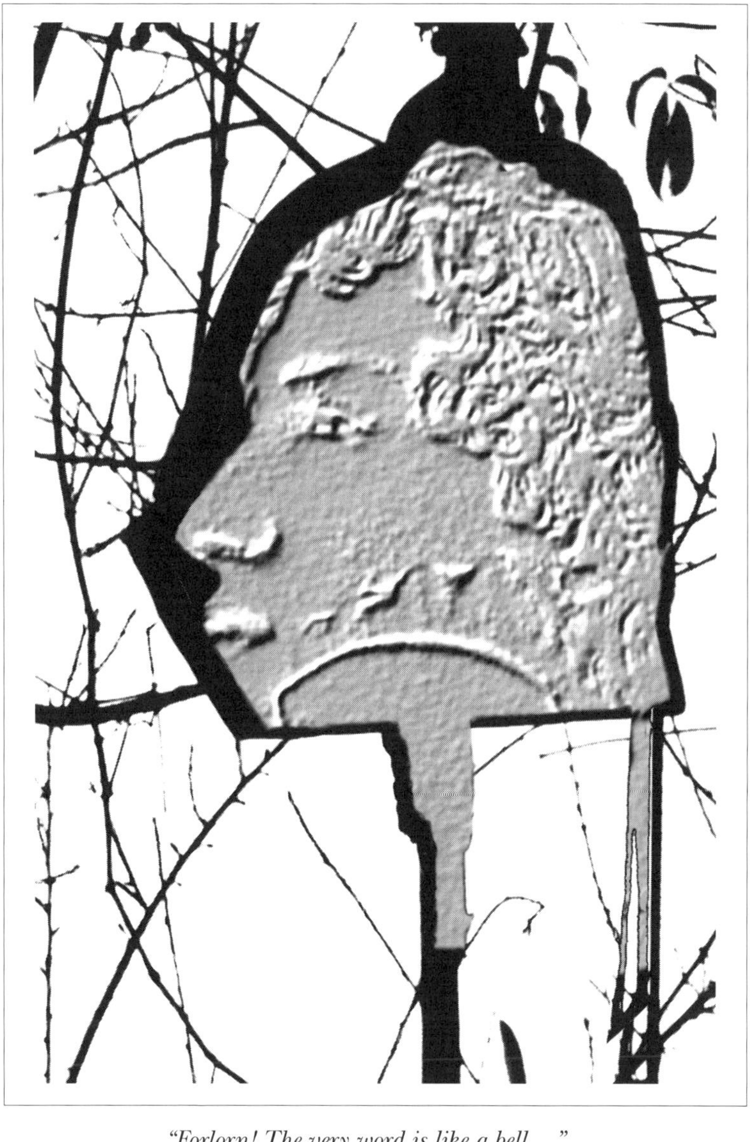

"Forlorn! The very word is like a bell..."

8

Free verse

That Mysterious, Elusive, Misnamed Thing

For those of you who aren't in the know, *free verse* is any poem that's not written in one of the traditional forms — that is, any poem that's unencumbered by or "free" of those forms. The following, by our three guest poets, arc all cxamples of *free verse*:

Handbag
by Ruth Fainlight

My mother's old leather handbag,
crowded with letters she carried
all through the war. The smell
of my mother's handbag: mints
and lipstick and Coty powder.
The look of those letters, softened
and worn at the edges, opened,
read, and refolded so often.
Letters from my father. Odour
of leather and powder, which ever
since then has meant womanliness,
and love, and anguish, and war.

Orlando
by Nina Cassian

He jumps from one mountain to another
the sky a scarf around his neck
stars on his face (dimples and scars)
he connects ideas like a UFO
he sings (voice of sirens, voice of coyotes)
he fills like air the space between the Parthenon's columns
his eyes are sparkling with tears

he is a woman.

Ministering Spirits
by Jeffrey Greene

What is the resistance to death of the ministering spirit
if not a mission between the sea and the wilderness
in the bare winter woods of New England,

where it was starving time and saints and strangers were
dying,
by twos and threes, until half were gone, and the rest
lay waiting, Captain Standish tending the fires and defenses

and with Brewster, the Elder, cleaning the filth of grateful
patients,
fearless under the peering hatred of the native ghosts
whose stores of colored corn had been raided?

While all three are examples of *free verse*, these poems are quite different from one another stylistically, wouldn't you say? Well, in case you didn't see that, take a moment to look at them now:

Exercise 1

Count up the number of syllables per line in each poem and look for major sound repetitions.

That should have done it, but in case it didn't:

Exercise 2

Read each poem aloud, one person to each poem if you're in a group, in different voices if you're alone.

Now you see it, yes? They are quite different from one another, aren't they? So-o-o, let me state this as a general precept: the style of a *free verse* poem is as unique to its poet as its content. True, you may at times find a poem by one person that stylistically resembles that by another, just as in your lifetime you may encounter people who look and/or think alike. It follows from this that there are as many different kinds of *free verse* as there are poets composing poems in it, so be sure to ignore any categorizations of them, as has been attempted from time to time by scholars who should know better. So which of the three poems do you like the best? Good, I'm happy for you..

Exercise 3

Mark the stressed and unstressed syllables in that poem, and then substitute cha-CHA's and OOM-pa's and so on, and read it aloud instead of the words.

This sort of takes the sting out of it, doesn't it? Now I'll give you a choice:

Exercise 4 (?)

Write a poem in place of the cha-CHA's and OOM-pa's you just wrote, or substitute nonsense words for them.

Care to read it aloud? I didn't think so.

Exercise 5

What do you say to a short poem in your own free verse idiom or burgeoning idiom. Do it on any subject you wish, including a response to one of the three poets.

Was it so bad? Tell me, whisper it.

Exercise 6

How about reading it aloud — I dare you.

If ever there was a misnomer, it's got to be the term *free verse.* Nothing in this world is "free" of rules and regulations; everything is subject to them. And while the rules for *free verse* may not be immediately apparent, they nevertheless exist. To think otherwise is to be like a kid craving release from onerous tasks like doing your homework and cleaning up your room that The Nagging World demands of you.

Those rules are very subtle and much stricter than the rules governing traditional verse because it's your inner self calling the shots. Take it from me, that self's voice, modeled (whether you're willing to admit it or not) on The Nagging World's, can turn out to be far more demanding and unreasonable than you'd imagine. Don't be surprised if, at some point, you find yourself wanting to hot-foot it back to the traditional forms for relief — much as Wordsworth found it comforting to be confined to the *Petrarchan sonnet*'s "scanty plot of ground."

We must distinguish between the origin of the term *free verse* and that of the thing itself. The term is of relatively recent coinage. It was a literal translation of *vers libre,* the name of a species of French poetry that originated in the late nineteenth century, which various English-language poets, like Ezra Pound and T. S. Eliot, applied to their own poetry in the early twentieth century.

There are a number of schools of thought as to how long *free verse* in English has been around. According to one of them — the one to which I subscribe — it has been in existence almost from the beginning, that is, almost as long as traditional verse itself. As the old adage goes, rules were made to be broken.

To me, the first major work in *free verse* was the Bible. You understand that this work, which was a compilation of many very ancient ones in tongues like Hebrew, was first translated into English in the fourteenth century by John Wycliffe and his followers and, after quite a number of other translations, appeared in a version sponsored by King James I in 1611, which English poets thereafter used as a literary bible. Consider the opening to our old friend Psalm 23 in that version:

> The Lord is my shepherd; I shall not want.
> He maketh me to lie down in green pastures: he leadeth me beside the still waters.
> He restoreth my soul: he leadeth me in the paths of righteousness for his name's sake.

Without belaboring the matter, this is certainly a far cry from the *dramatic blank verse* that was being written for and spoken on the stage at the very same time:

> To be, or not to be, that is the question:
> Whether 'tis nobler in the mind to suffer
> The slings and arrows of outrageous fortune,
> Or to take arms against a sea of troubles,
> And by opposing end them....

Milton in his *Samson Agonistes* was, to my way of thinking, the first English poet to try to break the shackles of *blank verse* and venture into something different that was all his own, and we've already seen an example of this in his use of sporadic rhymes in that work. Note in this rhymeless passage how he began with ten-syllable lines but quickly and unexpectedly went to considerably fewer, only to return to ten-syllable lines:

> O dark, dark, dark amid the blaze of noon,
> Irrecoverably dark, total Eclipse

Without all hope of day!
O first created Beam, and thou great Word,
"Let there be light, and light was over all";
Why am I thus bereav'd thy prime decreee?
The Sun to me is dark
And silent as the Moon
When she deserts the night,
Hid in her vacant interlunar cave.
Since light so necessary is to life,
And almost life itself, if it be true
That light is in the Soul,
She all in every part; why was the sight
To such a tender ball as th' eye confin'd?
So obvious and so easy to be quencht,
And not as feeling through all parts diffius'd
That she might look at will through every pore?

Exercise 7

You don't believe that an old-fashioned dude like Milton could commit such a sacrilege? Count them up and see.

If you're in a group, even of two, your results should lead to considerable discussion. Oooh, I just love discussions, don't you? If you're alone, do be sure to have a long think about these things. Talk to yourself. Yes, why not? Take my word for it, articulation about these things — saying them out loud — does make a difference.

Since the majority of lines in *Samson Agonistes* are in *blank verse,* very likely that's how we'd designate the verse of this work as a whole. However, if you were to consider the passage above alone, would you call it *blank verse* with many lines that are exceptions or *free verse* interspersed with some lines of *blank verse*?

A little after the middle of the eighteenth century, a trend counter to Pope and his *heroic couplet* began. Helping things along considerably was a curious individual named James MacPherson (1736-1796), who came out with supposed translations from the Gaelic of a poet called Ossian that soon proved to be forgeries — but not before they'd taken the English literary world and that of the Continent by storm. Here's a sample:

> A tale of the times of old! The deeds of days of other years! The murmur of thy streams, O Lora! brings back the memory of the past. The sound of thy woods, Garmallar, is lovely in mine ear. Dost thou not behold, Malvina, a rock with its head of heath? Three aged pines bend from its face; green is the narrow plain at its feet; there the flower of the mountain grows, and shakes its white head in the breeze. The thistle is there alone, shedding its aged beard. Two stones, half sunk in the ground, shew their heads of moss. The deer of the mountain avoids the place, for he beholds a dim ghost standing there. The mighty lie, O Malvina! in the narrow plain of the rock.

Those Ossianic "translations" proved of enormous influence on English poets for generations to come, providing a breath of fresh air and a viable alternative to what some might've begun to feel was stultifying tradition.

Other anti-Popean poets were influenced by the "untraditional" cadences of the Bible, which, it's important to realize, was an English child's First Reader. Among these was another curious individual named Christopher Smart (1722-1771), who wrote a long poem titled *Jubilate Agno* (Rejoice in the Lamb) while confined to a madhouse. Here's one of its most notorious passages:

> For I will consider my Cat Jeoffry.
> For he is the servant of the Living God duly
> and daily serving him.
> For at the first glance of the glory of God in the
> East he worships in his way.
> For is this done by wreathing his body seven
> times round with elegant quickness.
> For then he leaps up to catch the musk, which

is the blessing of God upon his prayer.
For he rolls upon prank to work it in.
For having done duty and received blessing he begins
to consider himself.
For this he performs in ten degrees.
For first he looks upon his fore-paws to see if
they are clean.
For secondly he kicks up behind to clear a
way there.
For thirdly he works it upon stretch with the
fore paws extended.
For fourthly he sharpens his paws by wood.
For fifthly he washes himself.
For sixthly he rolls upon wash.
For seventhly he fleas himself, that he may not
be interrupted upon the beat.
For eighthly he rubs himself against a post.
For ninthly he looks up for his instructions.
For tenthly he goes in quest of food.

William Blake (1757-1827), another pseudo-biblical apostate from tradition, made it known early on in his career that he was going to create a Bible of Hell and wrote, illustrated, self-produced, and self-published quite a few works with titles reminiscent of those of the books of the Bible, such as *The Book of Thel, The Song of Los, The First Book of Urizen,* and so on. For those works, he developed his own long line, as in the following from *Milton, Book the Second,* another work in that series:

Thou hearest the Nightingale begin the Song of Spring;
The Lark sitting upon his earthy bed: just as the morn
Appears; listens silent; then springing from the waving
Corn-field, loud
He leads the Choir of Day! trill, trill, trill, trill,
Mounting upon the wings of light into the Great Expanse:
Reecchoing against the lovely blue & shining heavenly
Shell:
His little throat labours with inspiration; every feather

On throat & breast & wings vibrates with the effluence
Divine
All Nature listens silent to him & the awful Sun
Stands still upon the Mountain looking on this little Bird
With eyes of soft humility, & wonder, love & awe.
Then loud from their green covert all the Birds begin
their Song
The Thrush, the Linnet & the Goldfinch, Robin &
the Wren
Awake the Sun from his sweet reverie upon the Mountain:
The Nightingale again assays his song, & thro the day,
And thro the night warbles luxuriant; every Bird of Song
Attending his loud harmony with admiration & love.

Exercise 8

It wouldn't hurt to do a syllable count, would it?

Somewhat later across the Atlantic in America, Walt Whitman (1819-1892) went down a parallel path with his own pseudo-biblical cadences, as one can see in the opening to his celebrated "Song of Myself":

I celebrate myself, and sing myself,
And what I assume you shall assume,
For every atom belonging to me as good belongs to you.
I loafe and invite my soul,

I lean and loafe at my ease observing a spear of summer
grass.
My tongue, every atom of my blood, form'd from this soil,
this air,
Born here of parents born here from parents the same,
and their parents the same,
I, now thirty-seven years old in perfect health begin,
Hoping to cease not till death.

Creeds and schools in abeyance,
Retiring back a while sufficed at what they are,
but never forgotten,
I harbor for good or bad, I permit to speak at every

hazard,
Nature without check with original energy.

Exercise 9

A syllable count would again seem to be in order.

How does your count compare with that of Blake's passage above, I wonder?

Meanwhile in the latter half of the nineteenth century in England, there was a tendency toward relaxation where the traditional forms were concerned, which we've already seen something of in chapter six in Tennyson's *variable refrain line* in the *blank verse* stanzas in "Tears, Idle Tears"; Browning's loose *heroic couplets* in "My Last Duchess"; and Hopkins's language distortion and forced accentuation in his curious *sonnet* "The Windhover."

To me, this relaxed tendency can best be summarized by what Matthew Arnold did in "Dover Beach," where the lines and stanzas are of unequal length, and the rhymes, while there, are rather bland and casual — that is, until the celebrated last stanza:

The sea is calm to-night.
The tide is full, the moon lies fair
Upon the straits; — on the French coast the light
Gleams and is gone; the cliffs of England stand,
Glimmering and vast, out in the tranquil bay.
Come to the window, sweet is the night-air!
Only, from the long line of spray
Where the sea meets the moon-blanch'd land,
Listen! you hear the grating roar
Of pebbles which the waves draw back, and fling,
At their return, up the high strand,
Begin, and cease, and then again begin,
With tremulous cadence slow, and bring
The eternal note of sadness in.

Sophocles long ago
Heard it on the Aegean, and it brought

Into his mind the turbid ebb and flow
Of human misery; we
Find also in the sound a thought,
Hearing it by this distant northern sea.

The Sea of Faith
Was once, too, at the full, and round earth's shore
Lay like the folds of a bright girdle furl'd.
But now I only hear
Its melancholy, long withdrawing roar,
Retreating, to the breath
Of the night-wind, down the vast edges drear
And naked shingles of the world.

Ah, love, let us be true
To one another! for the world, which seems
To lie before us like a land of dreams,
So various, so beautiful, so new,
Hath really neither joy, nor love, nor light,
Nor certitude, nor peace, nor help for pain;
And we are here as on a darkling plain
Swept with confused alarms of struggle and flight,
Where ignorant armies clash by night.

Did anyone notice the throwbacks to Milton in "Tremulous cadence slow" and "vast edges drear"? If you did, go to the head of the class, hoo-hah.

Exercise 10

Needless to say, count up syllables.

So would you call this passage *iambic tetrameter* or *pentameter*? Don't all answer at once.

Exercise 11

Is there any pattern to the rhyming, or do the rhymes just fall—like drops of ocean spray-ay-ay?

Clearly, between the relaxations that I noted and what Arnold accomplished above, the stage was being set for something new and different in English poetry.

In the first and second decades of the twentieth century, various English-speaking poets, some of whom were living abroad, sought to break away from the fixed forms that we covered in the last two chapters. These poets included Ezra Pound, T. S. Eliot, H. D. (alias Hilda Doolittle), William Carlos Williams, Carl Sandburg, and E. E. Cummings, among others. A brief encounter with a poem by each of them is in order.

If ever anyone lived up to that famous line of William Carlos Williams, "The pure products of America go crazy," it was Ezra Pound (1885-1972). The only child of a petty federal official, he grew up in suburban Philadelphia and attended a variety of schools before finally getting an M.A. from the University of Pennsylvania in 1906. Leaving for Europe that summer, he lived in England and France for a while, making brief visits back to the States now and then, and then settled down in Italy, there to remain, making propaganda broadcasts for the fascist government, until 1945. Captured by our troops, he was brought back to the United States to face charges of treason but was declared mentally unfit to stand trial. Confined to St. Elizabeth's Hospital for the Criminally Insane, Pound was released in 1958 and returned to Italy, where he spent the balance of his life, largely in silence.

Clearly a one-of-a-kind prodigy, Pound is reputed to have had a comprehensive knowledge of Classical Greek, Latin, Anglo-Saxon, French, Italian, Provençal, Spanish,

German, and Chinese, and he left behind a considerable body of poetry, including 800 pages of *The Cantos*, begun in 1915, as well as seventy books, contributions to seventy others, and over 1,500 articles. He managed to touch the lives of most of the poets listed above, as well as such figures as Robert Frost, Ernest Hemingway, James Joyce, D. H. Lawrence, and William Butler Yeats.

Pound's poem "The Return" (1917) is about combat soldiers returning home during World War I, and since no nationalities are mentioned, one can perhaps look upon it as opposed to war generally.

> See, they return; ah, see the tentative
>   Movements, and the slow feet,
>   The trouble in the pace and the uncertain
>   Wavering!
> See, they return, one and by one,
> With fear, as half-awakened;
> As if the snow should hesitate
> And murmur in the wind,
>   and half turn back;
> These were the "Wing'd-with-Awe,"
>   Inviolable.
>
> Gods of the wingèd shoe!
> With them the silver hounds,
>   sniffing the trace of air!
>
> Haie! Haie!
>   These were the swift to harry;
> These the keen-scented;
> These were the souls of blood.
>
> Slow on the leash,
>   pallid the leash-men!

It's possible that the line arrangements — the short first stanza; then the second, which is longest; then the single line "Haie! Haie!" followed by the three-line and then the two-line stanzas — owe something to the quirkiness of

Dada. The indentations on some of the lines urge readers to pause and consider on one level, and on another provide a kind of visual analogue of combat in World War I, which was one of quick and slow advances from one trench to another.

Word repetitions are one of the major features of this poem — "See, they return"; "see"; "one by one"; "These were"; "These"; and "leash" — and are reminiscent of those of "this" and "these" in the opening of Wordsworth's "Tintern Abbey," where they perform the same function of giving a sense of immediacy. Also, as if a hangover from Shakespearian *blank verse*, many of the lines end with polysyllabic words whose last syllable or syllables are unstressed: "tentative," "uncertain," "wavering," "awakened," "hesitate," "inviolable," "harry," "silver hounds," "scented," and "leash-men." There's another three-syllable terminal pattern in "and by one," "hesitate," "in the wind," "half turn back," "wingéd shoe," and "souls of blood."

The soldiers are likened to "hounds," who are "swift to harry" and "keen-scented," in other words, "souls of blood." They obey the commands given them with eagerness and alacrity, as trained hunting dogs will, and in the end, they obediently return to their leashes — nevertheless men pallid from battle. Here's a thought: could Pound, in his overly fertile mind, have created "dog-boys" from "dough-boys," that is, American soldiers?

The masterstroke of the poem is in the inclusion of "Haie! Haie!" Is it the dogs or men crying out, or is it perhaps the poet himself, at the horror of it all?

Exercise 12 (?)

> *Just for fun copy the poem out with a straight left margin and without any of the indentations.*

Now I ask you, does it or does it not deflate like a cold soufflé? What do those indentations accomplish then? Are they cues for reading aloud and / or comprehension?

Exercise 13

A counting of syllables per line will reveal other important features of this poem. This should be followed by a replacement of words with cha-CHA's and OOM-pa's and the like or nonsense words patterned after the disposition of syllables.

So when all is said and done, that is, your counts are in, what are those other features?

Born of a prominent St. Louis family that had originated in Boston, T. S. Eliot (1888-1965) went to school locally and then to Harvard, where he received a B.A. in 1909. Study in France followed, and in 1914 in London, he met and began a close association with Pound. Eliot's first volume of poetry, *Prufrock and Other Observation*s, appeared in 1917, and this was followed by *Poems* in 1919, which contained "Gerontion," a monologue in *blank verse.*

Then, in 1922, came the celebrated *Waste Land,* which had been cut from its original 800 lines to 433 at Pound's suggestion. Reflecting the fragmented experience of the twentieth century through rhetorical shifts and juxtapositions of contrasting styles, it was and still is today a difficult poem. In my own apprenticeship days, I suspect that everyone had trouble understanding it, even some of my professors. This was just after World War II, when Eliot was all the rage in New York following the success of his play *The Cocktail Party* on Broadway, and everyone was giving them or going to them and drinking those poisonous concoctions in rooms so full of cigarette smoke you could hardly see to the end of them. The in-word was "obscure," and poetry was valued, judged, and cooed over on that basis — via a phony British accent, of course. Critic Alfred Kazin, as I recall, used to go hotfooting it along the beach in Coney Island as a kid, selling knishes and chanting "Shantih, shantih, shantih!" from *The Waste Land.*

Exercise 14

Get hold of a copy of ***The Waste Land*** *and read it over, either in a group or by yourself and see if it means anything to you.*

If it doesn't, not to worry, screw it — I mean, skip it.

In 1927, Eliot became a British subject and, more important, was confirmed in the Church of England, and then followed poems in his mature style: "Ash Wednesday" (1930) and *The Four Quartets* (1936-1942). The latter won him the Noble Prize for Literature in 1948. This passage is the beginning of Part I of "Burnt Norton," the first of the quartets:

> Time present and time past
> Are both perhaps present in time future,
> And time future contained in time past.
> If all time is eternally present
> All time is unredeemable.
> What might have been is an abstraction
> Remaining a perpetual possibility
> Only in a world of speculation.
> What might have been and what has been
> Point to one end, which is always present.
> Footfalls echo in the memory
> Down the passage which we did not take
> Towards the door we never opened
> Into the rose-garden. My words echo
> Thus, in your mind.
>   But to what purpose
> Disturbing the dust on a bowl of rose-leaves
> I do not know.

Exercise 15

Be a good sport and count up the syllables per line, paying particular attention to the line endings.

So-o-o, would you or would you not label the passage *blank verse?* This calls for a more than casual discussion, no? Have one, either with another or others, or yourself. P. S: Did you notice that tendency of Eliot's there, as in Pound's "Return," to end his lines on a light stress, for instance, with "pur-pose" and "rose-leaves"? Could this be a conscious or unconscious throw-back to the Bard?

Exercise 16

Look for, diligently look for, sound-correspondences. What kinds did you find?

What do you make of them? Not all folks like them. How do you feel?

Exercise 17

Follow up by replacing the words with cha-CHA's and OOM-pa's and the like or nonsense words patterned after the disposition of syllables.

In Part II, Eliot began with a passage of short lines irregularly end-rhymed:

Garlic and sapphires in the mud
Clot the bedded axle-tree.
The trilling wire in the blood
Sings below inveterate scars
And reconciles forgotten wars.
The dance along the artery
The circulation of the lymph
Are figured in the drift of stars
Ascend to summer in the tree
We move above the moving tree
In light upon the figured leaf
And hear upon the sodden floor
Below, the boarhound and the boar
Pursue their pattern as before
But reconciled among the stars.

Note that he's not at all self-conscious about resorting to triplets in the manner of Pope in his pentameters. But does this add or detract from what he is saying?

Exercise 18

Do a count of the syllables on every line and take note of the sound-correspondences.

What do we have in this passage? How would you characterize it? Make a beginning at least, or try.

This passage was followed by a verse paragraph of very long lines:

> At the still point of the turning world. Neither
> flesh nor fleshless;
> Neither from nor towards; at the still point,
> there the dance is,
> But neither arrest nor movement. And do
> not call it fixity,
> Where past and future are gathered. Neither
> movement from nor towards,
> Neither ascent nor decline. Except for the
> point, the still point,
> There would be no dance, and there is only
> the dance.
> I can only say, there we have been: but I
> cannot say where.
> And I cannot say, how long, for that is to
> place it in time.

Exercise 19

Again, count up the syllables per line and pay particular attention to the line endings.

What makes this passage work?

Exercise 20

Try replacing the words with cha-CHA's and OOM-pa's and the like or nonsense words and read aloud.

This is by no means easy, and if it begins to floor you, cease and desist.

Exercise 21

Read the three passages aloud in three voices, that is, using a number of different people or your own different voices.

Clearly, this is the author of "Prufrock" grown older and meditative, and some will find this seriousness a little hard to take after the fun of "Prufrock" and the delightful clutter of *The Waste Land* — and who knows, quite possibly a future generation of critics will give Eliot's later works a "reassessment." Nevertheless, right now, here we are: this is Eliot, sure of hand, at his *free verse* best — with no devil whispering in his ear.

Another protégée of Pound in the early days in England was fellow Pennsylvanian, born Hilda Doolittle (1886-1961), to whom he gave the nom de plume H. D. They'd met in 1904, while she was a student at Bryn Mawr, and re-met when she traveled to England in 1911. Pound was at that time involved in the Imagist Movement with its emphasis on lean diction and carefully chiseled images, and H. D. quickly fell under its spell. He sent poems by her in that idiom to *Poetry* and published others in his anthology *Des Imagistes* (1914).

H. D., whose love relationships, both with women and men, became as entangled as Pound's political views, left behind seven volumes of verse. At this time her reputation as a poet rests largely on her first volume, *Sea Garden* (1916), and in particular on the oft-anthologized flower poems in it, including the lead one, "Sea Rose":

Rose, harsh rose,
marred and with stint of petals,
meagre flower, thin.
spare of leaf,

more precious
than a wet rose
single on a stem—
you are caught in the drift.

Stunted, with small leaf,
you are flung on the sand,
you are lifted
in the crisp sand
that drives in the wind.

Can the spice-rose
drip such acrid fragrance
hardened in a leaf?

One thing that I'm sure you noted is the absence of capital letters at the head of each line. They occur only as needed, after a period to signal the beginning of a new thought, indeed as they would in prose. As I'm sure you also saw, there are three thoughts. The first, which occupies the first two stanzas, concerns how the sea rose looks, and a comparison is made with the "wet rose," meaning earth-born rose sparkling with dew. The second thought, which occurs in the third stanza, follows the movement of the sea rose from its being "caught in the drift" to its being "flung on the sand." The third thought, in the final stanza, is a *rhetorical question* comparing the fragrance of the earth-born rose, here referred to as a "spice rose," to that of the sea rose. The resulting impression is one of casualness or informality, which causes one to dwell longer than one ordinarily might on the flow of ideas and what's being said — that is, to read and re-read, sort of ebbing and flowing with the poet's tide. That tide, with full stops after the second, third, and last stanza is reminiscent of the rippling waves of the sea or, perhaps, of an orgasm.

Exercise 22

Be that as it may, let's subject this poem to our old routine: a syllable count and a replacing of the words with cha-CHA's and OOM-pa's and the like or nonsense words, which, of course, you'll read aloud, yes?

Like the sea rose itself, the *sound-correspondences* in this poem are very subtle and muted, so much so that it's easy to miss them or, worse yet, dismiss them. There's a modest amount of word and phrase repetition: "rose" in the first stanza; "you are lifted" and "you are flung" and "on the sand" and "in the crisp sand" in the third stanza; "leaf" in the first, third, and fourth stanzas. There are also modest amounts of initial *sound-correspondences:* "marred" and "meager" in the first stanza; "single" and "stem" in the second stanza; "stunted" and "small" in the third stanza. But something more yet remains to be said about *sound-correspondences* in this poem:

Exercise 23

Look more closely at them than I have above. Hint: keep a sharp eye on the vowels.

Did you discover anything interesting? I bet you did.

In human terms, the sea rose is most rare, a far cry from the common earthly rose. Its leaf is hard, and it's this leaf, not the flower, that holds its fragrance. This fragrance is acrid but still a fragrance, and it drips. Clearly, as Blake would have put it, more is meant here than meets the eye, wouldn't you say?

Exercise 24

Read this poem aloud, and consider using three different voices when doing so.

Physician as well as poet, William Carlos Williams (1883-1963) was born in Rutherford, New Jersey, of an American father and a Puerto Rican mother; hence there's a Latino dimension to him, which makes him of particular interest nowadays. He was to make Rutherford his lifelong home.

A friendship with Pound and H. D. began in their undergraduate days in Pennsylvania; Williams maintained his connection with Pound into the 1920s while seeking for a distinctive American voice. He published his first book, *Poems,* privately in 1909; his second, *The Tempers,* came out in 1913 with Pound's help. In the end, his major work, *Paterson,* in five books (1945-1958), celebrated just what Eliot in *The Waste Land* had deplored: the search for a community and imaginative expression in the modern city. Williams, too, was the recipient of numerous awards, including a Pulitzer Prize.

Like H. D., but with much greater concentration, Williams zeroed in on the line, to the point where it became his primary poetical unit. His line-breaks came to work "against" a poem's phrasing or syntax and helped to lay bare meaning, like a surgeon's scalpel. Williams's poem "The Dance" shows him at his best in this:

> In Breughel's great picture, The Kermess,
> the dancers go round, they go round and
> around, the squeal and the blare and the
> tweedle of bagpipes, a bugle and fiddles
> tipping their bellies (round as the thick-
> sided glasses whose wash they impound)
> their hips and their bellies off balance
> to turn them. Kicking and rolling about
> the Fair Grounds, swinging their butts, those
> shanks must be sound to bear up under such
> rollicking measures, prance as they dance
> in Breughel's great picture, The Kermess.

At first sight, this poem seems to be brimming with no-noes and an awful mess: lines ending in "and," "the," "about," "those," and "such," to say nothing of "thick-"; no terminal punctuation except for the first and last lines; and no initial capital letters on the lines except for the first one. When one looks more closely, it turns out that the line with which the poem begins and ends — "In Breughel's great picture, The Kermess" — acts as both a refrain and a frame, and contributes both to the circular movement of the dance and to the physical roundness of the dancers. The run-on lines within the frame reinforce this and add a certain hilarity in their unpredictability.

Exercise 25

A reading of this poem aloud would serve to drive this home. Do it several times, each time faster.

Looked at more closely yet, the poem consists of two separate statements, the second one announced by a period after "them" on the eighth line and a capital letter for "Kicking," the word right after it. There are *parallelisms* in both statements, but they are rhetorical rather than grammatical, reminiscent a little of the middle stanzas of Blake's "Tyger" ("And when thy heart began to beat, / What dread hand? & what dread feet?"). Sound and movement are the orders of the day. All of the *parallelisms*, disjointed as they are, imitate the speed and frenzy of the dance, and the movement of the observer's eyes are downward, from bellies and hips in the first statement to butts and shanks in the second. The observer's imaginary ear also "moves," from "the squeal and the blare and the tweedle of bagpipes, a bugle and fiddles" in the first statement to "rollicking measures" in the second.

Exercise 26

Another reading aloud is in order here, with different voices.

Sound-correspondences are almost all internal:"round" and "around" are prominent, and so too are "Grounds" and "sound"; their mates "impound" and "about" serve to reinforce at the ends of lines. "Tipping," "kicking," "rolling," "swinging," and "rollicking" add to the movement; the pure rhyme of "prance" and "dance" toward the end of the second statement parallels its all winding down.

Exercise 27

How about another reading, with lots of body language?

If anyone begins to dance, that's okay — hey!

In the end, this work is not so much an anti-poem as it is an anti-pedantic one, that is, it pits itself against the dry discourse of museum catalogue copy, whose author, in Williams's day, all too often would have turned out to be a European or would-be European know-it-all.

Exercise 28 (?)

Somehow, off the top of my head, this poem invites comparison with Swinburne's "Roundel" on page 287.

Which poem expresses "roundness" best, or was I asking you to compare apples with oranges?

Bostonian E. E. Cummings (1894-1962) began life innocently enough with a B.A. and M.A. from Harvard and then, during World War I, went on to drive an ambulance in France, where he was interned for a while for being friendly with a subversive. In the 1920s and 1930s, he divided his time between Paris, where he studied art, and New York's literary circles.

His first volume of verse, *Tulips and Chimneys,* appeared in 1923 and was followed by eleven others through the years. Almost from the beginning his style was marked by eccentric typography and punctuation, which, it's often said, grew out of a love affair with the typewriter. But there was more to it than that: as a visual artist, his blank page was, in its way, as much an artist's canvas as something for a writer to put words on.

Cummings's playfulness is indeed fetching, but one must not lose sight of the fact that it can sometimes mask deadly seriousness. A good case in point is his poem titled "in Just-" which deals with a very real social problem in our society today, the preying on innocent children by those who pretend to be something other than what they are. Largely through his typography, Cummings presents a world of spring and new love and growth, of first friendships — "eddieandbill" and "bettyandisbel" — and of puddles and mud pies, marbles, pretend-games, hop-scotch, jump rope, and dancing. It should be of balloons and whistling, too, but the one is a lure, a come-on, the other innocent pretense with the devil lurking underneath:

in Just-
spring   when the world is mud-
luscious the little
lame balloonman

whistles   far   and wee

and eddieandbill come

running frommarbles and
piracies and it's
spring

when the world is puddle-wonderful

the queer
old balloonman whistles
far and wee
and bettyandisbel come dancing

from hop-scotch and jump-rope and

it's
spring
and
the

goat-footed

balloonMan whistles
far
and
wee

The varying number of lines per stanza — 4, 5, 1, 4, 1, 4, 5 — reminds one of a piece of chewing gum that one has been at pains to stretch out from both ends, and note that initially, vowels and consonants are used ironically to show how the balloonman blends in: "when the world is mud-/luscious the little/lame ballonman/whistles far and wee." Beneath the surface is the *ballad*-like repetition of the balloonman's whistling, which, as if mocking the Sacred Three, occurs three times, each time with a variation — from his being "little" and "lame" to "queer" and "old" to "goat-footed" (in other words, satyr-like). Needless to say, this is to indicate the increasing proximity of danger and a tragedy possibly about to unfold.

It takes a special gift to do this sort of thing and do it well. Besides a fine sense of irony, also required is one of proportion and taste. Nevertheless —

Exercise 29

This deserves a read-through, with several voices for the children and a few more voices of varying degrees of sinisterness on the refrains.

However you did it, I hope you captured the contrast between the children's innocence and the balloonman's essentially evil nature.

Exercise 30

What do you say to an imitation? I bet you can give Cummings a run for his money on a computer keyboard and screen. But do be sure you have a poem or some semblance of one down on paper or on screen to begin with.

Having taken a cue from Pound and H. D. and, doubtless, numerous lesser lights regarding that traditionally razor-sharp left margin with its capital letters, Cummings pointed the way toward a new dimension in poetry, or so it has seemed: the combining of text and design, which has been all the rage as of late and will be dealt with in the next chapter.

As William Carlos Williams was a native of New Jersey and remained true to it to the end, so Carl Sandburg (1878-1967) was regarding Illinois, which, it's important to note, has been the home turf of many of our country's great orators, including Lincoln first and foremost. Largely self-educated, Sandburg became a Chicago newspaperman in his early thirties and began writing poetry. Idealizing Whitman, he met with instant success with a group of Chicago poems, published in the magazine *Poetry* in 1914 and a few years later in book form. Two more books of poetry and a collected works plus two books of folks songs followed through the years, and a biography of Lincoln that earned him a Pulitzer Prize.

In "Chicago," the best-known of his works, Sandburg captured the exuberance and excitement of that big city those many years ago in its heyday, and certainly he says it all as far as his style of *free verse* is concerned:

> Hog Butcher for the World,
> Tool Maker, Stacker of Wheat,
> Player with Railroads and the Nation's Freight Handler;
> Stormy, husky, brawling,
> City of the Big Shoulders:

They tell me you are wicked and I believe them, for I have
 seen your painted women under the gas lamps luring the
 farm boys.
And they tell me you are crooked and I answer: Yes, it is true I
 have seen the gunman kill and go free to kill again.
And they tell me you are brutal and my reply is: On the faces
 of women and children I have seen the marks of wanton
 hunger.
And having answered so I turn once more to those who sneer
 at this my city, and I give them back the sneer and say to
 them:
Come and show me another city with lifted head singing so
 proud to be alive and coarse and strong and cunning.
Flinging magnetic curses amid the toil of piling job on job,
 here is a tall bold slugger set vivid against the little soft cities;
Fierce as a dog with tongue lapping for action, cunning as a
 savage pitted against the wilderness,
  Bareheaded,
  Shoveling,
  Wrecking,
  Planning,
  Building, breaking, rebuilding,
Under the smoke, dust all over his mouth, laughing with white
 teeth,
Under the terrible burden of destiny laughing as a young man
 laughs,
Laughing even as an ignorant fighter laughs who has never lost
 a battle,
Bragging and laughing that under his wrist is the pulse, and un
 der his ribs the heart of the people,
     Laughing!

Laughing the stormy, husky, brawling laughter of Youth, half-naked, sweating, proud to be Hog Butcher, Tool Maker, Stacker of Wheat, Player with Railroads and Freight Handler to the Nation.

Needless to say, the mainstays of this poem are *parallelism* and *anaphora*, but the poem's success depends on its creator's knowing when enough is enough or, more to the point, his ability to generate variety and at the same time the facility with which he was able to shift from one element of statement to another.

So what have we here? A stanza consisting of five lines followed by another of twenty lines. In the first of the stanzas, there's our old chum the *apostrophe*, five of them in fact. These are echoed in abbreviated phrases at the end of the poem, which all go toward giving the whole thing a shape, a structure.

The second stanza starts off with seven long lines consisting of three *parallel* statements beginning with "they tell," and this is followed by a transitional statement beginning with "And having answered…cunning," which ends with a full stop. The next two statements ("Flinging…" and "Fierce…") are also *parallel*, this by virtue of their initial *f*'s. The second of these statements sets the stage for the list of single words that follow, beginning with "Bareheaded" and ending with "Building, breaking, rebuilding."

The comma following "rebuilding" leads into a new set of *parallelisms*, which bring together a variety of repeated elements. There's the *couplet* beginning with "Under," and within it, the words "laughing" and "laughs." In the next line, comes "Bragging and laughing," and then in the next, "Laughing!" The same word leads off the final line before the *echo* of the beginning, where the initial *b* and *l* are brought together in "brawling laughter." In other words, there's nothing accidental about this poem. The artistry is in its appearing to be bustling.

I've found that this kind of verse has very strong supporters and equally strong detractors. Some think that it's the only way to write *free verse* — indeed, consider it synonymous with *free verse* — others that it's a cop-out. Either way, you should have some hands-on with it, if only just to say that you did.

Exercise 31

Read it aloud, omitting the first five lines, "Bareheaded" to "rebuilding," and the last three lines. Try it two more times, omitting two and then one of the items.

Before pushing on to the nitty-gritty, it's time to take a little stock. Go back to our modern *free verse* models and read them over again: Pound's "Return" on page 313; "Time present and time past" from Eliot's "Burnt Norton" on page 316; H. D.'s "Sea Rose"on page 319; Williams's "The Dance" on page 322; Cummings's "in Just-" on page 324; and Sandburg's "Chicago" on page 327. Which one do you like the best or seems as if it might hold out possibilities for you to pursue? Can you possibly guess what's coming next? Bet-bet-bet you can —

Exercise 32

Compose a response in the style of that piece. Twelve to fifteen lines will do it. When you're done, read what you've written aloud. This is a very serious matter, so be sure not to laugh or even smile at someone else's if you're in a group.

Do you feel comfortable with that poet's style or close to it in some way? Well then, it's time for a little in-depth pursuing of more poems by him or her in an anthology. You might at this time, if you haven't done so already, acquire one; if not, there's always the library. Either of the following will do: *The Norton Anthology of Poetry*, or *The Norton Anthology of Modern and Contemporary Poetry*. Once you've read that author's poems in it, you might, if you're still enamored, go on and get hold of whole books of his or her poetry, and do nothing but read-read-read, and this means absorb and think as well.

It's possible that you'll have found yourself thereby or discovered a "way in." But whether or not you have done so, you will certainly want to shop around some more and see what others wrote after the above-named poets. May I suggest the following as starters: works by John Ashberry, W. H. Auden, Elizabeth Bishop, Seamus Heaney, Ted Hughes, Denise Levertov, Robert Lowell, Charles Olson, Sylvia Plath, Adrienne Rich, Theodore Roethke, Anne Sexton, Wallace Stevens, Dylan Thomas, James Wright, and of course the beat poets Gregory Corso, Lawrence Ferlinghetti, and Allen Ginsberg. Nor should one neglect our guests — Ruth Fainlight, Nina Cassian, and Jeffrey Greene, whose books you'll find listed in my bibliography.

Exercise 33

At some point in your reading, you'll want to take another look at the poem you composed in the previous exercise or your response to one of the poems by our guests that you wrote in Exercise 5. Decide on one of four possibilities: leave it or them alone, thereby declaring it or them done; revise it or them; tear it or them up and start afresh; do nothing.

Sneaking Up On Your Own First Free Verse Poem

"'Tis not enough no harshness gives offense; / The sound must seem an echo to the sense." So said eighteenth-century poet Alexander Pope, as you'll recall. Well, all fine and good where traditional verse is concerned, but it's simply not enough when it comes to *free verse.* The appearance of a *free verse* poem as well as how it sounds must be harmonious with its meaning; indeed, both should be unique to that meaning.

It Has to Sound "Right"

In actual fact, where *free verse* is concerned, sounds should do a bit more than "seem an echo to the sense" in most cases. They should help establish a mood or contribute to a tone and thereby enhance your sense. Bear in mind, too, that the world is your apple where a choice of sounds is concerned, meaning that you, as a poet writing *free verse*, are utterly at liberty to use anything — yes, even complete rhymes as Eliot did in "Burnt Norton," if it happens to suit your fancy or purpose.

On the other hand, you mustn't become so enamored of the sounds you're using as to lose sight of your meaning. To do so would be tantamount to creating word-salad, and even as a form of rebellion, that won't do, it simply won't. Why? Because it's been done too many times already and by now it's just plain boring, as boring as saying the same word or a phrase over and over like a mantra. If people found it on a printed page, they'd simply shrug and move on; if they heard you reading it aloud, they'd just tune out. So what, some of you are saying? So plenty; you're supposed to be communicating — poetry is a special form of communication between yourself, the poet, and others who want to or may be persuaded to hear what you have to say in your language.

Let's take a look, for starters, at William Carlos Williams's "The Red Wheelbarrow":

so much depends
upon

a red wheel
barrow
glazed with rain
water

beside the white
chickens

Who would deny that this short, utterly simple statement works? The question is, in terms of Williams's choice of sounds, why does it work?

Sometimes it pays to mess up a pretty poem like this. Let me, yes? Look:

A really lot relies
on

a fiery wheel
barrow

shiny with rain
water

next to some white
chickens

Now there's a real ugly, wouldn't you say? And what makes it so? After all, I've written pretty much the same thing, haven't I?

One can only conclude that Williams chose his sounds and *sound-correspondences* with extreme care — with the aim of supporting the peacefulness of his scene. This meant opting for soft sounds like the *s* in "so" and "depends"; the *p* in "depends" and "upon"; the *uh* in "much," "upon," and "a"; the *oh* in "so" and "barrow"; the *ee* in "de" and "wheel"; the *eh* in "pends" and "red"; the long *a* in "glazed" and "rain"; the *r* in "red" and "rain"; the *l* in "wheel" and "glazed"; and the *w* and related *wh* in "wheel," "with," and "water." These tended to tone down or even mute the few hard sounds, like the *d* in "depends," "red," and "beside" and the *g* in "glazed." Note that his choices here are in stark contrast to those in "The Dance" above. Indeed, one cannot help but recall the opening stanza of the "Elegy Written in a Country Church-yard," where, as we've already seen, poet Thomas Gray created the same kind of peacefulness:

The curfew tolls the knell of parting day,
The lowing herd wind slowly o'er the lea,
The plowman homeward plods his weary way,
And leaves the world to darkness and to me.

Exercise 34 (?)

A comparison between what Williams did in "Red Wheel-barrow" and Gray in the stanza above might be in order here. Care to give it a whirl?

At the risk of belaboring, let's engage in a little more exploring with respect to this matter.

Exercise 35

Select one or more of the samples by Pound, Eliot, or H. D. that I gave above, and focus on their sounds.

Illuminating, wasn't it?

It sometimes happens, when one is in a group, that someone other than the author of a poem will come up with a word that seems to "work better" than the poet's choice. If this happened to you, be sure to chew on it, together or apart. It can get a little hairy, no? One begins to have a yearning to — to —

Exercise 36

Can you play around with, meaning juggle, the echoes in the following sentence to make it sound "better": "She sits with tears on her cheek, her chin in her hand, the child at the window, his nose pressed to the glass."

Bear in mind that there's no right answer as there'd be to a "problem" in math. Two people and, who knows, maybe more than that may come up with quite different results that are all striking in their way.

How do you know when the sounds are "right" in a poem of yours? Simply by working at them until you get a sense that something is settled. Less desirable but acceptable, obviously, would be a point when you feel that what you have is the best solution under the circumstances — something that's almost "right" but not quite.

Exercise 37

Take in hand that free verse poem of yours from Exercise 33 and look more closely at the sounds you chose. Is there anything you'd care to change? If so, change it. If not, try to reach some understanding with yourself as to why those particular sounds work.

Line Arrangement: It's Simply a Matter of Logic?

Before our modern era, poems were arranged by the typesetter, who also at times supplied punctuation. With the arrival of free verse, poets insisted on doing their own, as one can well understand. Take a moment to look back at the poems by Pound, Eliot, H.D., Williams, Sandburg, and Cummings in this chapter, and note how appropriate the arrangement of each is to the text and how different the arrangements are from one another.

Is there some rule of thumb to follow where the disposition of the lines in your own free verse poems is concerned? Yes and no. You are free to arrange your lines in any way you wish, and they may be of any length. The only consideration is that your arrangements support the sense of poems of yours, in other words that they feel "right" to you — though, of course, inevitably it becomes a matter of whether readers in the know agree.

Let's consider William Carlos Williams's "Red Wheelbarrow" again, and explore his idea of rightness where line arrangement is concerned by looking at his other options. Mind you, I'll not for a moment be suggesting that he went through any of what follows; I'm simply using the poem as an example. If you recall, "The Red Wheelbarrow" is a single sentence broken up into four stanzas of two lines each, the first of which in each instance consists of three or four syllables, the second of two:

so much depends
upon

a red wheel
barrow

glazed with rain
water

beside the white
chickens

Now let's go as far as we can in one direction: try the text written out as sentence:

> So much depends upon a red wheel barrow glazed with rain water beside the white chickens

It doesn't seem to say very much, does it? In fact, one's reaction is likely to be, "So what else is new?"

Nor does writing it out as a single stanza offer much of an improvement:

so much depends
upon
a red wheel
barrow
glazed with rain
water
beside the white
chickens

Those pauses between the stanzas are truly necessary, it would seem.

How about it if we were to get rid of all those short lines and create something like this:

so much depends upon
a red wheel barrow
glazed with rain water
beside the white chickens

No, that doesn't seem to do the trick either.

So, are all four of the poet's stanzas necessary? What about two instead:

so much depends
upon
a red wheel
barrow
glazed with rain
water

beside the white
chickens

That seems better, but there's an awkward split between the barrow and the chickens.

So how about this instead:

so much depends
upon

a red wheel
barrow
glazed with rain
water

beside the white
chickens

No, that's not IT either because now too much of the burden falls on the barrow and its glaze.

Four stanzas seem to be the answer, then, but what about the arrangement of words within each of them? Here are three possibilities:

1. so much
depends upon

a red
wheel barrow

glazed with
rain water

beside the
white chickens

2. so
much depends upon

a
red wheel barrow

glazed
with rain water

beside
the white chickens

3. so much depends
upon

a red
wheel barrow

glazed
with rain water

beside the
white chickens

Dizzying, isn't it? And sobering, I hope.

So what makes the arrangement that Williams opted for a successful one? Focus is the answer. And that focus cannot be too long any more than it can be too short; the following won't do either —

So
much
depends
upon

a
red
wheel
barrow

glazed
with
rain
water

beside
the
white
chickens

No, it must be just so, with the first stanza introducing —

so much depends
upon

— and those that follow each presenting a picture, a very precise picture, which it is necessary for readers or, if you will, partakers of his vision, to have a view of part by part —

a red wheel
barrow

glazed with rain
water

beside the white
chickens

Concomitant with this scene that Williams was inviting us to behold as he beheld it is the rhythm or cadence that results from each shorter line following each longer line — which seems to underline his vision, as if he were saying, "Look — LOOK!"

Exercise 38

Go back to one or more of the samples that I gave above by Pound, Eliot, or H. D. and try it or them out with different stanza and line arrangements as I did with "The Red Wheelbarrow."

Some people fail to realize that this matter of line arrangement in *free verse* is extremely critical in that it affects how a poem is going to be read and possibly viewed. So at the risk of belaboring:

Exercise 39

Return to Marianne Moore's poem "The Fish" on pages 156-157 and copy it out with all the margins flush left.

Do you see what I mean? What happened to those cutesies? Did they swim away, or what?

Sometimes it turns out that someone comes up with an arrangement of the lines of a poem that seems better than the original by the poet. This requires discussion, no? Bear in mind that the poet may well have thought of that arrangement, too, and rejected it for some reason. What could that reason have been?

Exercise 40

Take the following sentence or your revision of it in Exercise 36 and try three or four different stanza and line arrangements: "She sits with tears on her cheek, her chin in her hand, the child at the window, his nose pressed to the glass."

Each arrangement gives a different effect, does it not? Which one do you prefer? Why?

Exercise 41

Once more take in hand that free verse poem of yours from Exercise 37 and try various line and stanza arrangements.

Don't be surprised if, after seemingly endless shuffling around, you come back to the arrangement you originally had! It happens, it happens. . . .

Silent and Not-So-Silent Punctuation

When most folks hear the word "punctuation," their first reaction is to think "How boring" and begin heading for the hills. But do not do so, please. As you'll soon realize, punctuation, both real and understood, is a most necessary ingredient of poetry, especially of *free verse.*

As I'm sure you know, there are four main punctuation marks — a comma, semicolon, colon, and period — and there are four more — the question mark, exclamation point, dash, and ellipsis (three or four dots) — for use in special circumstances. In the olden days like, let's say, before the nineteenth century, poets often used the four main ones to indicate lengths of silence rather than grammatical relationships, so — I'm saying it — do feel free to use your arsenal either way.

You should bear in mind, though, that readers tend to pause at the end of a line, yes, even when there's no punctuation mark there — and even when the line's sense or grammatical structure is incomplete. And so, quite often the result is that each line tends to become a thing unto itself, a poetical unit, with its own internal rhythm and *sound-correspondences.*

Certainly something of the kind happens when one reads "The Red Wheelbarrow," which has no punctuation whatsoever. In case you didn't realize this, here it is yet once more:

so much depends
upon

a red wheel
barrow

glazed with rain
water

beside the white
chickens

Look more closely and you'll realize that in each stanza there's a different duration to the pause after the first and second lines; the pause after the second line is a trifle longer. The result is a kind of fine-tuning of the poem's separate images, as if Williams were giving us and we, as readers, were receiving via his hand — or sensibility, if you will — a last little turn to a pair of binoculars.

So should you or should you not use end-of-line punctuation marks? If you look back at the poems by our three guests at the beginning of this chapter and then at the samples by Pound, T. S. Eliot, H. D., E. E. Cummings, and Sandburg as well as at Williams's "Kermess," you will see that practice varies considerably. So as with them, you'll have to decide for yourself, but the important thing is that you do so consciously — and indeed, henceforth with each and every poem that you write.

A final word: each pause on a line, wherever it occurs and whether it be with or without punctuation, brings with it a silence, and in *free verse,* silences can be as much a part of sound as the utterances they come between, functioning much as negative space, or the space around, does in sculpture, both traditional and modern.

One can also speak of the qualities of a silence (as opposed to its duration), depending on the word or words that have come before and after it on a line or lines.

It's possible as well to speak of the additional sound-coloring that comes from ambient noises in a room — like a car horn blowing — when one is reading a poem aloud and even in one's head. Whew, heavy stuff!

To anticipate your questions here, in the next chapter we'll be considering a number of different ways of intentionally adding sound to your poetry.

Exercise 42

Time for another party! So find that stub of candle and light it, put a fresh flower in the little vase, and get out a bottle of wine. What else to do? Why read-read-read: all the poems in this chapter, out loud of course, keeping a sharp look-out for their silences. Do it in a group or with a like-minded friend or two, or even alone.

9

Getting it all together & Then Some

At a certain point in your reading of works by other poets, you should begin tapering off and then pretty much stop altogether so as to delightfully and deliciously concentrate on your own stuff. If this doesn't happen of itself, make it happen — just stop reading.

By this time, you should have decided on a place to work, Your Place as a Poet, and stocked it with the writing implement(s) and paper of your choice and at least a dictionary or *Roget's Thesaurus.* If you haven't done so, do it now, understanding that it's part of a contract with yourself regarding your seriousness of purpose as a poet.

Settle down in Your Place, and with your stuff at hand, go back to your answers to the critical questions that I posed in chapter one:

— *for whom do you want to write or are you trying to write?*

— *would you like to have or do you indeed have an agenda as a poet?*

— does your writing lean toward the formal (for example, Milton) or informal (for example, Wordsworth) side or would you like it so to lean?

Make changes to your answers if you feel like it; if you haven't answered the questions yet, give it a whirl now. Just remember that this isn't a school-test — indeed, the questions are much harder than anything you'd ordinarily find on such a test, aren't they?

If you aren't keeping your notes for poems that you'd like to write and early drafts in one place, like in a notebook, you should begin doing so now, and at the same time, you should get into the habit of spending some time every day in Your Place as a Poet, even if it's just to tinker or stare at a wall or out a window. Sooner or later — and this is likely to come about quite naturally — you'll select a passage from among your notes, even just a few words, and begin "working it up" by adding more words, substituting others, rearranging them, and so on. Sometimes, especially at the beginning, you may have to force the issue and deliberately select a passage to work on; don't be surprised if at a certain point you realize that what you selected isn't the Thing but that something else is. In other words, your initial selection may simply act as a catalyst toward influencing you to choose something else that is the Thing. You may also find yourself working on a poem to a certain point and then dropping it to work on another, and then going back to the first, and so on. It happens, take it from me, it happens.

In the end, you should feel that each word in your poem is the Right One and that it's in its Right Place, and that goes for punctuation marks, too. Where the latter's concerned, strive for a kinship with your readers through the clarity that periods, colons, semicolons, and commas can bring, but at the same time, don't neglect to use them to bring out your inner rhythms.

So when is a poem finished? It's usually when you feel a sense of completeness, like nothing more can be done to it. Is a poem ever Done in a first draft? I guess it happens, but I'd certainly be mighty suspicious of one that did. Give it the test of time, I say: that is, lay it aside for a while and then take it out and have a look to see if it is indeed cast in cement.

I asked our three guest poets about their practice regarding revisions and when they know that a poem is done. And here are their answers.

Ruth Fainlight wrote:

> There's no pattern for the amount of revision a poem might have. Sometimes – though rarely – after a few drafts a poem seems as finished as it will be. But usually, almost always, I might take it through as many as fifteen or even twenty drafts – and then, after it has "rested" for a while, find I still can do more.
>
> Some poems I work on even after they have been published. In a few cases, poems have been changed between first magazine publication and appearing in a collection, and then been altered again for a Selected (and I've had two Selected; I think I made changes to some poems between those two volumes). So – this moves into a reply to the second question – when do I know a poem is finished? The true answer is that it depends WHEN I ask myself that question.

As for when she knows a poem is done:

> There is a point when you can't do any more so you say it is finished – but then, later, you see things you want to change and can't believe you didn't notice them earlier.

Nina Cassian is her usual quixotic self, but can one really believe her:

> Generally I make very few revisions. Being an utterly spontaneous creature, I find that usually the first draft seems to turn out to be the right one.

And she added regarding completion:

> One never knows for sure if a poem is done — I just hope it is.

Jeffrey Greene was his usual serious self where the matter of revision is concerned:

> Revision is a mysterious, often more magical process than the original version/vision. I have never written an unrevised poem, and revisions can be relatively minor (a gift), to a decades-long process. The trick is simple: be outrageously passionate about what you write at first and then be willing to violate your most precious line for something special overall. Often that change will come from a close friend, editor, or a wonderful poet.

As for when he knows a poem is done:

> You should no longer interfere with a poem that has a life of its own, particularly if it's very special to you. You should write the next and the next.

So You're Writing Poems, What's Next?

In the good old days of my youth and before, a poet's options were extremely limited. One got one's poems accepted by a magazine, often by hook or crook, and then after one had a certain magical number of them in print, usually ten, one went on to find a publisher for a whole book. When it comes to hide-bound traditionalists, this is still the tried and true and only way to go. But, happily, it's not the only route that a poet of today can take. There are other options, as indeed there always have been, except that nowadays, thanks especially to recent developments in modern technology, there are many many more.

First of all, there are any number of things that you can write, besides poems intended for inclusion in a literary magazine, that is, short poems that can be read in a single sitting. For starters, you can write longer poems; in fact, what's to prevent you from writing a series of longer poems that can be brought together in a book or indeed a book-length poem? Your longer poem could conceivably be a made-up story with characters, dialogue, and description, in other words, it could turn into a short story or even a novel. After all, what else is that magnificent entity called *Paradise Lost* but a long story in verse? And if this is your bent, you should take some time out, before settling on this track, to learn more about fiction writing, namely how to create believable characters and realistic dialogue and description.

A play in verse is another possibility. Think of Shakespeare's plays and *Samson Agonistes,* and more recently, of T. S. Eliot's *Murder in the Cathedral* and *The Cocktail Party.* Once again, before venturing forth, this will require some study on your part, about such ingredients as structure and format as well as the creation of character and dialogue. Nor would you be limited to writing for the stage nowadays; film, television, and the Internet are also possibilities. Productions can be as simple as a single, spot-lighted actor standing on a stage in front of a video-projected set; on a computer, it would be simpler yet, with the whole "show" pre-recorded.

This is as good a place as any to mention another possibility: your creation of a *prose poem.* What is it? A *prose poem* is an entity defined as such by its author. Perhaps the most famous example of one from our modern era is Allen Ginsberg's (1926-1997) *Howl,* which is book-length. Here's a sample:

> I saw the best minds of my generation destroyed by
> madness, starving hysterical naked,
> dragging themselves through the negro streets at

dawn looking for an angry fix,
angelheaded hipsters burning for the ancient heavenly connection to the starry dynamo in the machinery of night,
who poverty and tatters and hollow-eyed and high sat up smoking in the supernatural darkness of cold-water flats floating across the tops of cities contemplating jazz,
who bared their brains to Heaven under the El and saw Mohammedan angels staggering on tenement roofs illuminated,
who passed through universities with radiant cool eyes hallucinating Arkansas and Blake-light tragedy among the scholars of war,
who were expelled from the academies for crazy & publishing obscene odes on the windows of the skull,...

I cannot here resist including one by me, written at age twenty-three and revised now at seventy-four:

Sundays in New York.

Empty bags in the wind and the dust flying. The streets hollow, futile, hushed, like a last-whispered prayer. Between the buildings scarred and mute, a cheerless sunlight filters. Sentinel ash cans mark the way for a solitary stroller walking his Sunday dog. From a distance and nearer, a lone jalopy jogs along full of family good-feeling. Soft-talking stragglers lingering on the steps of churches turn to stare at it, offended; while rollicking children, freshly released, bouncing balls as if their lives depended on it, scatter out of the path of the oncoming, clattering fenders.

In the houses all around, neighbors are sitting down to a leisurely Sunday breakfast; he, with his paper, she, with the small talk of days gone by. Dishes scattered about the table, papers rustling, talk. Soon, more dishes appear, new papers arrive, more talk. It's lunch-time...

The classical music on the radio, the ebullient church choruses, the soft and lilting popular songs that become louder, more raucous as Sunday blooms. All so far away, so so far away, even in their cacophonous blending far away…

Sundays in New York.

Gold dust on a heap of bricks or in the ruts of cobblestone streets. Or when it rains, and Christmas trees and trinkets dance, do a tumble of lights in standing pools. Or when it snows and spluttering ashes lemon and gray renew their death in a white fire.

Uptown, in the sixties, seventies, and eighties east and west, all the houses look alike, and all the people think alike, and the curtains all alike are drawn. And you'd wonder if you were to pass, whether there were any in there, whether there were any alive in there at all.

Hey you! Are you alive in there? Wake up! What are you trying to hide in there, what shut out! Hey! Are you dead in there or what! Hey!

Sometimes out of a dark and forlorn alley a bewildered, bewhiskered Rip Van Winckel wanders. People call him a bum, a beggar, a derelict, a tramp, a homeless, but with eyes wide and glittering, and despite a scrawny finger poking through a tattered glove, he'll tip his dusty hat to you, smile at you and bid you a good day as if he'd discovered a new universe…

Sundays in New York.

Along Fifth Avenue up and down, people clean- smelling, clean-looking, happy (oh happiness sublime), strolling, talking, dreaming, strolling. The shop windows displaying the latest death heads and priapi. Strolling arm in arm. Chatting.

O stroll into my heart, why don't you!

Or better, peep into my guts — dirty to you, I guess. Smile then if you can; pull your gloves on and off with that oh so mechanical fluster!

How I've longed sometimes to walk off the earth, to be alone in space, free-flowing — to be. Yes, to be…

Sundays in New York.

And here even the Gods receive no mail.

And so you get up, and it's late, and so you're sick, and it's the same as always. And you say to yourself that it was he last night, he, or she. And then that expectation (always the same) of a hand, a human hand on your shoulder, some warm and living presence nuzzling close to you, some almost human whisper in a tone of consolation. But he, she has fled, probably to church — there was the mark the head made on the pillow — and you are once again imprisoned, alone, in Sunday.

I tell you it's the same as someone fucking you and screaming curses at you, this Sunday with its whirring silence and muffled car horns and neighbors clattering dishes in their kitchens!..

Sundays in New York.

With a will, life is done.

In the museums, the pristine museums, always the same stony facades. The same intonations, inflections, the ah's, the oh's, the beyootifuls, the grands. The same little boys chasing each other down the glowy marble halls; the same little girls tittering at the detumescent penises of glad-eyed Apollos; the same Brooklynites speaking French and making themselves feel foreign and important; the same students bent in musty corners, examining with furrowed brows a broken pot.

But after all, consider: Plato didn't fling away his millions to found a Republic. Also, the Knights Templar always managed never to draw blood; they just stunned their prey with a cudgel the same way you'd swat a nasty fly on a hot summer day…

On the one hand, polytheistic and hilarious; on the other, pensive and methodical. Dionysian, Apollonian. Manic-depressive.

In his cell the creature sits, gazing out of green eyes—at nothing in particular. His chin rests on his paws, the ends of which dangle limply over the side of his bunk. Suddenly, he rises, glides easily, muscle by muscle, to the ground, looks scowlingly at his audience amidst ohs and ahs, paces up and down to consider the matter, then deflates all at once into an impassive heap, licks a sleek black paw, blinks an eye, rolls his head from side to side, has one more long and weary gaze at his peanut-wielding benefactors, and then like "a good kitty" falls into a deep and enviable sleep…

Sundays in New York.

Uptown in Harlem, the good people go to church and the bad people go to church and everybody else in between. Bible thumpers and sermon-quoters, and the original Uncle Tom, so help me. Another, swaying on a street corner, overcoat all awry, arms shot out in a tragic pose, eyes bulging bloodshot out of sockets, will commend the day with a loud guffaw, flip away the time with a cigarette, either scrounged or collected with a careful fingernail from the gutterside, bow to the ladies with a noble demean, and chuckle at the hump-hipped coquettes whom he cannot, will never afford…

Muchacho, arriba! Time to go, time to go to work.

Hell no, it's Sunday! Muchacho, go anyway…

Senorita, give me your hand, your dark and dainty hand, and let's go for a walk — did I say, dance? — no, walk, in the Park…

Sundays in New York.

Downtown, where the streets are crooked and bent, and the houses are always redolent of the same dinners warmed over, an old shawled nana leans into the world from a flower-potted window sill. She used to be married to a guy named Pop, remember him? He was the one who had the candy store on the corner. You know which one I mean.

Up and down Houston, near Katz's, geezers rich geezers poor gently bob their chins at one another, discussing, sometimes not so softly, what's new, whatever is new, on this, the Sun's day — while among them, youth walks apart, its soul flung out like the first jubilant cast of a fisherman, making all the music in the world superfluous and all of the paintings a sham,

Along Canal, old-time Cantonese, Taiwanese, mainlanders, Koreans, Japanese, Burmese, Tibetans, and Filipinos from the north and south. Did I leave anyone out?

Hey, where do the Indians and Pakistanis hang?

Let's go eat...

Down by the Bowery, smoke-filled honky-tonks revive for a moment the glory of a golden past. All from yesterday and all the same, the alchies, the junkies, the two-bit con men, the punchies, the played-out fags, all wander in, have a beer and a lookaround, then wander out again to a place up the block just the same. Sometimes an old time gal wrapped in satin and lace will give you a slow, somnolent dance in ragtime, blow wisps of hair out of her face, flash you a smile as she passes. Her thighs, heavy once, knew how to grip a man, bold him down, and her breasts are so huge, you could bury your whole head in them, sob your heart out if you wanted to. For only a beer she'll sit beside you, pat your knee consolingly, and talk to you of yesterday...

Sundays in New York.

A family's off to visit the relatives in the suburbs. The mother bulging in her Sunday suit, keeping a wary eye on the children, straightening a hat here, a tie there, buttoning a coat, unbuttoning a coat, fingers busy, always busy, lips grim, pressed tightly together. The father languorous, leaning against a column, fumbling with a box of candy he doesn't quite know what to do with, dreaming of the many things he'd rather be doing, trying to make it appear as if he weren't with them, dreaming perhaps that he and they are in two different worlds, continua — not realizing that the dreaming that he loves so is lost without something to dream against...

A train arrives, whisking bits of paper, dust, ruffling hair. Again more buttoning, unbuttoning of coats. An awkward, frantic effort to drag the children on. Finally they board, are gone, whisking bits of paper, dust...

Sometimes I too have longed to ride the subway on a Sunday, have longed, with a flower-pot hat on my head, stockings sheer, shoes smooth suede brushed down, a simple suit set off by a simple sprig of flowers, to carry a box of candy too; have longed to ride out far somewhere where there are trees, real flowers; have longed to leave it there somewhere. Just this and nothing more...

The bars empty early in the evening. Monday's a serious day. The streets forlorn, asleep. Everything shut tight, bolted down as if for good. Only a solitary stroller walking his Sunday dog.

Exercise 1 (?)

Writing prose poems *can be great fun — once one loses one's fear of them, or realizes that one's got nothing to fear. How about it, care to give it a whirl?*

You may have begun wondering at this point as to how one distinguishes between what is and what is not a poem. Technically, one can call anything that one writes a poem, even a single word, even an *onomatopoeic* word like

"Baroom!" But-but-but — let me put it in a nutshell: you need at least one more vote besides your own, and I don't mean from the cat or the candle.

Another alternative to going the traditional print-publishing route as a poet is to combine your poems with music in some way. I've already mentioned song-writing, and you'll recall that we even took a whack at writing some lyrics in chapter seven. Of course, if you don't compose music yourself, there's a danger here that texts of yours will become a subservient part of a musical work listed as by the composer. The study of music is a long, involved process, and I don't recommend it unless it's really your bent. However, it's possible for a text of yours to be read against music or with music in between, and you don't necessarily have to use live music; with permission, you've got a whole world of CDs to choose from. You can even make a CD of your own of you reading your poems aloud with background or in-between music and even possibly put it all up on a website.

Exercise 2 (?)

> *If you like what you did, consider recording it, which should be a fairly easy thing to do, considering how far you've come already.*

Combining your poetry with something visual is another route that you can take. And here I must warn you of a similar danger: that unless you yourself are graphically inclined, you run the risk of seeing your text overshadowed by someone else's design elements.

The simplest thing you can do respecting this sort of thing is to select a typeface and ornaments for your poems. I did this with some traditional poems in my novel *Bagatelle • Guinevere.* For example, here's one, utilizing a first line from Lorca:

VERDE, QUE TE QUIERO, VERDE

What's to stop you from doing something similar with your own poems? And you can go further yet: you can use graphic designs and photos with your poems to create a handmade book (called a *chapbook*) or put it all up on a website or on a DVD or both. Expertise with graphic design for this purpose is fairly easy to come by, provided, of course, that you have some talent in that direction

A *concrete poem*, where the visual shapes of the words make a picture, is yet another possibility. This has been around, in English at least, since George Herbert (1593-1633), and here's his most celebrated venture in this subgenre, "Easter Wings":

Lord, who createdst man in wealth and store,
Though foolishly he lost the same,
Decaying more and more
Till he became
Most poore:
With thee
O let me rise
As larks, harmoniously,
And sing this day thy victories:
Then shall the fall further the flight in me.

My tender age in sorrow did begin;
And still with sicknesses and shame
Thou didst so punish sin,
That I became
Most thinne.
With thee
Let me combine,
And feel this day thy victory;
For, if I imp my wing on thine,
Affliction shall advance the flight in me.

As you would very likely imagine, I'm not a great fan of this concrete sort of thing because *sound-correspondence* and rhythm, the two staples of verse, don't figure in it or do so only minimally.

Nevertheless, here's my opus:

r
 a
    i
        n

Exercise 3

Now where's yours? Use a line or word from one of your own poems if you wish or make up a suitable candidate.

I for one prefer stand-alone graphics to this sort of thing, and nowadays, thanks largely to computers, there are any number of things one can do with respect to combining text and graphics. Just for fun —

Exercise 4

Take one of your poems or a short piece of prose and select a picture or graphic to go with it; this can be by you or something you grab from a magazine or the Internet. Combine them in a tasteful way in a graphics program or just with paper and glue or plain old Scotch tape. If yours is a practical and down-to-earth nature, consider making a greeting card or postcard to send to someone close to you.

Finally, there's the possibility of creating multimedia works consisting of your poems along with both visual and musical content, and here I must warn you of another danger, that of losing focus. You must decide — and this must be fairly early on — if your multimedia work is or is to be a composite of poetry, music, and graphics, or is to be poetry supported by music and graphics. DVDs and the Web, including your own website or blog, are the obvious venues for this sort of thing, but one mustn't rule out live performance at local cafes and the like.

For some of you, especially those just starting out as poets, all of the above may be a little premature; understandably, you may want to get some finished poems under your belt first. Others among you, regardless of where you're at, will immediately see that this is the way, and in that case, what can I say, but GO TO IT!

Sharing Your Work with Others: AKA (That Dreadful Word) Publishing

As a poet, your career begins as *Paradise Lost* ends — the world is all before you — and as I have indicated above, there are many roads to follow. In other words, I've defined "publishing" broadly to mean getting the word out about your work. Every route is fraught with some difficulty; the important thing is to persevere and not give in to despair – unless, of course, it feeds, delightfully, into your work.

Let's begin with print publishing, and for a comprehensive overview, may I recommend *Poet Power*, by Thomas A. Williams. As I said, one normally begins by getting poems into magazines, by which I mean literary magazines, especially those devoted to serious contemporary poetry, as opposed to more popular mass-market types like women's, sports, outdoors, or hobby magazines. Exhaustive lists can be found in the latest editions of the *Dustbooks Directory of Poetry Publishers* and *Poet's Market;* there's a more selective list in *The Literary Press and Magazine Directory,* put out by the Council of Literary Magazines and Presses (CLMP). The Reference section of any well-stocked public library should have all three, but if you're planning on a long campaign or do things at odd hours like me, it might be worth your while to invest in your own copy of one, two, or all three. In Appendix II, I've included a list of literary magazines culled from the latest *Dustbooks Directory* who say they're willing to publish new poets, that is, those who haven't had a work in print yet. However, be aware — painfully aware — that literary magazines are known to have a very short life span, generally because the editors have moved on to something else or the movers-and-shakers have run out of money. So it's always a good idea to check the mag out first— either online or through a telephone directory— to make sure it's still a going enterprise.

Pinpointing the right magazines for your work is no piece of cake, by any means. Ideally, you should take a look at a copy of each prospective candidate, and if you're in or near a big city or a sizable college or university, you may find some at a library or in a literary bookstore. But the best way is probably going to be to order a copy directly from a magazine; no need to be completely up-front and tell them what you're after. When you've got one in your hands, examine it carefully and sensibly. Sometimes it helps to set a poem of yours in the font the magazine uses, print it out, and paste it onto one of the magazine's pages. Does your poem fit, does it stick out for the right reason (or reasons) — or wrong one (or ones)? Either way, don't be too discouraged or too sure of yourself.

With a list of likely candidates in hand, check their entries in one of the directories to see how many poems at a time each one recommends that you submit — usually it's three. If one of them doesn't specify, plan on sending it three for starters. Some magazines frown on multiple submissions, while others encourage it, and still others don't care. Carefully read the directory entry for each magazine you intend to submit to and be advised accordingly. If you do submit a poem to several places at the same time, keep a careful record, and if and when you receive an acceptance, notify the other magazines of it at once as a matter of courtesy, so they won't waste time reading and considering something they'll probably no longer be interested in. It's extremely bad form to have the same poem appear in two different magazines around the same time — some editors consider it an act of utter hostility on a poet's part.

Two enclosures, besides copies of your poems, are a must: a covering letter and a stamped self-addressed envelope, or as it's known in the trade, an SASE. The latter's not necessarily for the return of your poem; it could be used to inform you that it's been accepted.

The letter should be addressed to the editor in charge of poetry submissions or, failing that, simply the editor or the head of the organization with the person's title. Bear in mind that it may be the first thing from the envelope that the person reads, so it should accurately and seriously represent you. If need be, you can easily create a letterhead for yourself in a word-processing program on a computer; besides a telephone number for your home, include a cell-phone number and an e-mail address, if you have them. By all means, make sure that the text of your letter is spelled correctly and that the grammar is up to snuff; when in doubt, have someone else proofread it, hopefully someone else who knows better.

Your letter should consist of three paragraphs, and be direct and to the point. You should indicate at once that you're submitting x-number of poems for their consideration, and give their titles. It would be a good idea to indicate in the next paragraph that you're familiar with some of the poetry in their magazine and think that yours would be of interest to their readership, too; feel free to enlarge upon this somewhat — but only somewhat — meaning always let your poetry speak for itself. If publication in their magazine would be your first, that fact should go in your next paragraph, or if your work's been published before, briefly list what, where, and when. End the letter with a short paragraph thanking the person for his or her time and consideration, and that you've enclosed an SASE.

Each poem should appear on a separate sheet of plain white paper, in a familiar typeface that's easy to read, like Times Roman, at a point size that is no smaller than 11 and no larger than 12, unless there's a good reason to do otherwise. Unless the magazine has other instructions in their directory listing, type your full name in the upper left-hand corner, and if your poem runs to more than a page, type the page number of the pages after the first one in the upper right-hand corner. The title should appear about an inch down from the top, centered on the page, and your poem should begin two spaces down from that — again, unless there are special instructions.

Achtung! Before sealing your envelope, make absolutely sure that you have not parted with the only copies of your poems!

As soon as you've sent poems off to the various little magazines, get busy on something else. Some well-meaning folks are fond of saying "Get started on a new piece," but I've never been that stoical or calloused. So if you're like me and can't write under those circumstances and time hangs heavy on your hands, do busy work, clean out drawers, closets, etc. But whatever you do, DON'T take to looking out the window or up the street for the mailperson, because you may have a long wait. The waiting period for work submitted will usually be spelled out under each entry in your directory, and it can vary from several weeks to several months and maybe even longer — sometimes as long as six months or more. Bear in mind that little mags are notoriously short-handed; indeed, sometimes they're basically run by one person, maybe with members of his or her family and friends lending a hand now and again.

If there's no word from one of your recipients after three months, you could send them a query by mail (with another SASE) or e-mail or even phone them, but if it were me, I'd give up on them and cross them off my list. Here and there will be found a mag that's run, alas, by a child posing as an adult who gets a kick out of making people, especially vulnerable people, feel ill at ease, if not downright miserable, and you may have unwittingly stumbled onto one of those unfortunates.

If a poem has been accepted, they generally tell you which issue it will appear in and that you'll be getting at least one copy of the mag. Do everyone a favor, including yourself: order a few more copies, sending along a check, of course, and toward the end of the year, have someone send them a contribution, if they accept same, or else take out an ad. No one is in mag-publishing to make money, but the movers-and-shakers in such a venture have to come close to breaking even just to stay afloat.

If handwritten comments regularly appear on rejection slips from one of the mags you send to, that's a good sign. It probably means that they liked what they saw but not enough to print it, so keep sending things to them, and if after a while, you still haven't met with any success, get hold of a few more copies of the mag and see if you can figure out just what it is they'd be pleased with and then see whether you've got something like that in your growing arsenal to send. At the same time, if you haven't done so already, get those pieces of yours they liked but didn't like enough right out again to someplace else.

In addition to magazines in print, there are also others online, which are called zines, and these seem to exist in the zillions. Many of them appear to be catering to and looking for amateurs and seem to be interested mostly in poems about love, nature, etc. Others go in for combinations of graphics and poetry, about which I'll say something more later on in this chapter. For what it's worth, try the Open Directory Project, which lists poetry zines galore on its website. Just go to — http://www.dmoz.org?Arts/Online Writing/E-zines — and lotsa luck.

Whether you choose to send your poetry in the direction of the print or web or both, it's important to keep a stiff upper lip and not be discouraged easily. You may not luck into acceptance anywhere right away. You may not even get a single scrawled "Try again" right away. Does that mean your work's no good? Not at all. It's possible that you're doing something different that the editors you're coming into contact with, who are after all human beings like you and me, simply don't get the hang of. Literary history is full of horror stories of writers — sometimes glorious ones like Blake — who didn't find acceptance right away. For some, it happened in another country first; for others, it took more than a lifetime.

At the same time that you're trying to get published, you could begin giving readings of your poems, which is actually another form of publication, isn't it? But of course you have to decide very coolly and calculatingly if this is a way for you to go. Not everyone's works lend themselves to being read aloud. Look, for instance, at those by Pound, Eliot, H. D., William Carlos Williams, Sandburg, and E. E. Cummings in the last chapter. Probably they'd all fare pretty well via a microphone on a stage except for Cummings's. Why not his poem? Because the visual element in it is uppermost; that's where its strength lies, not as much or not nearly as much in how it sounds.

If you feel that your work communicates when being read aloud, my feeling is that it's best to start out modestly, like in your living room, and see how it all goes. Begin with your friends, even if poetry's not especially their thing, and make that debut of yours into a festive occasion with yummy things to eat and drink afterward. If you have a lot of friends, don't invite everyone, lest they all show up and you can't accommodate them comfortably. If you know very few people, urge them each to bring someone as a favor to you. Needless to say, meanies and overly critical folks with or without belly-ache are to be avoided at all costs. Extend your invitations by writing or calling; if you feel squeamish about doing this, draft a friend.

You'll also need someone — a pleasant, but not overly gushy or somber person — to act as a greeter and usher. If you own a computer and printer or you have a friend who does, you can create a simple hand-out program with a sheet of paper in landscape orientation. Put a title page on one side and a list of poems to be read on the other, fold, and voilá, you're "in business!" One important piece of advice regarding this "document" and your invitation too, if you make or have one printed, as well as anything else coming from you in behalf of your work: it should look like what it is, and it should represent you as you want to be seen.

At the performance, be sure to have a glass of water ready to hand for yourself. Some people like to read from a lectern, others from sheets of paper in their hands; you should decide on your preference beforehand. Your audience's seats, whether chairs or floor-cushions, should be arranged in a circle or in rows; either way, there should be enough room for you to come and go. If you wish, set up a simple tape recorder and an unobtrusive microphone to record yourself. To get really fancy, you can create a spotlight for yourself with a simple slide projector and a cardboard template placed over the lens.

You would have rehearsed your reading several times over the course of the week before, possibly with help or advice from a drama teacher at your local community college or high school. Nevertheless, you'll be nervous, but just remember: those are your friends in the audience, and they're there to show support for you in this endeavor. Come out from somewhere as if onto a stage, say hello to everyone, and thank them all for coming. If you feel so inclined or you think it makes "brownie points" for you, say that you're dedicating the event to someone present who's been of enormous help or is an inspiration. But don't make a big to-do out of it; get right down to business. Announce the title of each of your poems to be read in a clear voice, pause a moment, and then begin reading slowly and expressively, looking up at your audience now and then, especially at key moments in a work. At a certain point in your reading, announce a short intermission so folks can powder their noses and also have a breather — which, take it from me, people need even with the greatest poetry in the world.

After it's over, either ask for comments or invite everyone to partake of the refreshments, which should be decoratively laid out on a table along with plates, cutlery, napkins, and glasses and should represent you, not what you airily imagine poets should offer. Be sure to make the rounds and say hello to everyone, conscious that this is also part of your performance. Expect all kinds of reactions, including someone's complaining that they didn't understand or challenging some view expressed by you, or possibly even declaring that they didn't like your work or, in their humble opinion, that it sounds just like so-and-so's stuff, which you heartily dislike or even downright loathe — and be prepared to deal with each and every one. Even the best of friends can sometimes say the damndest things and with the greatest of good intentions. Look at the greater picture: they mean well or, pretending to be friends, are eaten up with envy.

Out of this debut of yours, all kinds of good things could happen. Fellow poets might like what you've done enough to ask for your help in organizing a reading for them — and there you will have the beginning of a poet's circle or literary society. Well-wishers might encourage you to get out and read at other places, like cafes and restaurants and local libraries, and even offer to make the connections for you. By all means jump to whatever opportunities present themselves — but only if you yourself had a good feeling about your reading.

If you do decide to go on and do readings in places outside of your home, you're going to have to "case" the "joints" first, meaning attend some readings at them to see what goes on and connect with the person or people in charge. Readers at such things fare best if they bring a little cheering section with them, so as the time approaches, be prepared to ask friends to pitch in.

To return to your crusade to get your work in print, once ten or so poems of yours have appeared in mags or zines or both, you should apply for membership in Poets & Writers, the national organization of same, which furnishes all kinds of information and services, including a directory in which you'll be listed. (See Appendix 1 for their address and phone number and those of other potentially helpful organizations.)

As you continue writing and submitting to mags or zines, you should begin looking for a publisher for a book of your poems. This should be done in much the same fashion as your quest for publication in mags and zines. Go back to your directory or directories and ferret out book publishers that have published poets whose work has appeared in the same mags and/or zines as yours or whom you've encountered in the course of your readings. Some book publishers are affiliated with certain mags or zines, so check to make sure that this is or isn't so with those that have published your work. Make a master list of likely candidates, and then try to get hold of a book put out by each of them to see what it looks like physically. Cross off your list any company whose practice is to issue things like computer printouts on cheap paper. You'll also want to rule out vanity presses, which will publish anything for cash, but not book publishers who ask for some up-front money.

Most book publishers want a query letter first, sometimes with some poems enclosed, but sometimes not; be sure to follow the rules. This letter should be in the same basic format as your query letter to mags and should be as direct and to the point as possible. Your first paragraph should clearly and succinctly state what you want: their consideration of your poems for a book. The next paragraph should include a list of places where your works, with titles, have appeared; mention those that have been enclosed with date and place of publication. This should be followed by a paragraph about you, especially you the poet, giving details that you think would be of interest to the person on the other end, including your friendships with one or more of their other poets, if such happens to be the case; avoid extraneous things like your hobbies and the foreign languages you know, unless it's pertinent. If anyone of note has made favorable comments about your work, a brief summary belongs in the next paragraph. Bear in mind, where this paragraph and the preceding one are concerned, that books are expensive to produce, and you'll want to show an editorial board that you as a poet, as well as your work, will spark interest among their readers. Your final paragraph should express the hope that they'll respond with a request to see the rest of your work and should mention that an SASE is enclosed.

Once your book of poems is off the press, your publisher is going to try to get it reviewed, but you should also do your part. Let's face it, even under the best of circumstances, publishers of poetry need — indeed, have always needed — all the help they can get, so dooo be prepared to give it to them, including, as I said above, a little up-front money. Yes, indeedee, the days of being an author with one's head in the clouds are a thing of the past. In fact, given my own past experiences with so-called literary agents — some of them nightmarish — I sometimes wonder if those days ever really existed.

Reviews are now considered glorified forms of advertisement, especially by publishers; they were originally intended to tell what the book is about and make a recommendation as to its purchase. But nowadays even a bad review sells a book, they say. So don't be concerned about sending copies to potential reviewers who might be unkind. Do be concerned about making a review copy of your book count — that is, getting it to the attention of a newspaper or magazine whose audience is larger, at least a bit larger, than its staff.

After the review copies are out, the first thing you'll need is a pub party, which the publisher will generally host. But if this isn't possible, see if a local literary bookstore will do one as a promotional event or if a friend or friends will give you a blow-out in one of their homes. Worst-case scenario: you do it yourself. What happens at a pub party, besides relatives and friends eating and drinking? Your new book is on display on a table with copies of reviews if they're available — only good ones, of course — and you get to read from your book, people buy copies, and you autograph them for the buyers.

After your pub party, consider going back to your local literary bookstore, with or without reviews, and feel them out to see if they'll handle the book and, having heard of the success of the first pub party, offer to give you a second. You should also do your part in promoting your new book by getting out and doing readings at neighborhood libraries and schools, and even senior housing, hospitals, and nursing homes. Poets & Writers provides small matching grants to poets for readings if the organization that you do a reading at pays you.

Small press book fairs, both on a local and national level, should not be neglected either. Urge your publisher to rent a table or consider going partners on one with another small publisher in the same situation. Be sure that he/she has excerpts from the reviews of your book on display with it. Also, your publisher should list your book with online bookstores like amazon.com, which encourages readers to review your book and prints the reviews.

This is as good a place as any to mention contests and grants, of which there are quite a few both in the print and web worlds. A list of both in the print world, as well as conferences and workshops, can be found in separate chapters of *Poet's Market.* Online, the following may prove fruitful for contests: http://www.poetry.com; http://www.poetry-contest.com; and http://www.writing.com. Another site — http://www.foetry.com — maintains an ongoing list of fraudulent contests, including some real shockers the last time I looked. Grants are best applied for after your book is in print, and don't hesitate to try for them. You've got nothing to lose and you might just get lucky. One fruitful grant-giving agency is your local arts council. Check out Poet and Writers, which has a goodly number of such organizations on its list.

Boo-Hoo, No One Wants You-ou-ou!

Well, it's no laughing matter. On the other hand, no need to carry on so. This is still a wonderful country in which a wonderful system prevails at what's still a wonderful time. Let us suppose that after a goodly number of submissions to magazines, you don't find a taker and no one scrawls even so much as a "Sorry" or a "Good luck elsewhere" on their rejection slip or — the worst — doesn't even include the obligatory slip when sending your poems back. What to do then? Why, it's very simple. You found your own literary mag or zine! That's how a fair number of those now in existence got their start. Why not you too?

Make no mistake about it, this isn't an enterprise that one enters into lightly. It's hard work, and it costs money. So before going at it full throttle, best think it over very carefully or at least take a deep breath and count to ten. A joint enterprise with like-minded friends, especially if they're poets or serious creative writers, would seem to be in order here, but a decision to invite them on board depends upon how well you're capable of working with others. Me, I'm a loner; always have been and always will be; I'd find having to pool ideas before each and every decision has to be made very trying, and lots of meetings, phone calls, and emails, even with people I like and respect, would drive me up a tree. But that's me; another person may welcome the challenge or take comfort in the shared responsibility.

Before you even go to Square One, may I strongly recommend that you acquire and selectively read *Starting and Running a Successful Newsletter or Magazine* by Cheryl Woodward. It's geared toward a commercial market but covers all the high points, including zines. I also urge you to take a look at different mags, especially those whose formats you especially like, and examine them carefully to see what makes them work. Brace yourself: unless you're loaded with money to hire service people, you're also going to have to acquire a hefty load of new skills, including type-specing, layout, and design, if you don't have them already, and to invest in some new equipment, like a deluxe printer or two, depending on how fancy-schmancy you want to get. You might find a book specifically on design useful here, such as *Newsletters from the Desktop* by Joe Grossman and David Doty.

Your first order of business will be to come up with a name for your mag or zine, and you'll have to make sure that it's not one already being used by another periodical. This you can do by checking the directories and the Web. Next, if you've chosen to establish a mag, you're going to have to decide who your mag's prospective readership is going to be, how many copies of each issue you'll turn out, and how often it's going to come out, like once a year or month and so on. And then there are a multitude of decisions that you'll have to make relating to its physical appearance, such as its dimensions and how many pages it will consist of. When it comes to design, happily, thanks to computers, it's a very simple matter. Programs such as Adobe's *InDesign* and *QuarkXpress* come with style sheets and grids, so all you'll have to do is decide which one you want to use, call it up, drop in your text from *MS Word*, and you're off and running.

Lest you find this a trifle discouraging, bear in mind that many community colleges and evening divisions of four-year colleges offer courses of various kinds to help you along the way. Also, if there's a fairly well-established little mag in your neck of the woods, consider it a potential source of sound, practical advice. Quite possibly the editor or someone else on the staff might be willing to hear you out on a specific production problem and offer suggestions for the price of a lunch. A search of the Internet, while possibly time consuming, is also a potential source of help in matters of print production; I found *In-Design* expert David Bergsland in that way. On the other hand, I found graphic designer Lisa Tait of Silvertop Graphics quite by accident through a wonderful brochure that she created for the Delaware County Historical Society (NY).

Founding a zine is certainly a much more economical way to go, by comparison, and certainly gratifying if you're environmentally-minded. Also, you can include poets reading their poems as well as the texts in print, and at the same time go absolutely nuts with photos and graphics, and add music and all sorts of sound effects. There's a big danger in this in your getting lost in the visual or auditory aspects of the thing and putting poetry on a sort of back burner — much as concrete poetry encourages one to do, in my opinion. But I'm inclined to think that the zine-way is okay as long as you're aware of what you're doing and are sure that it's what you, consciously, want to do. Needless to say, before taking a leap in this direction, make a list of the zines you like and take a good, long look at each of them, as well as listen, to fathom what makes them tick.

Finding an audience for your zine will be one of your major considerations; I'm told that it's not all that easy, even when one pays up-front money to the search engines for a special listing. But first things first: you're going to have to establish a website for it and be able to maintain it — meaning, for starters, that you'll need a more than passing familiarity with web design and layout programs like Macromedia's *Dreamweaver* and *Flash.*

Some of the same skills necessary for mag production, like type-specing, layout, and design, are also of paramount importance here. However, even with fabulous image-editing programs like Adobe *Photoshop* and audio-editing programs like Adobe's *Audition,* getting things up on a site to look and sound as you want them to is, as of this writing, fraught with all sorts of perils. Still, one of the advantages of the zine is that once the necessary skills are acquired, you can at least take steps toward going multimedia.

I mention this because for me it seemed to be a Way to go early on, when the Web was still in its infancy, and now looking at the multitude of multimedia zines to be found there, it clearly was. May I recommend that you take a look, with audio on, at the works in the Gallery of my performance group, The Lark Ascending — http://www.thelarkascending.org — especially at *Black on Black / 13* and the *Cries of Cassandra,* where you'll see what I've done visually and sound-wise with Wallace Stevens's "Thirteen Ways of Looking at a Blackbird" and Hart Crane's "To Brooklyn Bridge."

Well, it takes all kinds, doesn't it, and after all that's been said about the negative sides of self-this and self-that, is there someone loony enough to want to found their own small publishing company — fondly referred to as a small press — and put out their own book? If the truth be known, I'm one of those fools.

In 1980, totally out of options after thirty-odd rejections, I founded The Twickenham Press and published my first novel, *Klytaimnestra Who Stayed at Home.* Since it was considered a shame and a disgrace to do such a thing at that time, I created a fictional owner of my press, Barbara Beesley, and I even provided "her" with a fictional Uncle Alex, a rich one. Anyone who's aware that the great eighteenth-century English arch-satirist Alexander Pope lived in Twickenham would've gotten the joke; alas, very few did. After putting out my second novel, *Bobe Mayse: A Tale of Washington Square,* in like fashion, I decided to design and typeset my third, *Bagatelle • Guinevere,* myself, which necessitated my creating a fictional designer Karla Kraus (after pre-World War II Austrian man-of-letters Karl Kraus, who wrote many of the articles for his literary journal *Die Fackel* and signed them with different names). You can read the whole story plus a bio of me with photos and see reviews of all three books, I mean the whole blood-and-gut things, not benign excerpts, on the website my designer Lisa and I made for the Twick: http://www.twickenhampress.com.

Happily, nowadays there's no shame and disgrace attached to doing what I did, which is the way it should be. If you've got the money or can raise it and are willing to work your ass off — go for it if that's the only way left to you or you'd rather do it yourself. In case you should choose that route, my bible in those days was Dan Poynter's *Self-Publishing Manual,* which I still recommend. This book takes you through the whole process of book publishing from the proverbial soup to nuts, even providing model letters and so on, and I'm happy to see that, in its present edition, Dan is very positive about the future of e-books, tantarrah! Also helpful were Malcom Barker's *Book Design & Production for the Small Publisher,* which gives an excellent overview, and Stanley Rice's *Book Design: Text Format Models,* whose chapter seven, by the way, covers the typesetting of poetry.

And now, without any further ado, it's only fitting that our guest poets have the final word. First, here's my dear friend Ruth Fainlight with one of my favorite poems by her — and do take note of how the *s*'s in the first stanza are picked up here and there in the other three, and how in the second and third stanzas, she discreetly uses *anaphora* and *consonances* like the *b*'s in "by" and "bodily" and "because" and "but":

Stubborn

My Stone-Age self still scorns
attempts to prove us more
than upright animals
whose powerful skeletons
and sinewy muscled limbs
were made to be exhausted
by decades of labour
not subdued by thought,

despises still those dreamers
who forget, poets
who ignore, heroes
who defy mortality
while risking every failure,
spirits unsatisfied
by merely their own
bodily survival.

I know her awful strength.
I know how panic, envy,
self-defence, are mixed
with her tormented rage
because they will deny
her argument that nothing
but the body's pleasure,
use, and comfort, matters.

Guarding her cave and fire
And implements, stubborn
in her ignorance,
deaf to all refutation,
I know she must insist
until the hour of death
she cannot feel the pain
that shapes and haunts me.

And here's one of my favorites by Romanian-born Nina Cassian. Notice how expressive she can be in English when she's unselfconsciously her Romanian self:

The Sow Is Dead in the Barn

This rather depressing Romanian saying
means, of course, that it's over —
nothing else to be done now
(certainly not for the sow):
we have to part, to leave,
to quit, to resign, to give up — what?
Memory tells us once there was a feast
ending with heavy, sumptuous clusters of grapes,
that we rinsed our fingers in perfumed, oily water,
counting our achievements,
feeling proud of ourselves
(maybe also a little drunk).

Our memory is malicious: it reminds us
of so many functional embraces,
voluptuous promises of eternity.
— "What a shame," the sow would grunt
were she still alive.

Now here's my cousin Jeffrey Greene with surely one of his best and most memorable poems. I find the final repeated "claw" absolutely devastating; probably you will, too. Notice how his repetitions of "sea" in the first and third stanzas, "light" in the fifth stanza, and "where" in the next-to-last and last stanzas anticipate it:

Night Dive

The seabeds are nocturnal.
Even on the searocks in the shallows
green crabs cling in starlight.

Boys pull on their neoprene suits
and arrive in the black ocean
looking down for lobsters.

Getting it all Together

The sealife slows under their lanterns.
In the same way the moon
would jacklight us on the bare shore.

In your right hand you can hold a lantern,
and with your left hand
you can touch the blind fish.

This is the element you love so well,
your body without light
in the ocean without light.

Tonight, Mother, I could lose you
as you sleep under the clear surface
of an oxygen tent.

I have come back to New England,
to this house where now there is no one.
I turn on lights and the rooms go on sleeping.

This is the night dive
where the slow halibut lifts like a table,
where the eel swims from a bed of skins,

and where the lobster
goes forward with its one crushing claw
and its one tearing claw.

APPENDIX 1

USEFUL ORGANIZATIONS

The number of organizations out there offering some kind of help or service to poets is mind-boggling. Here's a short quick-and-dirty-type list, which obviously is far from exhaustive (and exhausting).

ACADEMY OF AMERICAN POETS

Supports poets at all stages of development by administering major awards such as a first-book prize, a lifetime-achievement award, and about 200 college prizes. It also aims to foster the appreciation of contemporary poetry through Poets.org; National Poetry Month (April); the Online Poetry Classroom, which provides free poetry lesson plans and other tools for teachers; the Poetry Audio Archive, a collection of nearly 500 recordings dating back to the 1960s; and *American Poet*, its biannual literary journal and magazine for members. Membership is open to all.

Address: 588 Broadway, Suite 604, New York, NY 10012 - 3210

Phone: 212 - 274 - 0343.

E-m: academy@poets.org.

Website: www.poets.org.

ASSOCIATION OF WRITERS AND WRITING PROGRAMS

Is higher-education oriented and has as its aim to foster literary talent and achievement, advance the art of writing as essential to a good education, and serve the makers, teachers, students, and readers of contemporary writing. Membership is open to the independent writer or one affiliated with an institution of higher learning.

Address: Mailstop 1E3, George Mason University, Fairfax, VA 22030
Phone: 703 - 993 - 4301
E-m: awp@awpwriter.org
Website: http://www.Awpwriter.org

Author's Guild
Provides legal assistance and a broad range of consulting services about practical matters to its members, who must have authored at least one published book.
Address: 31 East 32nd Street, 7th Floor, New York, NY 10016
Phone: 212 - 563 - 5904
E-m: staff@authorsguild.org
Website: http://www.authorsguild.org

Council of Literary Magazines and Presses
Acts as an umbrella organization for and disseminator of information to book publishers of and magazines offering serious fiction, poetry, and prose.
Address: 154 Christopher Street, Suite 3C New York, NY 10014-9110
Phone: 212 - 741 - 9110
E-m: info@clmp.org
Website: http: // www.clmp.org

Litline
A not - for - profit website for the independent literary community that provides links to small presses, journals, organizations, and what have you.
website: http: // www.litline.org

National Federation of State Poetry Societies
Is an umbrella organization for state poetry societies and includes twenty members.
Address: 2712 Scott Avenue, Fort Worth, TX 76103
Phone: 817 - 535 - 7304
E-m: JFS@flash.net
Website: http: // www.nfsps.org

Poet's House

Has a 45,000-volume poetry collection that is free and open to the public, and it includes books, journals, chapbooks, audio tapes, videos, and electronic media. Each year the House offers over fifty public programs, including panel discussions and lectures, as well as seminars and workshops. In addition, it sponsors readings in public parks and public libraries throughout the city and a festival, The People's Poetry Gathering, which celebrates poetry's roots in popular oral traditions from around the globe.

Address: 72 Spring Street, New York, NY 10012
Phone: 212 - 431 - 7920
E-m: info@poetshouse.org
Website: http://www.poetshouse.org

Poetry Society of America

Tries to extend an awareness and appreciation of poetry throughout the country and includes poets and readers as members.

Address: 15 Gramercy Park, New York, NY 10003
Phone: 212 - 254 - 9628
E-m: poetrysoc@aol.com
Website: http://www.poetrysociety.org

Poets & Writers

Provides information, support, and guidance to creative writers. Among its activities are: Poets & Writers Magazine; Poets & Writers Online; a Readings/Workshops program, which funds writers in New York, California, Atlanta, Chicago, Detroit, and Seattle; and Information Services, which provides answers to questions writers may have about publishing and edits and maintains PW's Directory of American Poets and Fiction Writers.

Address: 72 Spring Street, New York, NY 10012
Phone: 212 - 226 - 3586
E-m: admin@pw.org
Website: http: // www.pw.org

ShawGuides

provides a variety of guides to help you find writers' conferences, workshops, seminars, and art colonies.

Website: http: / / www.Shawguides.com/writing/

The Poetry Project at St Marks Church

Is a forum for public literary events and a resource for writers. It boasts a Wednesday night reading series, a Monday night reading/performance series, a Friday late-evening events series, four weekly writing workshops, an annual literary magazine, a quarterly newsletter, a biannual four-day Symposium, tape and document archives, and an annual New Year's Day Marathon Reading.

Address: 131 East 10th St., New York NY 10003
Phone: 212 - 674 - 0910
E-m: info@poetryproject.com
Website: http: / / www.poetryproject.com

US Copyright Office

Provides general information on issues and laws and downloadable versions of forms.

Address: 101 Independence Avenue, SE, Washington, D.C. 20559 - 6000
Phone: 202 - 707 - 9100 and 202 - 707 - 3000
Website: http: / / www.lcweb.loc.gov / copyright /

Verse Daily

Is an independently owned daily publication of quality poetry on the Internet that republishes one new poem each day from some literary magazine or book of poetry along with information about the poet and the publisher, including how to purchase the book or subscribe to the publication. Selections are made from the review copies of magazines and books it receives.

Website: http: / / versedaily.org

Web Del Sol

Also on the Internet, exists to promote, fund, and support the writing, publishing, and reading of contemporary literature in electronic media and has as its aim to foster collaboration between the literary arts and new forms of artistic and literary expression such as hypertext, film, and photography.

Website: http: / / www.webdelsol.com

"I celebrate myself..."

Appendix 2

Mags and Zines

The following is a list of literary magazines that I carefully selected from CLMP's *Literary Press and Magazine Directory* and Dust Books's *Directory of Poetry Publishers.* All of them have been around for a good long time, and most are based at a college or university; more important, they all recently responded to a query of mine indicating that they are open to works by new poets. All want submissions by regular mail as outlined by me in chapter nine. Begin by sending for a copy of their mag and/or going on their website as I suggested there. If you experience difficulty with any of them, please don't hesitate to contact me and let me know.

AGNI
Contact person: Sven Birkerts, editor
236 Bay State Road
Boston, MA 02215
617 - 353 - 7135
http://agni@bu.edu
Submission period: 9/1 — 6/1
Number of poems: no more than 5

ARTS & LETTERS
Contact person: Martin Lammon
Campus Box 89
Georgia College and State University
Milledgeville, GA 31061-0490

478 - 445 - 1289
http://al@gcsu.edu
Submission period: 9/1 – 4/1
Number of poems: 4 —8.

ATLANTA REVIEW
Contact person: Don Veach
Poetry Atlanta
POB 8248
Atlanta, GA 31106
http://atlantareview.com
Submission period: open
Number of poems: up to 5

BOSTON REVIEW
Contact person: Joshua Friedman
30 Wadsworth Street
E53 - 407 MIT
Cambridge, MA 02139
617 - 253 - 3642
http://bostonreview.mit.edu
Submission period: 9/15 — 6/1
Number of poems: open

BYLINE
Contact person: Sandra Soli, poetry editor
Po Box 5240
Edmond, OK 73083 - 5240
405 - 348 - 5591
http://ByLineMag.com
Submission period: open
Number of poems: 1 — 3

CHICAGO REVIEW
Contact person: Eirik Steinhoff
5801 South Kenwood Avenue
Chicago, IL *60637*
http://humanities.uchicago.edu/review
Submission period: 9/30—5/31
Number of poems: 3 — 6

THE COMSTOCK REVIEW
Contact person: Peggy S. Flanders, managing editor
4956 St. John Drive
Syracuse, NY 13215
http://comstockreview.org
Submission period: 1/1— 3/15
Number of poems: 5 — 6

THE CONECTICUT POETRY REVIEW
Contact person: J. Claire White and Harley More, editors
P.O. Box 818
Stonington, CT 06378
Submission period: by October 1
Number of poems: 3

CONNECTICUT RIVER REVIEW
Contact person: Tony Fusco, editor
311 Shingle Hill Road
West Haven, CT 06516
anthony.fusco@yale.edu
Submission period: 10/1 — 4/15
Number of poems: 3

COTTONWOOD MAGAZINE
Contact person: Tom Lorenz, editor
1301 Jayhawk Blvd., Room 400
Kansas Union, University of Kansas
Lawrence, KS 66045
Submission period: open
Number of poems: 4 - 6

CRAB ORCHARD REVIEW
Contact person: Jon Trible
Department of English
Southern Illinois University
Carbondale, IL 62901 - 4503
618 -453 - 6833
http://siu.edu/~crborchd/
Submission period: 9/1— 4/30
Number of poems: 3 — 5

THE CREAM CITY REVIEW
Contact person: Beth Bretl
University of Wisconsin
English Department, P.O. Box 413
Milwaukee, WI 53211
414 - 229 - 4708
http: / / uwm.edu / dept / english / ccr
Submission period: 9 / 1 — 4 / 30
Number of poems: 3 — 5

ELEMENTS MAGAZINE
Contact person: Bernard Washington, poetry editor
2901 - 1/2 Truxillo Street
Houston, TX 77004 - 5459
713 - 614 - 8389
b.washington53@hotmail.com
Submission period: open
Number of poems: open

THE GEORGIA REVIEW
Contact person: T.R. Hummer
012 Gilbert Hall
The University of Georgia
Athens, GA 30602 - 9009
760 - 542 - 3481
http: / / uga.edu / garev
Submission period: 8 / 16 — 5 / 16
Number of poems: 3 — 5

THE GETTYSBURG REVIEW
Contact person: Peter Stitt, editor
Campus Box 2446
300 North Washington Street
Gettysburg College
Gettysburg, PA 17325 - 1491
717 - 337 - 6770
http: / / gettysburgreview.com
Submission period: 9 / 1 — 5 / 31
Number of poems: 3 — 5

THE GREENSBORO REVIEW
Contact person: Jim Clark, editor
MFA Writing Program, Department of English
134 Mc Iver Building, UNCG
PO Box 26170
Greensboro, NC 27402 - 6170
336 - 334 - 5459
http: / / uncg.edu / eng / mfa
Submission period: 8 / 15 — 2 / 15
Number of poems: 3—5

HANGING LOOSE PRESS
Contact person: Robert Hershon
231 Wyckoff St.
Brooklyn, NY 11217
http: / / hangingloosepress.com
Submission period: open
Number of poems: 4 — 6

HAYDEN'S FERRY REVIEW
Contact person: Salima Keegan
The Virginia G. Piper Center for Creative Writing
Box 875002
Arizona State University
Tempe, AZ 85287 - 1502
480 - 965 -1243
http: / / haydensferryreview.org
Submission period: deadlines 2/28 and 9/30
Number of poems: up to 6

HIDDEN OAK
Contact person: Louise Larkins
POB 275
Philadelphia, PA 19103
http: / / hidoak@att.net
Submission period: open
Number of poems: up to 4

HUBBUB
Contact person: Lisa Steinman
5344 S.E. 38th Avenue

Portland, OR 97202
503-775-0370
Submission period: open
Number of poems: up to 6

THE IOWA REVIEW
Contact person: David Hamilton
308 EPB
University of Iowa
Iowa City, Iowa 52242 - 1408
319 - 335 - 0462
http: / / uiowa.edu / ~iareview
Submission period: 9 / 1 — 11 / 30
Number of poems: up to 6

THE JOURNAL
Contact person: Kathy Fagan
Department of English
164 West 17th Avenue
Columbus, OH 43210 - 1370
614 - 292 - 4076
http://english.osu.edu/journals/the_journal
Submission period: 9 / 1 — 11 / 30
Number of poems: up to 5

THE KENYON REVIEW
Contact person: David Lynn, editor
104 College Drive
Gambier, OH 43022
740 - 427 - 5208
http: / / kenyonreview.org
Submission period: open
Number of poems: up to 10 pages

LUCIDITY POETRY JOURNAL
Contact person: Ted O. Badger, editor
14781 Memorial Drive #10
Houston, TX 77079 - 5210
281 - 920 - 1795

Submission period: open
Number of poems: up to 5

LYNX EYE
Contact person: Pam McCully
581 Woodland Drive
Los Osos, CA 93402
Submission period: open
Number of poems: up to 6

NATURAL BRIDGE
Contact person: Steve Schreiner
English Dept.
8001 Natural Bridge Road
University of Missouri
St. Louis, MO 63121
http://umsl.edu/~natural
Submission period: 7/1 — 8/31 & 11/1 — 12/1
Number of poems: 4 to 6

NORTHWEST REVIEW
Contact person: John Witte
369 PLC
University of Oregon
Eugene, OR 97403
503-346-3957
http://www.uoregon.edu/~nwreview/
Submission period: open
Number of poems: open

NOTRE DAME REVIEW
Contact person: Kathleen Canavan
840 Flanner Hall
University of Notre Dame
Notre Dame, IN 46556
219-631-6952
http://nd.edu/~ndr/review.htm
Submission period: 9/1 — 11/30 and 1/1 — 3/31
Number of poems: up to 5

POEM
Contact person: Rebecca Harbor
English Department
POB 2006
University of Alabama
Huntsville, AL 35804
Submission period: 9 / 1 — 5 / 31
Number of poems: up to 5

PRAIRIE SCHOONER
Contact person: Hilda Raz
201 Andrews Hall
University of Nebraska
Lincoln, NE 68588 - 0334
402 - 472 - 0911
http: / / uni.edu / schooner / psmain.htm
Submission period: 9 / 1 — 5 / 31
Number of poems: 5 — 7 poems

RED WHEELBARROW LITERARY MAGAZINE
Contact person: Randolph Splitter
21250 Stevens Creek Boulevard
De Anza College
Cupertino, CA 95014 - 5702
408 - 864 - 5629
www.deanza.fhda.edu / redwheelbarrow
Submission period: open
Number of poems: up to 5

REFLECTIONS LITERARY JOURNAL
Contact person: Tami S. Thrasher
POB 1197
Roxboro, NC 27573
336 - 599 - 1181
http: / / thrasht@piedmont.cc.nc.us
Submission period: July through December
Number of poems: 3 — 5

RIVERSTYX
Contact person: Melissa G. Bancks
3547 Olive Street, Ste 107

St Louis, MO 63103 - 1002
314 - 533 - 4541
http: / / riverstyx.org
Submission period: May to November
Number of poems: 3 — 5

SEWANEE REVIEW
Contact person: Bob Jones
735 University Ave.
The University of the South
Sewanee TN 37383 - 1000
931 - 598 - 1246
www.sewanee.edu/sreview/home.html
Submission period: 9 / 1 — 5 / 31
Number of poems: up to 6

SHENANDOAH
Contact person: Lynn Leech, managing editor
Mattingly House / 2 Lee Avenue
Washington and Lee University
Lexington, VA 24450 - 0303
540 - 458 - 8765
http://shenandoah.wlu.edu
Submission period: 9/ 1 — 5 / 31
Number of poems: up to 5

SYCAMORE REVIEW
Contact person: Sean M. Conrey
Dept. of English
500 Oval Drive
Purdue University
West Lafayette, IN 47907
765-494-3783
http://sla.purdue.edu/sycamore/
Submission period: 9\1— 3\31
Number of poems: 3 — 5

THIRD COAST
Contact person: Glenn Deutsch
Department of English
Sprau Tower

Western Michigan University
Kalamazoo, MI 49008 - 5331
616 - 387 - 2675
www.wmich.edu/thirdcoast
Submission period: open
Number of poems: 3 — 5

THE YALE REVIEW
Contact person: J.D. McClatchy
P.O. Box 208243
Yale University
New Haven, CT 06520 - 8243
203 - 432 - 0499
http://yale.edu.yalereview
Submission period: open
Number of poems: up to 5

ZONE 3
Contact person: David Till
POB 4565
Austin Peay State University
Clarksville, TN 37044
931 - 221 - 7031
Submission period: open
Number of poems: up to 5

Zines

There's so much out there that's bad and/or amateurish that I'm honestly reluctant to send you anywhere. The best place to start is with the *Electronic Poetry Center* at SUNY-Buffalo — http://wings.buffalo.edu/epc/ — which provides links to many zines' home pages. At any event, you're not likely to go wrong with the following for starters:

The Rose & Thorn: A Literary Ezine — http://members.aol.com/Rave763/index.html
Poetic Voices — http://poeticvoices.com
Poetry Daily — http://poems.com

Web de Sol — http://webdesol.com — hosts the websites of a number of literary mags like *Crazy Horse.*

"Do not go gentle..."

Bibliography

Anthologies

Costanzo, Gerald, and Jim Daniels, eds. *American Poetry: The Next Generation.* Pittsburgh: Carnegie-Mellon, 2000.

Ferguson, Margaret, et al., eds. *The Norton Anthology of Poetry.* 5th ed. NY: Norton, 2000.

Prufer, Kevin, ed. *The New Young American Poets.* Southern Illinois, 2000.

Ramazani, Jahan, Richard Ellmann, and Robert O'Clair, eds. *The Norton Anthology of Modern Poetry and Contemporary Poetry.* NY: Norton, 2003.

Waters, Michael, and Al Poulin, Jr., eds. *Contemporary American Poetry.* 7th ed. Boston: Houghton, 2001.

Our Guest Poets

Cassian, Nina. *Call Yourself Alive? The Love Poems of Nina Cassian.* Tr. Andrea Deletant and Brenda Walker. Boston: Forest, 1988.

———. *Blue Apple.* Tr. Eva Feiler. Merrick, NY: Cross-Cultural Communications, 1981.

———. *Cheerleader for a Funeral.* Tr. Brenda Walker. Boston: Forest, 1992.

———. *Lady of Miracles.* Tr. Laura Schiff. Berkeley, CA: Cloud Marauder, 1982.

———. *Life Sentence*. Ed. William Jay Smith. Tr. various. NY: Norton, 1990.

———. *Take My Word for It*. NY: Norton, 1998.

Fainlight, Ruth. *Another Full Moon*. London: Hutchinson, 1976.

———. *Burning Wire*. London: Bloodaxe, 2002.

———. *Cages*. London: MacMillan, 1966.

———. *Climates*. London: Bloodaxe, 1983.

———. *Fifteen to Infinity*. London: Hutchinson, 1983.

———. *Moon Wheels*. London: Bloodaxe, 2006.

———. *Selected Poems*. London: Hutchinson, 1987, and Sinclair Stevenson, 1995.

———. *Sibyls and Others*. London: Hutchinson, 1980.

———. *Sugar-Paper Blue*. London: Bloodaxe, 1997.

———. *The Region's Violence*. London: Hutchinson, 1973.

———. *The Knot*. London: Hutchinson, 1990.

———. *This Time of Year*. London: Sinclair-Stevenson, 1994.

———. *To See the Matter Clearly*. London: MacMillan, 1968.

———. *Twelve Sibyls*. NY: Gehena Press, 1991.

———. *Twenty-One Poems*. London: Turret, 1973.

Greene, Jeffrey. *American Spirituals*. Boston: Northeastern UP, 1998.

———. *Glimpses of the Invisible World of New Haven*. Lawrenceville, GA: Coreopsis Books, 1994.

———. *To the Left of the Worshiper*. Cambridge, MA: Alice James Books, 1991.

Your Author

Bogen, Nancy. *Bagatelle • Guinevere by Felice Rothman*. NY: Twickenham, 1995.

———. *Bobe Mayse: A Tale of Washington Square*. NY: Twickenham, 1993.

———. *How to Write Poetry.* 3rd ed. Clifton Park, NY: Thomson. 1995.

———. *Klytaimnestra Who Stayed at Home.* 3rd ed. NY: Lintel, 1989.

———. *William Blake's Book of Thel: A Critical Edition with a New Interpretation.* Providence: Brown UP, 1968.

More Books About How to Write Poetry

Behn, Robin, and Chase Twichell. *The Practice of Poetry.* NY: Harper, 1992.

Boisseau, Michelle, and Robert Wallace. *Writing Poems.* 6th ed. NY: Pearson, 2004.

Drake, Barbara. *Writing Poetry.* NY: Harcourt, 1994.

Kowit, Steve. *In the Palm of Your Hand: The Poet's Portable Workshop.* Gardiner, ME: Tilbury, 1995.

Rhyming Dictionaries

Fergusson, Rosalind. *The Penguin Rhyming Dictionary.* NY: Viking, 1985.

Upton, Clive. *Oxford Rhyming Dictionary.* NY: Oxford UP, 2004.

Wood, Clement. *Complete Rhyming Dictionary.* NY: Doubleday, 1992.

Books about Prosody and Related Matters

Boland, Evan, and Mark Strand. *The Making of a Poem: A Norton Anthology of Poetic Forms.* NY: Norton, 2000.

Corbett, Edward P.J. *Classical Rhetoric for the Modern Student.* NY: Oxford, 1990.

Deutsch, Babette. *Poetry Handbook: A Dictionary of Terms.* NY: Harper and Row, 1974.

Fussell, Paul, Jr. *Poetic Meter and Poetic Form.* NY: Random House, 1979.

Harmon, William, and Hugh Holman. *A Handbook to Literature.* NY: MacMillan, 1986.

Kirby-Smith, H.T. *The Origins of Free Verse.* Ann Arbor: UPMI, 1998.

Malof, Joseph. *A Manual of English Meters.* Bloomington: Indiana UP, 1970.

McDowell, Robert, and Harvey Gross. *Sound and Form in Modern Poetry.* Ann Arbor: UPMI, 2000.

Oliver, Mary. *A Poetry Handbook.* NY: Harcourt, 1994.

Packard, William. *The Poet's Dictionary.* NY: Harper and Row, 1989.

Preminger, Alex, and T.V.F Brogan, eds. *The New Princeton Encyclopedia of Poetry and Poetics.* Princeton: Princeton UP, 1993.

Saintsbury, George. *A History of English Prosody from the Twelfth Century to the Present.* NY: Russell, 1961.

Turco, Lewis. *The Book of Forms: A Handbook of Poetics.* Hanover, NH: UPNE, 2000.

Manuscript Preparation and Book Design

A Manual of Style. Chicago: U. of Chicago, 1961.

Achtert, Walter S., and Joseph Gibaldi. *The MLA Style Manual.* NY: MLA, 1985.

Barker, Malcom. *Book Design & Production for the Small Publisher.* San Francisco: Londonborn, 1990.

Bringhurst, Robert. *The Elements of Typographic Style.* Port Roberts, WA: Hartley & Marks, 1996.

Nicholson, Margaret. *A Dictionary of American-English Usage.* NY: NAL, 1958.

Rice, Stanley. *Book Design: Text Format Models.* NY: Bowker, 1978.

Publishing

Bergsland, David. *Introduction to Digital Publishing.* Clifton Park, NY: Delmar, 2002.

Breen, Nancy, ed. *2006 Poet's Market.* Cincinnati: Writer's Digest, 2005.

Ciaravino, Helen. *How to Publish Your Poetry.* Garden City, NY: Square One, 2001.

Council of Literary Magazines and Presses. *The Literary Press and Magazine Directory: 2005/2006*. Brooklyn: Soft Skull, 2005.

Fulton, Len, ed. *The Directory of Poetry Publishers*. Paradise, CA: Dustbooks, 2003.

Grossman, Joe, with David Doty. *Newsletters from the Desktop*. Chapel Hill, NC: Ventana Press, 1994.

Poynter, Dan. *The Self-Publishing Manual: How to Write, Print, and Sell Your Own Book*. 14th ed. Santa Barbara: Para, 2003.

Ross, Tom & Marilyn, *The Complete Guide to Self-Publishing*. 4th ed. Cincinnati: Writer's Digest, 2002.

Williams, Robin. *Web Design Workshop*. Berkeley, CA: Peachpit, 2002.

Williams, Thomas. *Poet Power: The Complete Guide to Getting Your Poetry Published*. Boulder, CO: Sentient, 2002.

Woodward, Cheryl. *Starting and Running a Successful Newsletter or Magazine*. Berkeley, CA: Nolo, 2004.

Other Works Cited

Frye, Northrop. *Anatomy of Criticism*. Princeton: Princeton UP, 1957.

Hunter, William B. Jr., gen. ed. *A Milton Encyclopedia*. Lewisburg: Bucknell UP, 1978.

Melville, Herman. *Moby Dick*. NY: Norton, 1967.

Percy, Thomas. *Reliques of Ancient English Poetry*. London: Bell, 1900.

Santayana, George. *The Sense of Beauty*. NY: Modern Library, 1955.

Acknowledgements

With words we began, and with words we end. Where would this book be without them? Let me express sincere gratitude to one and all for their permission to reprint them.

Calabrese, Rosalie. "On Thursday" by Rosalie Calabrese. Copyright © 2007 by Rosalie Calabrese.

Cassian, Nina. "Night Must Fall," translated by Dana Gioia, from LIFE SENTENCE: Selected Poems by Nina Cassian, edited by William Jay Smith. Copyright © 1990 by Nina Cassian. Used by permission of W.W. Norton & Company, Inc; "Invitation au voyage," "Orlando," "The Sow Is Dead in the Barn," from TAKE MY WORD FOR IT, by Nina Cassian. Copyright © 1998 by Nina Cassian. Used by permission of W.W. Norton & Company, Inc.

Conway (Campana), Jean. "Celebrating the Best" by Jean (Campana) Conway. Copyright © 2007 by Jean Campana Conway.

Crane, Hart. "Proem: To Brooklyn Bridge," from COMPLETE POEMS OF HART CRANE by Hart Crane, edited by Marc Simon. Copyright 1933, 1958, 1966 by Liveright Publishing Corporation. Copyright © 1986 by Marc Simon. Used by permission of Liveright Publishing Corporation.

Cummings, E. E. "in Just-" Copyright 1923, 1951, © 1991 by the Trustees for the E.E. Cummings Trust. Copyright © 1976 by George James Firmage, from COMPLETE POEMS: 1904-1962 by E. E. Cummings, edited by George J. Firmage. Used by permission of Liveright Publishing Corporation.

Dickinson, Emily. "I Heard a Fly Buzz When I Died" by Emily Dickinson. Reprinted by permission of the publishers and the Trustees of Amherst College from THE POEMS OF EMILY DICKINSON, Thomas H. Johnson, ed., Cambridge, Mass.: The Belknap Press of Harvard University Press, Copyright© 1951, 1955, 1979, 1983 by the President and Fellows of Harvard College.

H. D. (Doolittle, Hilda). "Sea Rose" by HD (Hilda Doolittle), from COLLECTED POEMS 1912-1944, copyright © 1982 by The Estate of Hilda Doolittle. Reprinted by permission of New Directions Publishing Corporation.

Eliot, T. S. "The Love Song of J. Alfred Prufrock" and "Burnt Norton" by T. S. Eliot, from THE COMPLETE POEMS AND PLAYS: 1909-1950. Reprinted by the kind permission of Harcourt Brace & Company.

Fainlight, Ruth. "Four Pheasants" by Ruth Fainlight, reprinted from BURNING WIRE; "Stubborn," "Love Feast," and "Handbag" by Ruth Fainlight, reprinted from FIFTEEN TO INFINITY; "Blossom and Technology" and "The Japanese Bath" by Ruth Fainlight, reprinted from THE KNOT; "The Prism" by Ruth Fainlight, reprinted from THE BLOODAXE BOOK OF CONTEMPORARY WOMEN POETS, all by permission of Ruth Fainlight. "The Point of It All" by Ruth Fainlight, reprinted from SUGAR-PAPER BLUE by permission of Bloodaxe Books.

Fraser, Silvana (Guadagnoli). "Education" by Silvana (Guadagnoli) Fraser. Copyright © 2007 by Silvana (Guadagnoli) Fraser.

Ghignone, Lorraine. "Ballad of a Fallen Angel" and "Paradise Always" by Lorraine Ghignone. Copyright © 2007 by Lorraine Ghignone.

Gilbert, Ilsa. "Zoo International, Basel, Switzerland" by Ilsa Gilbert, reprinted from POEMS OF THE HUMAN AND ANIMAL KINGDOM by Ilsa Gilbert, copyright © 2007 by Ilsa Gilbert. Reprinted by permission of Ilsa Gilbert.

Ginsberg, Allen. "Howl" from COLLECTED POEMS 1947-1980 by Allen Ginsberg. Copyright © 1955 by Allen Ginsberg. Reprinted by permission of HarperCollins Publishers.

Greene, Jeffrey. "The Anatomy of Night" and "Night Dive" from TO THE LEFT OF THE WORSHIPER by Jeffrey Greene. Copyright © 1991 by Jeffrey Greene. Reprinted by permission of Alice James Books; "Ministering Spirits" reprinted from THE SEWANEE REVIEW 110:3 (Summer 2002), by permission of Jeffrey Greene; "The Evening of the Whale" by Jeffrey Greene, reprinted from AMERICAN SPIRITUALS, p. 11, copyright © 1998 by Jeffrey Greene, reprinted by permission of University Press of New England; "La Cluza," reprinted from CRAZYHORSE, Number 24, Spring 1983, by permission of Jeffrey Greene.

Greissle-Schönberg, Arnold. "Tell Me Where" and various Schüttelreim by Arnold Greissle-Schönberg. Copyright © 2007 by Arnold Greissle-Schönberg.

Homer. THE ILIAD OF HOMER, translated by Richmond Lattimore, excerpt from p. 249. Reprinted by permission of the University of Chicago Press.

Johansen, Gjertine. "Mortality" by Gjertine Johansen. Copyright © 2007 by Gjertine Johansen.

Kobayashi, Issa. "Shaking His Loose Skin" by Issa Kobayashi, translated by Peter Beilenson and Harry Behn, published in HAIKU HARVEST. Copyright © 1962 by Peter Pauper Press, Inc. Used by permission.

Lo Presto, Jody. "A Psychic Psyche's Vow to Cupid" by Jody Lo Presto. Copyright © 2007 by Jody Lo Presto.

Acknowledgements

Melendi, Ursula. "The Anti-Neo-Nazi Protest" and "Baker's Villanelle" by Ursula Melendi. Copyright © 2007 by Ursula Melendi.

Moore, Marianne. "The Fish" by Marianne Moore. Reprinted with the permission of Scribner, an imprint of Simon & Schuster Adult Publishing Group, from COLLECTED POEMS by Marianne Moore. Copyright © 1935 by Marianne Moore; copyright renewed © 1963 by Marianne Moore and T.S. Eliot. All rights reserved.

Rasmussen, Eugene. "An Unworthy Rhyme" by Eugene Rasmussen. Copyright © 2007 by Eugene Rasmussen.

Sandburg, Carl. "Chicago" and "The Fog" by Carl Sandburg from CHICAGO POEMS. Reprinted by the kind permission of Harcourt Brace & Company.

Siegel, Brenda. "On First Reading Arnold's 'Dover Beach'" and "Essay on Teaching Poetry in High School" by Brenda Siegel. Copyright © 2007 by Brenda Siegel.

Stevens, Wallace. "Thirteen Ways of Looking at a Blackbird," copyright 1923 and renewed 1951 by Wallace Stevens, "Sunday Morning," copyright 1923 and renewed 1951 by Wallace Stevens, "Peter Quince at the Clavier," copyright 1923 and renewed 1951 by Wallace Stevens, from THE COLLECTED POEMS OF WALLACE STEVENS by Wallace Stevens. Used by permission of Alfred A. Knopf, a division of Random House, Inc.

Thomas, Dylan. "Do Not Go Gentle into That Good Night" by Dylan Thomas, from THE POEMS OF DYLAN THOMAS, copyright © 1951 by Dylan Thomas. Reprinted by permission of New Directions Publishing Corporation.

Toro, Michael. "Lovers Within the Darkness" and "A Fantasy to Beyond" by Michael Toro. Copyright © 2007 by Michael Toro.

Wallace, Laura (Martino). "Free" by Laura (Martino) Wallace. Copyright © 2007 Laura (Martino) Wallace.

Walker, Susan. "Tears Roll" and spoonerisms by Susan Walker. Copyright © 2007 by Susan Walker.

Williams, William Carlos. "The Red Wheelbarrow" and "The Dance" by William Carlos Williams, from COLLECTED POEMS, VOLUME I, 1909-1939, copyright © 1938 by New Directions Publishing Corporation. Reprinted by permission of New Directions Publishing Corporation.

Yeats, William Butler. "Sailing to Byzantium" by William Butler Yeats. Reprinted with the permission of Scribner, an imprint of Simon & Schuster Adult Publishing Group, from THE COLLECTED WORKS OF W.B. YEATS, VOLUME I: THE POEMS, revised edition by Richard J. Finneran. Copyright © 1928 by The Macmillan Company; copyright renewed © 1956 by Georgie Yeats. All rights reserved.

INDEX

A

B

C

D

E

F

H

I

P

Q

R

S

T

Y

Z

Notes & Quotes